"The author of this aptly named book wants readers to see the Bible in new, yet very old ways. By recovering the Jewishness of Jesus and his world, by finding out why early Christian leaders practiced 'four-fold exegesis,' and by simply taking tensions, conflict, and even disagreement for granted within the New Testament, Byassee believes Bible-readers will once again be 'surprised by Jesus.'"

— MARK NOLL,
author of *Jesus Christ and the Life of the Mind*

"This is a book ministers, not to mention others, really should read. Jason Byassee's delight in scripture dances off every page of this well-informed but accessible book, informing and delighting us in equal measure as he leads us to look anew to where 'God is unendingly sharing the divine presence,' that is, in the scriptures."

— JANET MARTIN SOSKICE,
Jesus College Cambridge

"Allegorical interpretation has had a surprising number of defenders recently—surprising because its rejection by Protestant and modern critics could easily lead to the assumption that it was finished off, one more item for the dustbin of history. Those defenses, however, are almost always theoretical in nature, telling readers that we should retrieve it, not how to do so. Byassee has accomplished a remarkable achievement in this work, convincingly demonstrating how to interpret the Bible allegorically for preaching and teaching. I know of no other comparable work. It is a lively read, which could cause readers to overlook its profound theological and philosophical underpinnings. Anyone interested in preaching, biblical interpretation, theology, or church life should be reading this book."

— D. STEPHEN LONG,
Southern Methodist University

"Writing with clarity, profundity, and humor, Byassee draws on Augustine, Origen, and Gregory (among others) to help us recover reading habits that can help us become faithful readers of scripture. In particular, Byassee gives us an account of how and why a robust Christology requires Christians to recognize our need for those people called Jews. Byassee's argument is heavy, but this is a book that can restore the joy that is commensurate with reading God's word."

— STANLEY HAUERWAS,
author of *The Character of Virtue*

"After decades studying the works of ancient and modern interpreters of the Bible, Jason Byassee has come to the conclusion that 'the difference is in their delight.' Happily, in Byassee we meet an interpreter in whom diligence and delight are wedded. On every page of this learned and hopeful book, there is fresh instruction in the art of reading Israel's scriptures and fresh delight in seeing the Bible through the eyes of the whole church."

— CAROL ZALESKI,
Smith College

"Jason Byassee goes hunting in the church's past and discovers a long-forgotten and much-needed treasure for today. The treasure is richer ways of reading scripture than the dry, lifeless habits of reading that bewitch and bewilder the church with illusory, pointless, and life-sucking arguments. Others have discovered the same treasure, but Byassee's account stands out as a winsome invitation to an adventure with Christ. The adventure is to escape the spells of modernity and reorient ourselves to the life-giving power of scripture that flows from the Father, Son, and Spirit."

— JONATHAN R. WILSON,
Regent College

Surprised by Jesus Again

Reading the Bible
in Communion with the Saints

Jason Byassee

WILLIAM B. EERDMANS PUBLISHING COMPANY
GRAND RAPIDS, MICHIGAN

Wm. B. Eerdmans Publishing Co.
4035 Park East Court SE, Grand Rapids, Michigan 49546
www.eerdmans.com

Published 2019
Printed in the United States of America

25 24 23 22 21 20 19   1 2 3 4 5 6 7

ISBN 978-0-8028-7168-8

Library of Congress Cataloging-in-Publication Data

Names: Byassee, Jason, author.
Title: Surprised by Jesus again : reading the Bible in communion with the
    saints / Jason Byassee.
Description: Grand Rapids : Eerdmans Publishing Co., 2019. | Includes
    bibliographical references and index.
Identifiers: LCCN 2018059529 | ISBN 9780802871688 (pbk. : alk. paper)
Subjects: LCSH: Bible—Criticism, interpretation, etc.—History—Early
    church, ca. 30-600.
Classification: LCC BS511.3 .B93 2019 | DDC 220.609/015—dc23
    LC record available at https://lccn.loc.gov/2018059529

For Richard Topping

CONTENTS

CONTENTS

FOREWORD

When we look at the church today, in our increasingly polarized society, do we discover a refreshing oasis of delight across difference as members of Christ's body seek the truth together, wrestling with one another and with scripture in ways that display the beauty and reconciling power of the gospel? Or do we find national ideologies in theological drag, with every side demanding to be recognized as right, faithful, and true—delight and difference be damned? I suspect, given media's formative power over our imaginations, most of us will resonate more with the latter than with the former.

What would it take for things to be otherwise?

For starters, we could work to find friends like Jason Byassee, who may well disagree with you, but will do so with such grace and playful delight that you forget your fear and instead set off with him on an adventure, chasing Jesus instead of a cheap rhetorical victory. As a wide-eyed first-year seminarian at Duke Divinity School, I vividly remember my first significant disagreement with a teaching assistant in one of my classes. After reading some theologian's reflections on Dostoyevsky's "Grand Inquisitor," I mused on the problem of evil, entertaining a flirtation with process theology. The teaching assistant, with a puckish grin on his face, responded by suggesting that perhaps I wasn't the first person to have discovered the problem of evil and that I might consider looking backward toward the tradition with a bit more patience and charity before choosing to jettison it for some "new-fangled" idea. I was put off. Considerably. As someone quite used to being the teacher's pet, it struck me as rude, dismissive, and closed-minded. Perhaps perceiving my negative reaction at having my rather sensitive nose tweaked, the teaching assistant suggested a couple of essays by David Bentley Hart, offering an extra session or two to talk through the ideas I would encounter therein.

This little exchange set off a cascade of events in my life, scholarship, and career from which I've still not recovered—in the best sense of the phrase. The organization I'm now charged with leading, The Colossian Forum, is in many ways an extension of the adventure that began with those discussions with a playful teaching assistant. Learning to go back in order to go forward by looking to the radically different theological imaginations of the wider tradition with gratitude rather than culturally typical disdain, I took my first step toward engaging those who think radically differently from me today with gratitude rather than disdain. As you've probably guessed, that teaching assistant was Jason Byassee. And this book is vintage Jason, nose-tweak and all. Just as he did for me back at Duke, he now does in these pages as he helps us chart a way ahead by giving thanks for what's come before. And he does it where we need help the most—scripture.

Jason, still with that puckish grin on his face, invites us on an adventure of rereading the scriptures with those who are very different from us *in order to be* surprised and delighted by Jesus, again. Instead of wielding scripture against those whose political ideology we disagree with, we are invited to chase after Jesus together. What could be *less* interesting than a church mimicking the hackneyed politics of the left and right, when we've been entrusted with the beauty and reconciling power of the gospel? And what could be *more* exhilarating than engaging scripture, not so much to win an argument with those with whom we disagree, but to seek together to enflame love and worship of the Lamb who was slain?

That is why this book is so profoundly timely and important. Following Augustine, Byassee rightfully seeks to upend our typical intentions in reading scripture from *winning* to *worship*. Praise seeking understanding—in that order. Sounds simple, trite even. Kind of like "God is love." Easy to say, impossible to grasp in all its magnificent depths—depths Byassee helps us begin to plumb. Moving from winning to worship means learning to refuse our ugly habit of weaponizing scripture in support of our pet causes and, instead, having the courage to cultivate habits of measuring the efficacy of our scriptural engagement on whether it produces charity—*deeper love of God and neighbor.*

This criterion, this christological norm for reading scripture that Byassee puts back in our hands, is in many ways remarkably simple. It's something we all learned in Sunday school—loving God and neighbor. What would happen if we could remember that such love matters right in the middle of a fight? It is precisely because Byassee points us to such a simple, basic Christian commitment that this criterion has the surprisingly broad potential to do significant work for the church today. Indeed, since nearly all believers identify with the christological norm, Byassee gives us a way to hold each other accountable, not by browbeating each other with scripture, but by challenging each other toward delight. As we engage scripture, we're freed to ask each other honestly, as a moral claim upon one another, Does our reading helps us look, love, and delight more like Jesus or not?

Of course, reading with a christological norm takes courage because it seems to lack epistemological teeth, academic rigor, and critical edge. It provides no way of compelling intellectual assent, ending disagreement, or enforcing unity, certainty, justice, or truth. Which is just another way of saying it doesn't "work" in the sense of helping us win our argument and thereby evade the claims our enemies have upon us to treat them with the same charity God lavishes upon us.

No, engaging scripture in the way Byassee suggests doesn't win arguments. It is, in fact, a ridiculously scandalous way to read—unless Christ has already won. If the resurrection is true, then what better way for us to witness to Christ's victory than by laying down our need to win and seeking instead to live true lives with those with whom we disagree?

The "teeth" of the way Jason Byassee wants us to read actually sink far deeper into our lives and actions than the typical epistemological requirements. After all, Jesus refused to call down twelve legions of angels to prove his claim. Rather, in humility, gentleness, patience, and forbearance, he laid down his life, betting everything on the power of the Father's love to overcome the power of death. Surprise! What might we, and the world, see if we similarly followed Jesus's footsteps in the face of our enemies? What might we, and the world, discover if we followed the exemplars Byassee puts before us, seeking not to simply score a rhetorical point but to enflame love in those with whom we disagree?

Such a radical shift in reading scriptures is daunting. We've lost our imagination for it. And that is why this book is, again, so profoundly timely and important. By putting us in conversation with very "other" voices and their engagement with scripture, Byassee shows us how their otherness, when received with gratitude and delight, can become a pointer to the Otherness of God—our ultimate source of gratitude, delight, and, of course, surprise. Thanks be to God.

MICHAEL GULKER
President, The Colossian Forum

PREFACE

To be able to offer this book on reading the Bible with the church's tradition is a gift of grace for me. I have tried and failed two times before to write this book as a sort of sequel to my *Praise Seeking Understanding* on Augustine's way of reading the Psalms. A first effort was a more popular version of that book. A second was a more academic book on how to draw on the ancient church's ways of interpreting. Both volumes were presented to publishers under contract and mercifully turned down. Neither was good enough. If this one is, then I have several people to thank.

I must thank especially The Colossian Forum (TCF), founder Kurt Berends and present leader Michael Gulker. I so admire its vocation to help congregations run toward the sort of trouble that pastors and churches often run away from. To that end they have crafted a leadership training program to help churches and Christian organizations use the energy around polarizing topics as a catalyst for intergenerational spiritual formation and as an occasion to display the beauty of the gospel in our fragmented world.[1] Several of their offerings deal with the fracture between theology and science, toward which this book also gestures at the end.[2] TCF is convinced that much of that fracture is due to our misunderstanding what the Bible is, especially the purposes for which God has given it to us. The Bible can only be understood well when it is seen as a gift in the context of God's relentless work to make all things new.

---

1. For more information, see www.colossianforum.org.
2. See the much more developed volumes by Cavanaugh and Smith, *Evolution and the Fall*, and Smith and Gulker, *All Things Hold Together in Christ*.

As I was completing this book, I spent several days writing at Queen of Peace Monastery in Squamish, British Columbia, whose sisters I must also thank. While there I heard a homily from Don Goergen, OP, who preached to the sisters from the Sermon on the Mount. There Jesus swears he is changing nothing in the law—he is rather fulfilling it, raising its bar higher. In his words, "Whoever breaks one of the least of these commandments, and teaches others to do the same, will be called *least* in the kingdom of heaven" (Matt. 5:19). Moving on from interpretation to speculation, though guided by a conversation with a Matthew scholar, Father Don made a connection to St. Paul's comment that he is *least* among the apostles (1 Cor. 15:9). Biblical scholars debate whether Paul even knew the traditions that would become the gospels, so this is not strictly a historical observation. The linguistic connection is homiletically interesting—the wording is so similar: "least," something most people don't ever want to be, but that saints seem, oddly, to long to embrace. Matthew and Paul say quite different things about being "least," and about other things too: Matthew's Jesus insists on his law-abiding and law-heightening; Paul suggests that gentile Christians need not follow the Torah but rather follow the law of the Spirit. Father Don made this comment, appropriate to any order, any congregation, any family, any grouping of human beings striving for any corporate good: conflict is no bad thing. The New Testament blesses disagreement right within the church's first few generations. Matthew and Paul indeed seem to have quite different views of Israel's law and its place in the life of the church of Jews and gentiles worshiping the risen messiah, Jesus. And the Bible is not anxious about this conflict. It stands there naked, not tidied up, rough edges exposed for all to see. Not that the difference does not matter, not at all.[3] But scripture sees fit to include difficulties on its face to show us that God is not afraid of conflict. God in fact uses it to make us holy, to teach us to forgive, to show us that our grasp of truth is only ever partial, even as the Truth enfleshed in Jesus *has* grasped *us* entirely. The Colossian Forum has a similar view of conflict. It is nothing to run from, despite whatever pastoral instinct drives me to want to do precisely that. (What am I afraid of? Scaring off members? Missing budget? Where, chapter and

---

3. They can indeed be reconciled: Jesus is a Torah-observant Jew himself, but the gospel calls all nations, *as gentiles*, to covenant with the God of Israel, so we gentiles need not observe the whole Torah.

verse, does Jesus ask us to worry about such things?!) I am honored to be part of their work.

I have already tipped my hand as to who I am as an interpreter. My work has been a combination of journalism, scholarship, and preaching. I've been graced to write for the *Christian Century*, *Sojourners*, and other publications about God's renewing work in the church. As a journalist I love to ask interesting people big, nosy questions and then tell others what they say. Some of this journalistic approach is present in this book, especially in chapters 1, 5, 7, and the postlude. I've worked also as an academic, studying the ways that the early church's theology can inform the church's preaching today. I am trained in theology and not in history or Bible (as experts in those fields will be quick to point out!). I write, then, as an amateur in the etymological sense—a lover of these fields, not an expert. I do theology in conversation with saints living (chapters 3 and 7) and saints long dead (chapters 2, 4, 6, and 8). And I write as a lover of the church. This approach is present throughout all the chapters. I see preaching as an act of taking part in Christ's intimate wooing of his church and all people back to the love for God and neighbor for which God longs for all creation. My work is unapologetically homiletical, then. Arguably anybody putting pen to paper for any other reader is always already preaching. The difference here is that the first sermon is the one God preaches to us in Christ. The church's sermons participate in God's own preaching, enabled to do so by the Holy Spirit who brooded over the waters in the beginning and who is making all things new.

None of this makes scripture safe or easy. We biblical interpreters have to see how strange scripture is. Every Christian in every age has been tempted to paper over scripture's cracks, explain away its oddities, show it's no different or more demanding than what we hearers already think we know about God and the world. This is a mistake. Scripture is spectacularly odd. Preachers must point out these oddities—historical, cultural, temporal, practical, linguistic, the list is endless. And then we have to show how scripture refers to Jesus. Not woodenly or awkwardly, or it won't delight. But naturally, beautifully, on the other side of the oddity. It is a key contention of this book that discovering Jesus in his scripture is not a matter of "finding" someone smuggled in. When scripture is read aright, Jesus is already there, drawing all creatures toward himself. All creation is made in Christ, Paul argues (Col. 1:15–20). So all things reflect him in whom they are made. This can be hard to see. Creation is fallen. We creatures reflect Christ poorly at first. But over time we come to reflect him more clearly as we grow in holiness. Those training themselves to see Christ in all things see him first and principally in scripture, on the way to seeing him everywhere. This is also hard at first. Then we grow accustomed to it. And once we see him, we cannot but point him out to others. To do so is our delight, and theirs, and God's.

I also want to thank Eerdmans Publishing Company, which has been exceedingly patient waiting for this manuscript. I love Eerdmans's originally Reformed vision of the world in which God rules over all and is presently working to make all things new, not in any narrowly religious sense, but in every part of creation. Their Reformed vision is broad enough to include Christians of all types, and I'm honored to be among their number.

I am grateful to students and colleagues at the Vancouver School of Theology (VST) and Duke Divinity School on whom these ideas have been tried out and with whom they have been sharpened. Portions of the argument have been tried out with audiences at Regent College, St. Mark's College, Carey Theological College, Wycliffe College, and Asian Theological Seminary, and at continuing-education events with the Anglican Diocese of New Westminster, Grace Presbyterian Church in Calgary, and the Roman Catholic Archdiocese of Vancouver, and with the alumni association of Queens Theological College. I thank the people of Boone United Methodist Church, where my preaching was steeped in these views of scripture. I'm grateful to *Sojourners* magazine, where I was privileged to write lectionary commentary for its "Living the Word" section off and on from 2015 to 2017. Those very tight strictures—just a few hundred words!—reminded me that biblical interpretation need not be verbose. Inspiring others to read scripture well can come more in the form of poetry, just a few sentences even, a slight gesture rather than ponderous length or theatricality. If those reflections were any good to anybody, well, here are the hermeneutical presuppositions that birthed them.

As time goes on, I'm increasingly grateful to my teachers at Duke Divinity School: Will Willimon, Stanley Hauerwas, Reinhard Hütter, David Steinmetz, Geoffrey Wainwright, Richard Hays, Ellen Davis, and, though I knew them less than the others, Nicholas Lash, Kathy Grieb, Robert Wilken, Lewis Ayres, and David Hart, whose principal appointments being elsewhere than Duke meant that I only got to study for a short time with each. They showed me that the church has been interpreting the Bible for a very long time, and there is wisdom to be found in tradition, though it doesn't come easily. I am grateful also to my VST colleague Rabbi Laura Duhan Kaplan, with whom I taught a course on Jews and Christians that made me realize at once how strange Christians' way of reading the Bible is, and how delightful. Thank you to my research assistant at VST, Eliana Ku, who saved me from many mistakes. Adam Joyce's expert editing made this book much better than it would have been without his wisdom.

This book is dedicated to Richard Topping, the principal of the Vancouver School of Theology, whose gospel-infused cheerfulness as a preacher and leader I so admire, and for whose friendship I give great thanks.

This book is about interpreting the Bible as a mystery of seeking to be surprised by Jesus again. Historical criticism tries to read without surprise. All the evidence is in. All that needs to be done is sift through the layers of historical detritus, determine what is scientifically "true" or not, and then leave the wreckage of the archaeological tell after carrying off whatever treasures the museum wants. But for a people who believe in a living God this is not enough. God is constantly surprising us. Robert Jenson said the difference between a dead god and a living God is a dead god can't surprise you. This book tries to proceed as though God is constantly surprising us. It proceeds with chapters on ancient exemplars—Mary, Origen, Augustine, and Gregory the Great. It includes some chapters drawing on contemporary interpreters who try to read the Bible guided by ancient insight. I will sometimes agree and sometimes disagree. The book will conclude with a proposal for reacquaintance with the medieval pattern of fourfold biblical interpretation: literal, allegorical, moral, and anagogical. Biblical texts should be read for what they say, historically and on their face; then we read them for what they say about God, we read them for what they say about the moral life, and we read them politically—about the city of God that Jesus longs to birth in our world and is presently making real through the church. Not every text can support every sort of meaning. But what they hold together is this—Jesus is the Lord of the world, of the scriptures, and of the hearts of those who walk with him and burn with his fiery presence (Luke 24:13–35). If a reading of the Bible doesn't require a resurrected Jew to make sense, it's not a Christian one. We read instructed by this stranger on the road, who only reveals his identity to us slowly, waiting until we can hardly stand it anymore, and then . . .

1

Grafted In

Relearning God's Promises to Israel

It is the spring of 2017. I am co-teaching a class to a room of Jews and Christians. My colleague, Rabbi Dr. Laura Duhan Kaplan, and I are trying to talk about God again. For a millennium and a half or more, Christians and Jews couldn't talk explicitly about God. Jews mostly had to figure out how to survive Christian mistreatment. Christians launched evangelism efforts that didn't work and crusades and inquisitions and pogroms of which we're still ashamed. More recently, in modernity, as Christians recoiled and reassessed after the Holocaust and Jews in the West muscled in to a more secure place, we had conversations about things that matter: civil rights, human rights, justice around the world, Israel and its policies toward its neighbors and its protection.[1] These weren't always pleasant, but they were good. And they're not what I mean here.

In our class, Jews and Christians: A Theological Journey, we're talking about the God of Israel, who Christians believe has grafted us into his covenant with his people by grace. That's new, perhaps unprecedented since Christians took civic power in exchange for blessing the emperor in 313 CE. And it's really hard. Few of us are good at it. In my sentence above we would have to define and endlessly qualify some words: God, Israel, Christians, graft, us, covenant, people, and grace, for starters.

---

1. Michael Wyschogrod describes his disagreement with his teacher, Rabbi Joseph Soloveitchik, on whether Jews can talk with Christians about God (so Wyschogrod) or whether they should limit themselves to discussing the common good (so Soloveitchik). Wyschogrod not only thinks Jews can; he also argues that his teacher secretly agrees with him, whatever protests he might make to the contrary! See his "Jewish View of Christianity."

So there I was in class, giving a lovely talk (or so I thought) on the virgin birth. Our textbook's author, Michael Goldberg, had slid by this sticking point fairly quickly.[2] His book gives brilliant, sometimes breathtaking readings of Exodus and Matthew that show Christianity itself to be a reading of Judaism, a re-presentation of the Jewish people and story and God in a new setting. Some scholars, Christian and Jewish and secular, dismiss Matthew's quotations of Israel's scripture. Matthew tends to break out the trumpets: "Behold! This was done to fulfill . . ." The easiest response among modern critical scholars is to say, "Um, actually, Isaiah didn't mean that at all." I've heard one rabbi say that Christians' claims that Jesus fulfilled the law is a bit like shooting arrows into a forest, going and seeing where they stick, and then painting a bull's-eye around the arrow. He's not impressed. Neither have modernist biblical critics been. Isaiah 7 is not, on any reasonable grounds, about Jesus of Nazareth. As Jews pointed out millennia ago, when the prophet says an *almah* will be with child, it means, in Hebrew, simply "a young woman" (Isa. 7:14). The Jewish translators who created the Septuagint rendered the word in Greek as *parthenos*, a virgin. That's an acceptable translation, not just in Greek, but in many cultures. But then for Christians to take that word as a prophecy of a future virgin birth fulfilled in Jesus is . . . not convincing. Unless you're already convinced.

We Christians have had responses to this.[3] Isaiah 7:14 seems to blow its own trumpets: "Behold, a virgin shall conceive, and bear a son" (KJV). Why the excitement? It's not surprising that a young woman gets pregnant. Isaiah's own enthusiasm suggests something more is afoot than the birth even of a very special child. Jews would say: still not convincing. In class I wasn't trying to make the virgin birth convincing. It's not, on its own. You only believe in it because you already believe in Jesus. If you believe God is fleshed in this one Jew, you're ready to believe a lot more. My goal was to make it sound as not-ridiculous as possible. My colleague, Rabbi Laura, helped a great deal. "Matthew is just doing what we Jews always do," she said. "Reading the Bible in a new circumstance in surprising ways." She doesn't think the virgin birth is true, I imagine. She just doesn't think it's ridiculous.

I taught the virgin birth in as Jewish a way as possible. Think back over the history of Israel: Almost no important figure gets born without

---

2. Goldberg, *Jews and Christians*.

3. See Sawyer, *Fifth Gospel*, esp. 46, 66, 215. Also Wilken, *Isaiah*, esp. 98–101.

trouble. Every time, there is a problem getting them born. Abraham and Sarah cannot have a child at first. Now they have more children than anyone can count, more than the sands of the sea or the stars in the sky. Ditto Isaac and Rebekah, Jacob and Rachel. These are the children of Israel, among whom we Christians count ourselves in Christ. Hannah is desperate for a child. Her husband, Elkanah, comforts her tenderly, "Am I not more to you than ten sons?" (1 Sam. 1:8).[4] The text is too nice to say it, but Hannah must think, "Yeah, no, not actually." She prays feverishly. And she is given Samuel. Whom she immediately gives back to God. These stories show that God is the giver of life. They show that God understands women and men who wish to give birth more than they wish for air or water, but cannot conceive. They do not show that if we just pray enough, we will get a child, contrary to much pastoral malfeasance. They do promise that we can all bear miraculous fruit. We just don't get to determine in what form that fruit will be born: in physical wombs or spiritual. And a great mystery hangs over it all that no one can pretend to understand.

Then we Christians start up with stories that are fashioned in the forge of Israel but not celebrated by Jews as scripture (Luke 1:5–25, 57–80). Elizabeth and Zechariah want a child, like the matriarchs and patriarchs of old. Zechariah is a priest. And Gabriel turns up in the temple to tell him the good news: old as they are, God has heard their prayer and will grant them a miraculous child, who will make for rejoicing in Israel. Zechariah's response is priceless: "I work here every day, and one thing that cannot happen is an angel cannot show up and say a miracle is coming. I have a Master of Divinity degree to prove it" (I'm paraphrasing a little). The angel's response is more priceless still: "You claim to speak for God, but you can't listen when God has something to say back? You're not allowed to talk anymore." Zechariah is voiceless until the child's birth, and it all turns out as the angel said: Elizabeth becomes as great with child as she ever wanted. Their son announces the coming king of Israel, savior of the world, before whom idols fall and shatter.[5]

That's a Jewish story. Retold and treasured by what quickly became a largely gentile church, but that doesn't make it not-Jewish. We Chris-

4. Scripture quotations are from the NRSV unless I indicate otherwise.
5. I'm echoing Rowan Williams on the virgin birth as he echoes Rainer Maria Rilke in *Ray of Darkness*, 5–6.

tians are a Jewish sect at first. Israel's stories are not our stories orig-inally, as gentile Christians. The Bible is not our book. God is not our God. Only by grace, through Jesus, are we given access to Israel's stories, scriptures, salvation. And this is how that happens.

The same angel, perhaps still a little miffed from the visit with the priest, turns up to an unmarried Jewish teenager from the sticks. The angel tells Mary she'll have a child. And that child will be God's child. And will save the universe. All creation waits with baited breath for her reply. What will it be (Luke 1:26–38)? God will not force himself on any-one. God wants willing conspirators, not slaves. The entire hackneyed plan to save the world and make right all things humans have made wrong waits on the word of a teenage girl from a despised religion in an occupied backwater from which nothing good is supposed to come. What will it be?

OK.

Or, as the church has often rendered this in Latin, *fiat*, let it be. Just as God said when creation fell from his fingers: "Let there be light." Just as Abram said when God appeared to him to uproot and go away and become father to countless many . . . he doesn't say anything; he just goes. This is what God's people are to do. When God has a cockamamie scheme to repair the world, we roll with it.

Mary's miraculous pregnancy is a presentation-all-over-again of Israel's miraculous pregnancy tradition. It is, of course, re-presented with a twist—a fulfillment, we Christians would say. Sarah, Rebekah, Rachel, Hannah, and Elizabeth got pregnant miraculously, but a man was involved. Through the original cockamamie scheme God designed for us to be intimate with our spouse and bear the wondrous fruit of children, these women bore sons who tilted the world on its axis. Mary requires no man to get pregnant. Rowan Williams, former archbishop of Canterbury, points out that anytime anyone trusts the God of the uni-verse, new things get born.[6] Miracles happen. New ministries arise. The creative way of God in the world is unleashed anew and inexplicable stuff gets going. Mary trusts so much she gets pregnant. She is the first Christian. Salvation begins with her yes.[7] Ever since, Christians have tried to go on saying yes like her. We mostly fail. But that she did not fail

6. Williams, "Waiting on God," in *Ray of Darkness*, 13–16.

7. I take this language from Willie Jennings, for whom I was privileged to serve as a teaching assistant at Duke in 2002–2003.

means salvation is loose in her and then in our flesh. And the Holy One of Israel gets born.

St. Symeon the New Theologian in the eleventh century described the virgin birth this way: God had already made a person with no parents: Adam. God had already made a person from a man alone: Eve. God has made people from two parents: all the rest of us. The one thing God had not yet done was to make a person from a woman alone: Jesus.[8] What God started in the garden, God finishes with the annunciation. Note well: this proves nothing. There is no bull's-eye drawn around an arrow here. It just flirts with us. It's supposed to delight. It suggests God works in the most beautiful way possible. Like an artist finishing a canvas, God returns to the work of creation and finishes it in Mary's untouched womb. She is like the temple: filled with divine *Shekinah* (Spirit) that births holiness in the world. She is like the burning bush: filled with the fiery presence of God and yet not consumed. Christians have broken out some of our highest praise and our most Israel-infused language to speak of Mary. The doctrine of the virgin birth might be wrong, but it's not wrong because it's non-Jewish or anti-Jewish.

Learning from Jews about the Trinity

Not bad, eh? Did my best.

But the Jewish students didn't want to talk about Mary at all. They wanted to talk about . . . other things.

"So the virgin birth is a sign that Jesus is God, right?" one asked.

"Yes," I said, bracing myself.

"So how come you Christians have three Gods?"

"Yes!" our Hasidic rabbi intoned. "That's why I can go into a mosque and pray but can't go into a Christian church. You're technically tritheists."

"Pagans?" I ask. He nodded solemnly.

Two other Jewish students' hands shot up. I looked over at Laura for backup. She smiled but did not intervene, as if to say, "You're on your own, kid."

I flailed around a little and went away distraught, thinking. I'm still thinking now, months later. Do we Christians worship three gods? Of

---

8. St. Symeon the New Theologian, *On the Mystical Life*, vol. 1, p. 32.

course not, we have all always been quick to say. But Jews don't see it that way. Despite our disavowals, it sounds like we have three beings running around claiming to be God. That's polytheism. Paganism. Not the sort of thing the God or the people of Israel regard benignly.

And, so what? Who cares if Jews think we Christians are tritheists? The word *monotheism* is a modern, history-of-religions classification. Europeans in the nineteenth century came up with taxonomies to describe religions without confessional language and lumped those who claim to have one God into one category (the superior one, of course— religion scholarship had a long way to go then; still does). But perhaps we Christians should have never been happy with such a classification. We claim that Jesus is God. The Holy Spirit is God. And there is only one God—Father, Son, and Spirit. And we can't understand that. We can only adore. Jews say, "OK, fine. Just don't claim not to be tritheists."

This is a wonderful and blessed challenge, nearly unprecedented since the church's first generations. To have Jews nosing around in our stuff and diagnosing missteps is a treasure. And it made me ask, Why do I care whether God is one? Or whether Jews think we have the right answer to that question? All my theological concern is trained on those who deny Jesus's lordship, or the Spirit's divinity. Christianity falls apart without those beliefs, so I wrote a whole book to support them.[9] But what if it turns out that God isn't one, by Jewish or other lights? If we're not in the right place in German university professors' nineteenth-century taxonomy? If Jews can't pray in church and Muslims agree to kick us out of the one-God club? So what? Jesus saves, not proper categorization in the university or among our religious neighbors. Why not give up the oneness of God with a shrug?

Because the Bible will not let us. "Hear O Israel: The LORD is our God, the LORD alone" is Israel's most important affirmation (Deut. 6:4). To have other gods besides the Holy One of Israel is to undo our own Jewish foundations, to saw off the branch on which we sit. Israel's scripture has hints that there may be something like pluriformity within YHWH's oneness: "Let us make," God says in Genesis 1; Wisdom is an agent and deserves capital letters in some places (Prov. 8); Abraham's visitors by the oaks of Mamre are three and yet they are one "Lord" (Gen. 18). But no one would think this meant anything like a Trinity if they didn't already think that.

9. Byassee, *Trinity*.

These conversations with Jewish communities are driving Christian scholars to reexamine our own roots and remember that these are Jewish roots. What if our gospel is true—Jesus is Lord of all, not least of his own people, *and* God's covenant with Israel is unbroken? Can we redo Christian teaching around God's faithfulness to Israel? We have to, by the way. Because otherwise this is the gospel we preach: "This man loves you enough that he would leave his wife for you." Pause. Of course, if he's the sort of man who would leave his wife for another, why should you trust that man?[10] The gospel cannot be that God left Israel for the gentiles. If it is, why should we trust that God? Flighty and unpredictable and fickle. No thanks. What if instead God *has to* be true to God's own word whether we reciprocate or not? That's a God of grace, who chooses Israel, and then through Israel and church blesses the world.[11]

In the ancient church, a man named Marcion tried to rip up those Jewish roots. He insisted that nothing Jewish can stay. Jesus is so world-turning that the old is gone. Well, what about the Old Testament bits quoted in the New? They have to go too. The fact that you're left with little more than some scraps of the New Testament didn't stop Marcion. The church condemned him. We said no—whatever Jesus is, he has to be a fulfillment of the story of God's promises to Israel. This is not a new religion. It is the old re-presented in some way. It's Judaism for gentiles.

But then that's awkward. There are still Jews. Please, God, let there always be, and may they always flourish. Christians' relationship to the covenant has always been a contentious one. Because Jewish people already have a Judaism for gentiles. It's called *becoming Jewish*. Or honoring the Jews. The laws of Noah, given as his family and the animals disembark the boat in Genesis, are those that Judaism has taken to be for all people (Gen. 9:1–7). The book of Acts shows that the church codified a version of those laws for gentile followers of Jesus: don't worship idols, don't eat blood or anything strangled or anything offered to idols, and don't fornicate (Acts 15:28–29). This is embarrassing too: Christians don't even follow these few laws! Or if we have, we've attended to the ones about sex and dropped the ones about food. Jews have 613 mitz-

---

10. I am remembering this from a comment from Richard Hays in his New Testament introduction at Duke Divinity School, spring 1997. I mean here no blanket condemnation of those who divorce and remarry.

11. Peter Ochs expertly shows the work that several generations of Christian theologians have done to reform theology out of supersessionism; see his book *Another Reformation*, 127–63.

voth given by God to bless Israel and the world, and they do their best to follow them. I've seen Jews cover themselves in *tallit*, a beautiful prayer shawl, as a symbol for the whole Torah—all 613 commandments—under which they seek God's tender mercy and find it. We Christians can't handle five.

Christians looking back at our history find plenty of anti-Judaism for which to repent. And we find occasional sources of light. St. Paul himself, surprisingly, is one of the latter in some places. In Romans 9–11 he wonders how God is being faithful to his covenant to Israel. Most Jews are not interested in the messiah Paul preaches. And yet Israel's unfaithfulness is not a new theme. It's as old as Moses (see Exod. 32). The prophets would have nothing to say without this theme. But the covenant is not conditional. God does not promise to keep God's promises to Israel only if Israel is faithful. God keeps them whether Israel is faithful or not. God is married to the unfaithful spouse in Hosea. God is true even if every person is a liar (Rom. 3:4). How exactly will God keep God's promises to Israel to bless the whole world through them? Paul isn't sure. He collapses in doxology, exhausted after wondering at such questions. "O the depth of the riches and wisdom and knowledge of God!" (Rom. 11:33). Exasperated doxology is not a bad place to finish. Or start.

Paul says other things elsewhere. In Galatians he sounds like the law is only there to trip people into realizing they can't do it. It's to show our need for grace. It's a law of death on its own (Gal. 2:19). Martin Luther, reading Galatians well, describes the enemy defeated in the gospel as sin, death, the devil, *and the law*. This is not helpful for conversations with Jews today. It never was. Of course, Paul is writing to gentiles who claim, in Christ, to be in surprising relationship to the God of Israel. It is such gentiles who do not have to follow Torah. As for him and his fellow Jews, we have no reason to think they must abandon the law. Michael Wyschogrod, a Jewish scholar who has learned a lot from and taught a lot to us Christians, argues that Christians had better be open to Jews practicing the law while being Christian.[12] If we think Judaism is incompatible with baptism, then Jews are in trouble. But if we are flexible enough to bless daughters and sons of Jacob as they practice Torah and confess that Jesus is Lord, Jews in general have less to fear.

What is the most important thing about Judaism? That God chooses a people through whom to bless and repair God's creation. The only God

12. See, for example, his remarkable "Letter to Cardinal Lustiger."

there is intervenes in history personally, to free slaves.[13] Then he forges them into a holy people, a priestly nation, for the rest of us. He sends prophet after prophet to insist on his people's and the whole world's holiness and mutual love. He gives scripture to suffuse our lives with story and poetry and law and apocalypse. Israel shows there is a God who chooses and will not unchoose, a God who creates and furiously loves creation, a God who wants us to recognize the dignity of all people and love them. "Do not oppress the sojourner and the foreigner in your midst," God commands. "Remember that you were a slave in the land of Egypt" (see Exod. 22:21; 23:9; Deut. 10:19; 15:15 and dozens more places like it). Every Egypt will be thrown down. And every enslaved people will be given their humanity back.

That's the light in which we should view the more conditional-sounding places in Israel's scripture. An example is Deuteronomy 28, written like an ancient treaty, detailing the benefits of obedience and the dangers of infidelity. Such places in scripture sound quite conditional: "If you will only obey . . ." and "If you will not obey . . ." (Deut. 28:1, 15). What we know of God's faithfulness despite human unfaithfulness shows how to read such passages that seem, on their face, to present the covenant as something more like a contract. As a Christian, I have New Testament promises with which to say that in Christ all God's promises are yes (2 Cor. 1:20). Israel is a sort of test case for Paul's claim. Is God's election of Israel irrevocable? Or is God's patience exhaustible? If the latter, we should all stop talking altogether. If the former (and Jews have their own resources with which to say that God's grace overrides human frailty), we must read passages like Deuteronomy 28 literally, obediently, and in some deeper manner than the letter itself.

Preachers: go and show us how to do this. Know that your prede-cessors have often failed, falling into anti-Judaism ("they failed, so God moved on") or moralism ("do good and God will bless you"). This book argues that neither heresy is acceptable. Instead, God is faithful. God's laws are a beautiful and graced way to live. Jesus submitted gladly to them. We submit gladly to Jesus, who is making all things new, including his own relationship to his fellow Jews. Don't disrespect that law, what-ever you do. We need its comfort, its shade, its delight.

---

13. I take this formulation from Rabbi Jonathan Sacks. See his "Philosophy or Prophecy? (Va'etchanan 5777)."

Learning from Mary

That's the gospel that Jesus learned on Mary's knee. The gospel that he *is*, nurtured in Israel's womb, born in the church. We Christians have often overstated the degree of the change in Jesus's teaching. Not a thing he says is without a footnote to Israel's scripture. Not a thing. I used to think "love your enemies" was, but even that is born in the command to love neighbor, to love the sojourner, to love even the oppressor in Babylon. When ancient Jacob finds himself carried by family and circumstance to Egypt, he lifts his aged hands and blesses old Pharaoh himself—the embodiment of evil in Israel's imagination (Gen. 47:7, 10). God is not flighty or capricious. Jesus is the God of creation and covenant fleshed. And he learned his gospel *somewhere*—Israel.

What's actually *new* is Jesus's life. His actions. His sacrifice of himself for Israel and the world. His dramatic reorganization of Israel's symbols and stories around himself. He chooses twelve disciples—he is reconstituting the twelve tribes. He sends out seventy disciples—a number that in Israel represents the whole world and echoes the seventy elders who help Moses in his work and who also receive the Holy Spirit and become prophets (Gen. 10—the rabbis have always counted seventy nations there). At his Last Supper, Jesus raises bread, blesses it, breaks it, gives it, and says to us it is his body. He does the same with a cup and declares it his blood. We Christians say this is communion, and without it we have no part in him (John 6:53). But where'd he get it? Israel. This is a Passover. And he is the lamb. Israel's story is entirely true, faithfully rendered, *and* it is entirely reworked here around Jesus. All its chief symbols are filled with the content of Christ. It might be wrong for us to do so. But it's not ridiculous. And it's not not-Jewish. It is Judaism redone. For gentiles. And, surprisingly, even for some Jews who come to believe in him. We can't rule that out, impolite as it may seem among modern religious types committed to interreligious dialogue (though in my experience gentiles seem as likely to convert to Judaism as anything). If you build bridges, some people walk over them. In both directions.

And this is where my Jewish students get most nervous. I spoke of Mary as the burning bush and showed an icon of her with her son in the fire before which Moses takes off his shoes. A student in the class has the name Mary. Her family was trying to hide her Jewish identity from the Nazis. It may have worked for her. It did not work for most of her family, who perished. Historians debate the influence of Christianity on the Nazis' Final Solution. Some Protestants with higher Christology resisted Hitler's claims to ultimate power (I just wish there had been more Bonhoeffers and Barths); Catholics of a traditionalist sort also had some resources with which to resist. But most Protestants, Catholics, and gentiles in general did not. What is undebatable is that many millions of baptized people willingly joined in with the murder of many millions of Jews. If there is a murderous flaw at the heart of Christian faith, I want no part of it. And if the logical outcome of Christianity is the gas chambers, then neither should anyone else want any part of it. Some Jews and others see Christianity as nothing other than this—millennia of pogroms ending with the greatest scar of a very greatly scarred century. And the loss of Mary's family. And much of Abraham's.

When I compared Mary (in the Bible) with the burning bush, Mary in the flesh in class responded with anger. You Christians can believe whatever you want, that's your business, she said. But don't take our symbols. Don't appropriate our stuff. That's *our* burning bush. The next step after taking our stories is taking our lives when we won't convert. Trust me, my family has experience with this.

I was struck by how different our experiences are. Folks speak of "Judeo-Christian" as if it's a thing. But this is one Jew and one Christian and one unavoidable accusation: what your people do is torture and kill my people. For me, the gospel is lifesaving. It introduced me to a God who loves infinitely, unreservedly, undeservedly, unendingly. It gave me life and meaning and something to live for and friends and confidence and a career and kids and daily worship and prayer. I preach that Jesus will give life to anyone who asks, and then to all creation one day. When I see that "every knee will bow" to his lordship, as Philippians 2:10–11 reads Isaiah 45:23, I am filled with joy. Mary is repulsed. And who could blame her?

My work is dedicated to showing Christians how to read Israel's scripture in light of Christ. Mary's query reminds me to ask, How is this not theft? That is, are we Christians up to our old trick of taking Jewish things and lives? Well, I said, my only access to your scripture, your God, is in Christ. He's the one by whom I can read this book, celebrate these stories, worship this God. I have no insight on how Israel ought to read its Bible. For gentiles grafted in Christ into Israel, we read scripture through the one by whom we are grafted in. In other words, I can't have the burning bush directly. But in Mary's boy, even I can listen there. And take off my shoes.

The other Mary didn't seem satisfied, but class was over. And really, she shouldn't be satisfied. Christians have developed such bad habits over millennia of thinking something is good, true, or beautiful precisely to the degree that it is *not* Jewish. Another time in the class I was explaining a fairly recondite Christian doctrine. And as I was doing so, I remembered that in the history of intra-Christian debate over this, each side accused the other of being too Jewish. Carnal. Literal-minded. I should've shut up just then. We Christians think things are true because they truly refer to God and God's world. Not because they're not-Jewish! Wyschogrod writes of Christianity and Judaism developing in "mutual recoil"—seeing the other's beliefs and practices and presuming that doing the opposite is faithful.[14] One Jewish student in the class pointed to the Passover tradition of holding up the matzah and saying, "This is the bread of affliction!" That is, this is *not* the body of Christ. Wyschogrod notices where Christians have emphasized parts of Israel's heritage and driven Jews to deemphasize them. But something is not true just because it is *not* Christian. It is true because it is true. And there we Jews and Christians have enormous overlap, similarity, which can make for contestation but can also make for friendship, mutual discovery, and joy.

That wasn't the end of my learning from Mary, thankfully. She had me over for tea one afternoon and fed me matzah. Passover was just completed and was now leftovers in the fridge. I'm glad to take the crumbs from Israel's table (Matt. 15:21–28). She told me of her family and showed me a picture—dozens of faces in stiff formal dress in a Polish photographer's studio three-quarters of a century ago. She is one of three who survived the Shoah. She did so because her parents spoke German without an accent, could pass themselves off as Catholics, left their village (where they could be identified), and scavenged for food until a Jewish relief organization could spirit them out of Soviet-dominated Poland (the second anti-Jewish empire to reign over her homeland in her childhood).

Mary didn't just have me over. She came to church. The whole class did (except for the aforementioned Orthodox rabbi, who could not for his aforementioned reason). And as she climbed into the pew beside me, I thought she was coming in for a hug. I realized only too late she was not—she was just sliding by. So I went from hugging back to trying to pretend I was not. She had noticed by then, however, and started the

14. See, for example, his "Jewish View of Christianity" and "Incarnation and God's Indwelling in Israel."

12

hug I originally thought she was initiating. We ended up slow-dancing in the pew for what felt like forever. She alleviated my awkwardness: "I'll hug you anytime," she said. There is more grace than we might expect.

But then awkwardness returned, in spades. It was Lent. The lector at our lovely evangelical church started to read the story of Jesus's trial from John 18:28–38 in which "the Jews" did this and that awful thing to Jesus. Medieval congregations heard these words and went out to stone Jews and set fire to synagogues. I listened and fumed. Afterward, in conversation with my pastor friends, Mary fumed. "That was very hurtful," she said, and she was right. Professor Duhan Kaplan and I had asked the church not to change anything that day for our class's visit, but now I wished the church leaders had. Some tried the standard apologetic responses: John is not denouncing the Jews for all time. Jesus himself is Jewish. His earliest followers all are too. True, all, and nearly irrelevant. This is where overlap is painful, contentious. But as ever, the Jews, pilloried in the New Testament text, spoke up and offered grace. Rabbi Laura pointed out that when the class attended synagogue, we heard a Torah portion in which the Jews, newly liberated from slavery, are given instructions on how to manage their slaves (Exod. 21:1–11). Awkward! What if folks listening thought Jews still approved of slavery? Another Jewish student pointed out that neither Jews nor Christians have any process by which to de-canonize a text: we call our respective canons "scripture" *because* they're altogether God's word and not open for editing by us or anyone else. He could not be more right. And it's true whoever is listening, however awkward that makes us feel.

One thing Christians simply must do is learn from actual Jewish friends, not just from Jews in history, Jews writing scripture, Jews as we imagine they "should" be. We can continue to pursue crumbs under the table of Israel (Mark 7:24–30). Since we hadn't gotten to worship together, I asked the Orthodox rabbi, Jay, if he would take me to synagogue. He was overjoyed, provided me with books, and asked if I had questions. He loves his faith and loves seeing others come to love it too. I found the familiar butterflies in the stomach that come whenever you attend another community's house of worship (and note: I do this for a living!). I found, bizarrely, that when I came into the synagogue I wanted to genuflect! I'm so much more practiced attending Catholic Mass that I instinctively took the butterflies as a sign of needing to do Catholic things. Thankfully, I thought better of it in time.

In synagogue I was struck by the differing assumptions operative than the ones with which I try to lead worship. As a pastor, I work to make everyone feel comfortable, to greet new people, to preach in a way that makes Christian beliefs as accessible as possible. The synagogue was plenty friendly, but not interested in boiling down their particularity so I could access it. They worshiped in the language and forms and songs of Israel. If I want to do the work to learn it, they have ways to make that accessible. But seeker-sensitive this was not (other synagogues would present themselves differently to new people, of course).

Yet it was also full of joy. A boy being bar mitzvahed was peppered with candy by his friends. What gives? Well, a son of the law should have a sweet life, Rabbi Jay said. And the shawl that symbolizes Torah should protect him from the sweet wiles of the evil one. He went on to say they have trouble knowing how to raise their children in love with their Judaism. "You don't say! Not us!" I joked. He laughed. Then we broke open a text together—Malachi 3–4—and I was struck by how many Christian things I saw patently on the page. The declaration that the Lord changes not (Mal. 3:6). The text beloved or loathed by every preacher facing a stewardship campaign, about the way God wants to overwhelm us with blessing if we would only bring in the tithe (Mal. 3:10). The prophetic passage that Christians refer to John the Baptist, which, in fact, is the reason we have Malachi last among our Old Testament books (Mal. 3:1–4). And the description "sun of righteousness," which Christians have long applied to Jesus (Mal. 4:2). Jay could tell I was staggered. "I just see Jesus everywhere. But I don't want to poach on your stuff." You're not, he reassured me. This isn't a zero-sum game. For me to believe a scripture is true doesn't require you to be interpreting it wrong. "It's just so odd, reading this, in this house." Well, we can fight if you want to, he joked. Indeed. Why should we? We can instead argue, in the most blessed, Judaism-inspired, scripturally based way possible. We can love the scriptures together. We can bless one another's houses of worship. We can garner scraps from under one another's table or even offer one another a seat of honor. And we can pray that God's messiah would come soon.

Abraham Joshua Heschel, the great Jewish intellect and soul who marched with Martin Luther King Jr., liked to say this to Christian audiences about the messiah: We all agree the messiah is coming. When he comes, we can ask if he's been here before. Pause for laughter. And then Rabbi Heschel plans to run up and whisper in the messiah's ear, "Please, for God's sake, don't answer." That sort of story did a great deal of work in an era when Jews and Christians just started to walk side by side, to march for justice. We have done that for a few generations. Now, I think, we can sit side by side in worship. Argue about God and scripture and everything else that matters. Dance awkwardly. Love one another by name and face. And ask big, nosy, open questions that leave us open to learning, vulnerable to being changed.

Israel's Scripture and Jesus

Here are a few more things we Christians *have* to do. *We have to read Israel's scripture.* Much of the Christian Church, especially Protestant churches, have left the Old Testament closed. We refer to the bits you can put in needlepoint, but we leave off Leviticus, many of the psalms, huge swaths of the prophets. We do this because we have lost confidence that we know how to read it. And the more inclusive we pride ourselves on being, the more sure we are that something horrible will be said there that we'd rather avoid. Isn't Leviticus against gay people? Isn't there a god of wrath and judgment in the Old Testament, best avoided with nice and gentle Jesus? How sad. This is the word of God. In this book God speaks to us, creates the worlds, summons a people, plans to bless the world. And we yawn, or recoil, and close the book. Christian theology traditionally was nothing other than the reading of the Old Testament with reference to Christ. We don't do that now so much because we fear it will be anti-Jewish. But we must read it. Not to is to let Marcion win. It is to cover our ears when God wishes to speak. It is to cut off the Jewish trunk into which we gentile branches are grafted. It is to lose everything.

And we Christians must read Israel's scripture *with reference to Jesus*. He's the one who calls us into relationship with God. He's the one in whose company we are becoming holy. He's the one who dies for us, rises for us, and promises to return to repair the universe. We are looking for him absolutely everywhere, because he is our Lover and we are desperate for more of him. We look without apology in nature, in one another's faces, in the recesses of our souls, in the enemy. How then can we not look for him in scripture? It's his book. Scripture is the mother, the matrix, in which Jesus is born. Without it he makes no sense. Without him we have no access to it. With him everything is illumined. And there is no end to his truth that can be found there and everywhere. Ancient Christians are rarely anxious about whether Israel's scripture is obscure, or even seemingly immoral. Those are signs God has left a surprise for us. We have to read more deeply—God is winking at us just there. Ancient Christians pile on interpretation after interpretation to respond to these "problems." Their desire is to delight us hearers—as God delights us in Christ, perhaps especially in places where we think God can't be at work, can't be delighting, can't can't can't. No, this is the God of the universe. He can take anything broken and make it beautiful. Watch. That's all God does in fact.

And we must read Israel's scripture with reference to Jesus *in the company of Jewish friends*. They show us how often our thoughts have been developed in recoil against Judaism. I told a friend and fellow pastor I'd been to synagogue, and his first response was "Was it really legalistic?" Actually, it was filled with joy and light. I wish I knew my own history and heritage and family like Jewish communities do. But we Christians have often acted like we needed Judaism as a sort of negative against which to build our positive. We do this because of Jesus. And Paul. Our earliest teachers are Jews who argue strenuously with their own people. What's a more Jewish thing to do than that?! And argument is frustrating. And they are often frustrated (take a peek at Matthew 23). But if we read those texts with Jewish friends, we'll read them differently. Because Judaism is meant to be for the repair of the world. Christians think we, the church, extend Israel's blessing to the world. How can we do that if we curse Israel from which we came? If, however, we talk with living Jews about the Bible, we will do a thing that Jesus and Paul constantly did. And we will find our theology more likely to be shorn of anti-Israel prejudice, unconsidered cursing, untruthful tropes, and lies. Not that it will be easy! I have no idea how to talk about Zionism, say, or about what Jesus's lordship means for forgiving enemies in the Middle East. But I don't have to in advance of friendship. It's good to do it over food too. Knowing the names of one another's kids. And loving one another.

Finally, we have to read our own scripture counter-literally at times. We have already seen this with Deuteronomy 28. Another simple example and then a hard one: In Acts 15 we see the first council of the church. Similar councils happened later to codify the Trinity, Christology, all the big stuff we believe. This first one had to decide whether gentiles claiming to come close to the God of Israel via Jesus had also to take up the yoke of the Torah. Wyschogrod points out that Jews who believed in Jesus must have still been obeying Torah.[15] Why else would anyone ask whether gentiles had to? The elders at the council decided that gentiles' salvation in Christ did not mean we had to obey the law. We simply have to avoid fornication, blood, strangled animals, and anything sacrificed to idols (Acts 15:28–29). Yet most Christians don't follow these laws. We have fixated on the fornication at the expense of the food laws perhaps precisely because the food laws lost out. Paul won. For him, an idol is nothing, and so food from sacrificed animals is perfectly reasonable, as long as it does not scandalize anyone's conscience (1 Cor. 8:1–13). I never think twice before eating a rare steak. So what do we do with this passage? It's still scripture, we have to honor it. To turn up the intensity further, we Christians believe a great number of things about blood. The blood of Christ saves us. How can we fail to respect the biblical teaching that the life of a creature is in the blood (Gen. 9:4; Acts 15:20)? We can take this admonition more seriously and watch whether that might help our conversation with Israel. Malcolm X tells of his brother writing him in prison, "Don't eat pork. I'll explain later." We Christians stand to learn a great deal from practicing first and reflecting later.

That was the easy one. Brace yourself. There is nothing good that we can do with Jesus telling some Jews "who believed in him" that they are from their "father the devil" (John 8:31, 44). Nothing. We have to read this counter to its letter. To do this is to honor and love Jesus, whose word is not dead, encased in amber in the pages of the Bible. It, or rather he, is a living Word, providentially guiding the cosmos, leading the church, currently bringing about repair of the whole world. That repair includes the repair of the church's long-vexed relationship with Israel. We do not worship the Bible. We worship Jesus, who shows us how to read the Bible. We read it with reference to him—and he commands us to love our enemies. There are texts that bubble over with love for Israel. And there are those in which God pulls his hair out with frustration over Israel and all people. We know this God. We have met his gracious face in Jesus. And we know that, as furious as he can get, mercy triumphs over judgment (James 2:13). Always. And if we say otherwise, it is not the gospel

15. Wyschogrod, *Abraham's Promise*, 232.

of Jesus we are preaching but that of some other god. There is only one true gospel, after all.[16]

The Bible is full of stories of elder and younger brothers. In most cultures the elder is preferred, given more inheritance, blessed. But in the Bible's stories the younger is, counterintuitively, blessed (see Gen. 25:19–28). In some ways more than the elder. God has this habit of choosing the lesser, contrary to all expectation, to show God's glory. The church has often seen itself as the younger, supplanting the elder, like Jacob over Esau. You can see this in the prodigal son story in Luke 15: the elder brother is Israel; the younger is the church. In so seeing ourselves, the church has grown unimaginably big and powerful. Now we are sliding out of that power, at least in the European and colonial West. This allows us to wrestle anew with our elder sisters and brothers in faith, Israel. There is only one God. He has only one covenant. Who is the rightful heir of that covenant? Israel, we say. And, astonishingly, by grace, we who wrestle with God in Christ think we're also part of this covenant with this God. We will work hard for the blessing of our elder sibling. And through him for the whole world.

For Further Study

Frymer-Kensky, Tikva, David Novak, Peter Ochs, David Fox Sandmel, and Michael A. Signer, eds. *Christianity in Jewish Terms*. New York: Basic Books, 2002.

Jewish theologians take on, engage, appraise, and critique traditional Christian doctrines, with responses by Christian theologians. This is the sort of mutual learning that is made possible when we push past polite avoidance.

---

16. Christopher Blumhofer's recent dissertation, *The Gospel of John and the Future of Israel*, has helped me here a great deal. He argues that the *Ioudaioi* in John are a rival group of Jews to those addressed in John's Gospel, and neither group ought to be equated with Judaism as such—both are wrestling for the mantle of continuity with Abraham. Further, the *Ioudaioi* who had believed in Jesus (John 8:31, 44) may have once *begun* to believe in Jesus without reorienting their life and practice of Judaism around him, as the writer of John demands (Blumhofer, 77, 262–66). To plot murder is to show that one's father is not Abraham at all but is instead the devil. The implication is clear: when Christians twist this text into a violent claim against Jewishness as such, we too show that our father is not God or Abraham at all.

Goldberg, Michael. *Jews and Christians: Getting Our Stories Straight; The Exodus and the Passion-Resurrection*. Eugene: Wipf & Stock, 2001.

Often we race past the most obvious resource for Jewish-Christian dialogue: the Bible. This book simply reads the scriptures, Israel's first and then the New Testament, and shows how each tries to bear witness to the God who makes and keeps covenant.

Wyschogrod, Michael. *Abraham's Promise: Judaism and Jewish-Christian Relations*. Edited by R. Kendall Soulen. Grand Rapids: Eerdmans, 2004.

For a Christian reader exploring the overlap between Judaism and Christianity, these essays are positively electric.

2

Origen

Blush While You Read

Ponder with me, gentle reader, the peculiar artifact of the Gideon's Bible. These tiny little scriptures, passed out by well-meaning men in suits on college campuses, inserted unasked into hotel rooms, often have only a New Testament. Some also have the Psalms tacked on. It is as if the Gideons realized, Wait, if we give them the whole Bible, they'll read the first part first, but the first part isn't best. Let's give them the best. They can meet Jesus, and then go back and read the first. For an analogous experience, try sitting down and reading the Qur'an from the beginning. You won't make it far.

Yet Israel's scripture is the bulk of Christianity's scripture, more than two-thirds of them. We had ancient church councils rule that you can't excise that first part or else the second is meaningless. Who cares if the God of Israel has acted anew if we don't know who the God of Israel is? A teacher of mine says we really only have one holy book—the Bible of the Jews. And we Christians have an appendix, called the New Testament, that shows us how to read it.

Origen will show you what I mean.

In most of this book we will be looking at companions who bear the proud moniker "St." by their names. This is a sign that the church has judged them not only worthy intellectuals but holy people whose lives we should imitate. Protestant churches changed the rules on this a bit, preferring, with St. Paul, to call everyone in the church "saint," and then expecting us all to act like it. The jury is still out on whether that decision was wise.

One man with whom we will read the scriptures in this book was a candidate for those letters before his name, yet no one now refers to him as "St. Origen." In fact, the way the church has treated the memory of Origen of Alexandria (ca. 185–250 CE) would lead us to think he should be called "the cursed Origen" rather than "the blessed." As a brilliant young teacher in Alexandria, he provoked the jealousy of his bishop, so he left Egypt (and referred ever after, in biblical parlance, to his deliverance from Egypt) and settled in Palestine. He taught the scriptures so extensively and so well that his bishop there ordained him. Yet his bishop back in Egypt raged that this ordination was irregular, and indeed he was right. Catholic missals today—that is, books that direct communal prayer—aren't even sure whether to call Origen a priest or not.

Not long after his lifetime Origen's works were attacked by others in the church: he is not sufficiently clear that the Son and the Spirit are divine, he disparages the letter of scripture, he seems to think human souls preexist our bodily lives, and he holds out hope that even the devil will be saved. Most troubling of all: he seems to have castrated himself in response to Jesus's odd words that some are eunuchs for the kingdom of heaven (Matt. 19:12). (The inevitable joke: for someone who taught us to take so much scripture allegorically, why did he choose *that* one to take literally?) In the sixth century a church council condemned Origen and his followers, and the emperor did his best to see that all extant copies of Origen's works were burned.

To a degree, in this chapter we read with a heretic.

But only to a degree. The council that condemned him in 553 CE had a poor grasp of his actual thought and was not particularly well-heeded in the west, which continued to hold Origen in high regard. Further, it's not fair to condemn someone for heresy who cannot defend himself. Technically, a heretic is not someone with wrong ideas in his or her head. That would make us all heretics—who can comprehend God or the world fully? A heretic is a church leader who teaches incorrect doctrine, is corrected by the broader church, and continues to do it anyway. That is, heresy is a sin of pride. A heretic claims to know better than the communal wisdom of the church and will not submit to the good of the whole. Origen never had the chance to heed the wisdom of the whole. Modern critics of faith tend to think of ancient Christians as heresy-obsessed, and there is some truth in that. But Augustine, no friend to heretics, actually thanks God for them. Without wrong teaching, how would we learn what is right? Heresies show us what doesn't work. Some of what Origen taught doesn't work. Vastly more does. On some matters, including the nature of God and the interpretation of scripture, we may not yet have caught up with his brilliance.

For example, the church gathered at Jerusalem for worship around the year 240.[1] Ordinarily bishops in the ancient Christian church did not pass the responsibility of preaching to mere priests. But this time the presiding bishop did pass the buck. You would too if Origen were present and available to preach. And a chapter of 1 Samuel just read included the astonishingly strange story of Saul's consultation of the recently deceased Samuel with the help of a medium at Endor. Origen needn't have asked which passage from the four chapters the bishop wanted to hear exposited, but he did. "The one about the necromancer," he was told.[2]

Now, the nice thing about having a low doctrine of scripture is that you don't tend to lose sleep over passages you can't square. The higher your doctrine of scripture, the more explaining you have to do in places like 1 Samuel 28. Origen saw this clearly. While trying to buy time to think of what to say, he held forth on biblical hermeneutics first: "Is it true or not? To say that it is not true encourages faithlessness, and it will come back to haunt [!] those who said so, but if it is true, it is a problem that requires investigation." No kidding. The obvious question that follows: Is holy writ itself suggesting that however forbidden the pagan practice of consultation with the dead may be, *it actually works?*

Origen figures out a way that a text about a medium summoning the spirit of Samuel can actually be about Jesus. The question for interpreters of his day was whether the witch of Endor summoned a demon pretending to be Samuel, or Samuel himself. And if the latter, what on earth was the prophet doing in hell? The answer: he was doing what prophets do, which is to make ready the way of the Lord. Samuel was in hell "to announce my Lord in advance." What could be scandalous about the prophet going where Christ would not disdain to go? And how could Christ not empty himself to the bottommost level of God's creation to restore all things to God? Origen concludes, "Let physicians go to the places where soldiers suffer and enter the place of their stench and wounds; this is what medical benevolence inspires. So the Word has inspired the Savior and the prophets to come here and to descend into hell."[3]

Origen shows here the right sort of freedom and boundedness. Bound by the gospel of Jesus, he is free to interpret the very oddest of

---

1. These next paragraphs draw on my piece "If Death Is No Barrier."
2. Homily 5 on 1 Samuel, in Trigg, *Origen*, 199–210.
3. Trigg, *Origen*, 205, 207.

passages in ways that edify the church. Not that it always turned out well for him personally, or for his legacy.

God's Kind Speech

Origen's story demonstrates an adage I've heard many a Christian recount: the church is the only army that shoots its own wounded. This is a man without whose thought it is impossible to imagine the shape of Christian theology for the next two millennia. He died after torture under the persecution of Decius. He coined the description that the Son is "eternally begotten" of the Father. This creedal language seems natural, yet it solves a deep problem in biblical interpretation on the nature of God. How can Jesus be both divine (hard enough in itself!) and "less" than his Father (John 14:28)? Origen spoke of the Son as indeed begotten of the Father, as the Bible told him he must. Yet he made the genius speculative innovation to say that that generation is eternal. From before all time the Father begets the Son. One comes from the other, but not in time—eternally, always present tense. Genius! Unfortunately, Origen couldn't check with postbiblical tradition in quite the way we can, and he continued to speak of the Son as less divine than the Father in ways that later heretics would find congenial. The orthodox later felt they had to condemn this near martyr-theologian without whose teaching there would be no orthodoxy. As Henri de Lubac, Origen's greatest twentieth-century interpreter, put it, those who condemned his work in 553 "have served the enemies of Christian civilization well."[4]

So, too, in biblical interpretation. In his great work, *On First Principles*, Origen explains his approach to scripture: "We must explain to those who believe that the sacred books are not the works of men, but that they were composed and have come down to us as a result of the inspiration of the Holy Spirit by the will of the Father of the universe through Jesus Christ, what are the methods of interpretation that appear right to us, who keep to the rule of the heavenly Church of Jesus Christ through the succession of the apostles." That's it: the only task that matters for the theologian and Bible scholar. If we believe this book

---

4. Introduction to *Origen: On First Principles*, viii. A major effort to reappropriate Origen's work for biblical interpretation is Greg Boyd's recent two-volume work, *Crucifixion of the Warrior God*, with which we will deal in chap. 8.

is authored by God, who is saving us in Christ, and we adhere to the creed, how do we make sense of these words on the page before us? Many answers were on the table before Origen. For some, the words on the page were plainly abhorrent, and many of them, especially in the Old Testament, should be rejected. How can we think of God having physical parts and changing? Of light and dark being created before there are day and night? Of illicit sexual liaisons between the very people whose faith we are supposed to imitate? For another group, the text should be taken literally. What's to stop someone from departing from the letter altogether, claiming "allegory" as a justification to make the text say whatever *you* want it to say? Critics of Origen's from the ancient church to now find allegory to be a sort of sleight of hand, a trick for reading, a lie, a denial of the historical narrative.

Origen had a pair of opponents with regard to their approach to the Old Testament. One was made up of "gnostics," Christians who believed that the Old Testament represents a second, lesser deity. They rejected this inferior god and urged other Christians to do the same. The other antagonists Origen refuted were the Jews. He had more respect for them as readers of the Bible whom he could cite approvingly on many important matters, but he balked at what he called their "literalism"—that is, their objection that Jesus had not fulfilled the messiah's role according to the letter.[5]

Origen split the difference between these options. For him, you must read the Old Testament. And you must read it with reference to Jesus Christ.

He was not a pure trailblazer in this way of reading: St. Irenaeus of Lyon before him had argued convincingly that the saving work of Jesus Christ in our flesh and the Old Testament scriptures that point forward to his coming are a package deal. You cannot throw out "the archives," or Judaism, or the flesh of Jesus, without throwing out our salvation itself. As he interpreted the Old Testament, Irenaeus mostly leaned on passages already familiar to and beloved of Christians, especially those quoted in the New Testament: bits of Genesis, Exodus, and Deuteronomy, certain psalms, the latter parts of Isaiah, and Zechariah. Irenaeus taught that there is an *economy* to how God speaks. God speaks in a way appropriate for the age we are. We understand this for children—you

---

5. Martens describes Origen's engagement with gnostics and Jews in *Origen and Scripture*, chaps. 6 and 7 (107–60).

don't speak to an infant the same way you do to a preteen or to a sullen and underemployed adult moved back into the basement. For Irenaeus, God accommodates himself perfectly to our spiritual state. God speaks to Israel in an appropriate way, and then to church in an appropriate way. The differences in scripture aren't a sign of divine clumsiness. They're a sign of divine kindness.

Origen takes this wise and tender observation a step farther. He takes the way of reading scripture in the New Testament and expands it to all parts of the Old Testament. And he reads them all with reference to Jesus Christ—that is, allegorically. In so doing, Origen saved the Old Testament for Christian interpretation.[6] Over against efforts both ancient (gnosticism) and modern (a sense that we have progressed past it) to jettison the Old Testament from the canon, Origen showed how the church has to be a people committed to searching out its every line and adoring the Old Testament like the body of our Savior.[7] He showed how the entire testament participates in God's saving work among us and so should be read as a witness, revealing more of who God is. And yet he is remembered as a heretic.

The striking thing about Origen's mixed reputation is just how influential he is. For a millennium and a half in the church, almost no one read Christian scripture without his influence. Origen's checkered reputation was somewhat restored in the twentieth century. Historians and theologians have looked again, and often now stand in awe. This can be traced almost entirely to the man I mentioned before, the French Jesuit Henri de Lubac, and four simple words he uttered in a crucial directive: "Watch Origen at work." Whatever you have heard about Origen's speculative theology or his slipshod hermeneutics, lay that aside for a minute. Watch him read the Bible. And see if you don't fall in love with him.

---

6. I lean here on Joseph T. Lienhard's description in "Origen and the Crisis of the Old Testament in the Early Church." See also Joseph Trigg's long introductory essay in *Origen*, 3–66. A very helpful recent description of Origen's approach to the Bible is Martens, *Origen and Scripture*. An older but still useful study is Karen Jo Torjesen's *Hermeneutical Procedure and Theological Structure in Origen's Exegesis*.

7. Ellen Davis speaks in moving terms of the loss of the Old Testament as the loss of a friend. The fact that such a description feels more moving than to say such a loss is a threat to our salvation speaks to the diminished state of our God-talk. See "Losing a Friend."

Watch Origen at Work

One mistaken way we speak of scripture is to speak as though we can come to the text fresh. We don't. Ever. And this is good news. Long before we get to a text, the Bible has already interpreted it, or shown us how to. As Origen says, "The right way . . . of approaching the scriptures and gathering their meaning . . . is extracted from the writings themselves." Scripture interprets scripture. While it is not intuitive for us that Isaiah would throw light on Matthew, it is for Origen. For example, he quotes Solomon about how to read the Bible: "We find some such rule as this laid down by Solomon in the proverbs concerning the divine doctrines written therein: 'Do thou portray them threefold in counsel and knowledge, that thou mayest answer words of truth to those who question thee.'" Scripture, like a human being, has a body, a soul, and a spirit. The "flesh of scripture" is "the obvious interpretation," while a reader who has made "some progress may be edified by its soul," and "the [person] who is perfect" has access to the spirit of the text, in a manner described by Paul in 1 Corinthians 2:6–7: "We speak wisdom among the perfect . . . God's wisdom in a mystery, even the wisdom that hath been hidden."[8] Much of scripture is plain and clear and can be followed by the simplest believer. Much more is obscure, difficult, and requires perfection in the soul of the reader before it can be read at all.

It leaves you asking—just who is this perfect reader? For Origen, it is a saint. The Bible is *there* to cure souls; its best readers are those who are fully suffused with love of God and neighbor. Reading is not about intellectual information. It is about growing into the radiance of love.[9] Later, Athanasius would agree with Origen: if you want to know the mind of the saints, you have to live the lives of the saints. Scripture is trying to make us holy.

---

8. *Origen: On First Principles*, 275 (§4.2). Interestingly, the NRSV translation of Prov. 22:20 asks, "Have I not written for you thirty sayings of admonition and knowledge?" Later medieval interpreters vastly multiplied the number of possible readings of scripture. For Jewish midrash, my colleague Laura Duhan Kaplan says that every passage has seventy interpretations. Seventy! A number that represents the whole world, based on the seventy nations described in Gen. 10–11.

Throughout this section I cite G. W. Butterworth's translation. I wish I had had the benefit of John Behr's magisterial new translation of *On First Principles*, but it appeared after this book was completed.

9. This is the thesis of Martens's book, *Origen and Scripture*, with its subtitle *The Contours of the Exegetical Life*. See especially chaps. 8–9 (161–226).

To the end of making us holy, scripture is a variegated landscape. Much of it is made for simple walking. Much more is territory into which you do not descend without grappling hooks and pulleys and experienced climbers alongside to help. Scripture's landscape demands progress from us. A proper assessment of an incorrect reading of scripture is that the reader has not yet progressed in holiness enough to read that text. Yet Origen is not asking anything of any interpreter through which he has not passed himself, and through which he does not think all Christians should pass: "One must portray the meaning of the sacred writings in a threefold way *upon one's own soul.*" Modern, technique-based ways of reading have their place, but reading scripture is not complete until the church loves God and neighbor more.

For Origen, the Holy Spirit's purpose in authoring scripture and enlightening those who read it is that they should come to know God and to be like God. "The aim of the Spirit" is that the reader should "become a sharer of the Spirit's knowledge and a partaker of his divine counsel." The goal is not just information or even knowledge but participation in God's very own self-knowledge, sharing in God's very nature. Yet the Spirit also has a second aim with scripture: *to conceal meaning* (sound like a certain Galilean rabbi?). Those who are unable to seek out the deep things of God ought not to be led to think they can.[10] So the Spirit imposes "stumbling-blocks," "hindrances and impossibilities" into the law and history. God himself, in other words, sticks out a leg to trip us when reading, with historical stories that "did not happen, occasionally something which could not happen, and occasionally something which might have happened but in fact did not."[11] Who could possibly think God couldn't find Adam and Eve (Gen. 3:9)? Origen asserts that the gospels are full of "thousands" of passages with such historical absurdities as claiming the devil could take Jesus to a place where he could see all the kingdoms of the world with his bodily eyes.[12] By the time Origen reassures us that "the passages which are historically true are far more numerous than those which are composed with purely spiritual meanings," it is almost too late for us to believe him.[13]

10. *Origen: On First Principles*, 284.
11. *Origen: On First Principles*, 286.
12. Martens points out Origen is here dueling with gnostics who think the New Testament superior to the Old: no, he says, the two testaments, read incorrectly, are equally morally treacherous.
13. *Origen: On First Principles*, 295.

Origen might seem a friend here of modern liberal interpreters who insist that nothing be taken "literally." But he will soon be a challenge to them too: he reads Jesus and Paul as literally as he can—they show him how to read the rest of scripture figurally. Origen thinks he is just reading scripture the way scripture reads scripture. St. Paul, St. John, St. Peter, and others are right in *how* they read the earlier portions of the Bible. As Origen puts it, "Paul . . . understood what Moses wrote much better than we do."[14] When St. Paul reads "Jerusalem" as a reference to "our mother above" (Gal. 4:26), or when the author of Hebrews sees Mount Zion as the "city of the living God" (12:22–23), Origen sees a pattern for how to read, not idiosyncratic and unfortunate hermeneutics to be avoided.[15]

De Lubac describes Origen's understanding of reading and its intertwining with the Christian life this way: there are two advents of the Logos in our lives. In the first we come to see the external truth about Christ, and that's good but not enough. The second advent corresponds to Christ's coming advent in consummation of his saving work in the world. To someone who reaches the first perfection, Christ "appears transfigured in his beauty and his glory." Then we no longer reject the deepest mysteries of the faith, from the incarnation to the cross, and we no longer accept them superficially. We come to fathom them, to steep in them, and have them seep into us, to understand them in the deepest sense, and at the same time, to love and adore them. The soul's faith then "becomes luminous."[16] As we progress to such a place, we become able, as Rowan Williams puts it, "to make plain the hidden harmonies" of God's work in scripture, in history, in our own souls, and in all the world.[17] Reading scripture is as difficult as becoming a Christian. It requires a drowning and a resurrection. Or to shift to another of Origen's favorite images: there are low rungs on the ladder, which some of us need all the time and some of us need only at first. We all must hope that some among our number can progress to a place of holiness from which to be able to explain to us the more profound truth of our faith—to drag us up the ladder with them.

14. Origen, *Song of Songs*, 25.

15. *Origen: On First Principles*, 300 (§4.3). Richard Hays has provided the biblical scholarship necessary to see the integrity of learning from the Bible how to read the Bible; see most recently his *Echoes of Scripture in the Gospels*. Hays would have voluminous disagreements with Origen on particulars, of course.

16. De Lubac, *Medieval Exegesis*, 2:xxi.

17. Williams, *Christ on Trial*, 30.

We are far past liberals' suggestion that we take scripture "seriously but not literally," or conservatives' that it all has to be one-dimensionally true, like a newspaper or science book. Here Christ's word has to become true *in us*. Origen's acts of interpretation show that to be open to the words of scripture is to have one's own soul laid bare, operated on, and returned to wholeness. No wonder liberals, conservatives, ancients, and moderns alike are uncomfortable with Origen. He points out that Christ is wielding a scalpel. And we're the ones under the knife.[18]

There is much to treasure about modern historical-critical ways of reading the Bible. Origen would have loved just a semester in any of our academies. But then, after we have established the language, the pre-history, the competing influences behind a text, we have to *read* it. Interpret it. And we have to read it as those with whom God is in love. For example, *The New Interpreter's Study Bible* comments on the beginning of the Song of Songs this way: "The woman yearns for her lover." Thanks! I couldn't see that as she cries, "Let him kiss me with the kisses of his mouth!" (1:2). Even better, the note says the superscription—"The Song of Songs, which is Solomon's" (1:1)—is "doubtless a later addition to the poetry."[19] The modern obsession with historical layering knows no ends. Here in the jewel in the crown of all the Bible—that the Logos wants to marry us, the bride *demands* that the bridegroom kiss her—the interpreter wants to talk about text transmission. Origen writes this: "Let it be the Church who longs for union with Christ." More erotically still, he paraphrases, may he "now no longer speak to me only by His servants the angels and the prophets, but may [he] come Himself, directly, and kiss me with the kisses of His mouth—that is to say, may [he] pour the words of His mouth into mine, that I may hear Him speak Himself, and see Him teaching."[20] If you

18. St. Augustine often describes salvation in medical terms, with Christ as the physician, us as the patient. One has to remember this is an ancient medical image: no anesthesia—you only ask to be cut open or to have something extracted when the pain is worse than the scalpel. But don't worry, it's Jesus cutting.

19. Roland Murphy, "Song of Songs," in *New Interpreter's Study Bible*, 945. Murphy, author of the notes on the Song, was himself a great practitioner of spiritual as well as critical exegesis. He writes in an excursus on the history of interpretation of the Song that "traditional interpretation, stripped of its extravagant allegorical details, can be defended as a valid surplus or supplementary interpretation" (953). This is like saying that a passionate romance, shorn of its extremes, is an acceptable manner of propagating the species. No word yet on whether modern critical scholars are willing to strip their work of its extravagant habits of historicist skeptical inquisition.

20. Origen, *Song of Songs*, 59–60.

can read the Song of Songs without blushing a little, you're doing it wrong, and Origen wants us to do more than blush.

In the Song of Songs, we see there is always "more" to be learned about Jesus. We are like a lover who only belatedly comes to realize there are parts of our beloved's body that we have not yet adored. Our beloved's face is beautiful and worthy of gazing upon eternally, but look here, there are other limbs we have not even begun to explore yet! As his contemporary and sometime critic St. Jerome said, "While Origen surpassed all writers in his other books, in his *Song of Songs* he surpassed himself."[21]

What Intimacy Is For

In the prologue to the Song commentary, Origen describes not only what this book of the Bible is for and what his commentary is for; he also describes the nature of God, humanity, and the love meant to bind them. And he gives a brief account of love, working from John's Gospel and Letters, that rivals anything we have in the Christian tradition. Wherever scripture speaks of any sort of love, we ought to think of charity,[22] for that is what God *is* (1 John 4:8). Charity is also *of* or *from* God (1 John 4:7), and since the Son is also from God (John 16:28), the Father and the Son are both charity: "It follows, therefore, that the Father and the Son are one and the same in every respect." This riff on the theme of love by way of John's Gospel and Letters is not just about the Trinity; it is also about us: "Because God is Charity, and the Son likewise, who is of God, is Charity, *He requires in us something like Himself*; so that through this charity which is in Christ Jesus, we may be allied to God who is Charity."[23] The Charity who knits Christians together into one body also loves all peo-

21. Origen, *Song of Songs*, 265. This volume includes the fragment we have of Origen's commentary and also two homilies on the Song translated by Jerome and preserved in Latin. This line comes from Jerome's prologue to those two homilies.

22. "Charity" is an older English translation of love that can cause confusion now: it doesn't mean only the narrow task that Christians understand as almsgiving to the poor, but love in every sense, the love that God *is*, in which we take part. The Latin *caritas* was often a translation of the Greek *agapē*, so it worked for Latin-aware English readers for centuries. The problems with our word *love* are so bad that perhaps we should use *charity* again.

23. Origen, *Song of Songs*, 32. Hereafter, page references from this work will be given in parentheses in the text.

ple as neighbors. Salvation, and indeed all of human life, is a matter of turning that passionate love toward God and neighbor.

What we are is lovers: those who have had the capacity for passion implanted in our souls as a gift from our good Creator. This is not a generic love, just as a woman looks for not just any old man to be intimate with (scripture has harsh words for such an indiscriminate lover). Origen and the church look for our specific lover: the triune God, fleshed in Jesus, poured in our hearts by the Spirit. With an eye trained for finding this God, an ear tuned to his voice, we learn to find him again and again. Every beloved loves her lover in his specificity—his face, his hands, his voice—and love leads her to "act in all respects and regulate her every movement in a manner designed to please the man she loves" (37).[24] Origen notes this love can be diverted, to avaricious ends or vainglorious ones, or to manual crafts or branches of learning, or, he helpfully adds, to "the art of wrestling . . . and track running" (36). But the "only laudable love is that which is directed to God and to the powers of the soul." That is what God, the Word, seeks to do with us through this biblical text.

It is very, very hard to direct love. I mean, have you ever tried to love someone you don't? So the Word goes to dramatic, kenotic, self-abasing extremes to bring about this right response of love from us: after an apology for why the Word is described biblically as a lamb, a vine, bread, and now in the Song an apple tree, Origen explains, "The Word of God becomes all these things to each and every one according as the capacity or the desire of the participant requires" (198). He charges after us, leaping the mountains, skipping over the hills (the prophets) to meet us. The result for us will be passion, desire, often unrequited, but occasionally satisfied on the way to ever greater satisfaction. We will, at times, be embraced by his right hand, his divine economy before he took flesh, and his left hand, his work through the incarnation (Song 2:6). At other times, we will be wounded with memory of a love beautiful and fair, remembered but now absent, leaving us pierced with "a certain dart and wound of love" (29). Origen continues, "If a man can so extend his thinking as to ponder and consider the beauty and the grace of all the things that have been created in the Word, the very charm of them will so smite him, the grandeur of their brightness will so pierce him

24. Origen often runs afoul of our norms for speaking of gender, difference, and love. I have found it cumbersome to try to update him, so I leave his language as it is in the translation.

as with *a chosen dart*—as says the prophet—that he will suffer from the dart Himself a saving wound, and will be kindled with the blessed fire of His love" (29–30). This last quote points to one of the most unnoticed aspects of allegory: it depends on a robust doctrine of creation. The only way that apple trees, lilies, marriage and sex, gender and procreation, or even Bibles or language can reveal to us so much about the nature of God is that they're good gifts that bear the imprint of their divine Maker. Origen himself stops to explain this sacramental vision of all knowledge via the created order this way: we "cannot receive the naked and plain wisdom of God, but [we] behold the invisible and the incorporeal by means of certain analogies and tokens and images of visible things" (234).

I was once in a conversation about the Italian film *A Great Beauty* with a proudly secular crowd at a Canadian university. One participant pointed out that the protagonist fails to find the beauty he seeks precisely because he is rootless. "If he were rooted somewhere, he could reach for transcendence again," she said, making an argument more Christian than she knew. That's precisely it. Roots and transcendence go together. Deracinated, we cannot reach. Planted in the soil of Israel, we stretch upward toward God. And we will find that he has already stretched downward far lower than us, in love.

Training to Read and Be Read

Origen sees that our senses have to be trained in order to delight aright and love God properly. The physical senses by which we experience the world are, for him, a metaphor for the spiritual apprehension by which we come to experience God. So the sensual, almost luxurious nature of the Song is perfect for him—it teaches us to look, listen, smell, feel, and even taste the incarnate Word. Song 1:3, "Thy name is as ointment emptied out," leads Origen to think of the way the Savior's name is now spread abroad throughout the world through the church's ministry, and of Paul's olfactive comparison, that "we are the good odour of Christ" (2 Cor. 2:14–16).[25] The chorus of maidens praising the Bridegroom will smell "the pleasantness of His sweetness" and will "hasten to the odour of His sweetness, not at a slow pace" (76). The entire Song of Songs commentary is a matter of attuning our senses to the Word made flesh. The

25. Translations of scripture in this discussion are from Origen, *Song of Songs*.

Word gathers up the sensual way we engage with the world and habituates us to see him there: our "senses are acquired by training, and are said to be trained when they examine the meaning of things with more acute perception" (79). For Origen, a good way to understand any impenetrable biblical text is to pray more deeply, to love someone you'd rather not. Only one who has advanced far enough can see Christ and be changed in these words. Such a one has their senses attuned aright in recognition that Jesus "leaves none of the soul's faculties empty of His grace" (162).

But it is not enough just to perceive God through the incarnation, rapturous as that clearly is. We must also be transformed through so perceiving. One reason we misunderstand allegory is that we moderns think that reading is a matter of garnering information. For ancient Christians, reading *scripture* is a matter of being changed from one degree of glory to another, of being transformed (2 Cor. 3:18). Origen wants us to behold God throughout scripture and creation, and then he wants us changed into the holiness that God is, in order to be embraced by the incarnate Word. Another way of putting it is that we moderns ask whether knowledge is true of events "out there," on the page, in history, in the manuscript tradition, in other languages. Origen cares passionately about those questions too. They're necessary, but not sufficient. The subsequent question we moderns rarely ask is whether the words of scripture are true "in here." Have they done the spiritual work on us that God means them to do? As Origen insists in one of his homilies on the Song, with reference to the maidens and groomsmen: "You must not look without for the meaning of these; you must look no further than those who are saved by the preaching of the gospel" (267).

Origen then finds patterns of holy progress throughout the Song. In one elaborate reading, he describes the Song of Songs as the seventh song in Israel's scripture. For us to sing this marriage song, we first have to sing the songs of Moses and Miriam in Exodus 15, liberated from bondage in Egypt with our sins dead by the seashore. We must then sing Numbers 21, where princes and kings dig a well in search of living water. Next, we sing Deuteronomy 32, teaching the law to our children, singing that even the heavens might hear. Then Judges 5, a song of victory and deliverance. Next, a song from the book of Kings about the enemies David vanquishes. Then, a song from the book of Chronicles that calls on all the earth to sing praise to God's name. Finally, now, we can sing the Song of Songs. Origen marvels: "See with what stately steps the Bride, as she makes her entrance, attains by way of all these to the nuptial chamber of the Bridegroom"

(47–50). To read like Origen is to constantly look for such "stately steps" in scripture. The point is less to say that step six must follow step five, as though Chronicles can only be mastered after Kings. It is more to say that the spiritual life requires progress, order, and that God's Spirit makes that progress through scripture possible, with ever more stately steps.

Our wedding day is coming. We desire the spotless beauty the Bridegroom desires of us.

Christological Literalism at Work

It is important to gain a sense of, a feel for, how christological interpretation of the scriptures works out at length. All interpreters cherry-pick their subjects' best lines—but how does this way of reading wear over time? I encourage readers to consult the suggestions for further study below. For now, I would like to linger a bit on Origen's interpretation of the Song of Songs, which laid the groundwork for passionate unveiling of the christological import of the Song for more than a millennium. We will look at a series of verses that Origen interprets, beginning with these two:

> For thy breasts are better than wine. (Song 1:2b)
> The vineyards have yielded their sweet smell. (Song 2:13)

Origen speaks often of texts having three levels, on analogy to a human being with a body, a soul, and a spirit, or, more charmingly, to an almond with a shell, a rind, and a nutritious interior.[26] Scholars still debate the way he treats these three levels and whether the first two are left behind. I think they often are, in ways the church would need to correct later. The body, the exterior, is part of God's good creation and so is full of beauty. Breasts and wine, vineyards and sweet smells are good things. Yet Origen shows us how to do something we have forgotten as we have insisted on the value of the letter and the body—he invites us to push deeper. Yes, these are good. And they also refer to even deeper goods.

In these verses of the Song, the bride has been praying and seeking the kisses of the bridegroom's mouth, and suddenly, "even as she began to utter those words, the Bridegroom was present and standing by her

---

26. Martens, *Origen and Scripture*, 199.

as she prayed, and . . . He revealed his breasts to her . . . and even as she spoke He offered her the thing for which she asked" (63). In this instance, the revelation of Jesus's breasts is an image for prayer: seek and ye shall find, as long as what ye ask for is the breast of Jesus. As a Baptist minister from my home state is purported to have said: God gives us what we want, after God changes our "wanter" around. God plants desire in us to meet it, surpass it, deepen it, delight us in it. But only when we desire the one thing worthy of human desire: God. Who is no thing at all.

This is all a literal approach to the biblical text, mind you.

Next, Origen reads ecclesiologically. He may call this approach doctrinal or mystical, but more accurately he reads with reference to the church, or the economy of salvation. This can be seen more clearly by contrast with his third approach: a reading with regard to the individual soul. Origen reads at the second and communal level quite briefly, as here he finds reference to a perfect soul like a Nazirite, who will drink no more wine. That second reading takes a paragraph; the third and individual level takes seven pages in English translation.

First Origen stops and considers all the ways both breasts and wine are used in the scriptures. The breast is where the heart is, biblically speaking. And the pure of heart see God (Matt. 5:8), and with our heart we believe and are saved (Rom. 10:10). More evocatively still, it is on the heart of Jesus that the beloved disciple rests, reclines, seeking there "the treasures of wisdom and knowledge" hidden in the bosom of Jesus (John 13:23; Col. 2:3). The breast and shoulder are the portions set aside for the priests in Leviticus.[27] By saying *these* breasts are better than wine, the church is saying that the new teaching that comes from Jesus's breast is better even than the marvelous teaching that gladdened God's people's hearts before his coming. Notice how much richer this image is than most Old Testament/New Testament contrasts, especially in the ancient church: the teaching we had before was delightful, drunk-making wine; that which we have now is, unfathomably, even better. As we drink from the Savior's breast, we find him "mingling the new things that flow from His own breasts with the wine of the ancients," as when Mary and Joseph find him teaching in the temple (not lost at all, in fact, but right at home), and as when he preaches, "You have heard it said . . . but I say to you . . ." We receive something new, yet that newness does not denigrate what came before. In fact, what is "superior" is measured against that "which

27. This is based on the Vulgate's reading of Lev. 10:14.

she had been gladdened as with spiritual wine served to her by the holy fathers" (65). It's not a bad image for comparing the old and new covenant: one is wonderful; the other is, staggeringly, even better (John 2:10).

But Origen is not finished telling the whole gospel through the image of wine. It is not enough to find God in the created order. We must find ourselves there too. Later in the commentary, the bride of the Word dwells in his house and is taught "whatsoever things are stored and hidden within the royal court and in the King's chamber." The King's house includes a cellar, where "she becomes acquainted with that wine which is extracted from the holy wine-presses, the wine that is not only new, but also old and sweet." Origen knows full well that older wine is better. Now that we are married to the King, resident in his house, we drink this older wine and discover its treasures: "The teaching of the Law and the Prophets" (231–32). In rapturous love with the Word, moved into his house, we find the best wine and drink deep.

Now we are ready to read Israel's scripture.

> My spikenard has yielded its (or His) odour. A sachet of a myrrh-
> drop is my Nephew to me. (Song 1:12–13)[28]

Origen faces a text-critical problem here. Some manuscripts say "its," while others say "his." In seminary I was taught a set of critical skills with which to find the most original reading—choose from the best manuscripts, choose the most awkward reading (because editors tend to tidy things up). Origen prefers "his," with a different rationale, for in this reading "something still more divine emerges." Namely, the perfume has taken on the scent of the Bridegroom rather than the reverse: "Its natural odour has been mastered by the Bridegroom's fragrance" (159). (Note: this is the literal reading!) Origen reads this as a charge for the church to take on the character of Mary Magdalene, who anoints the Lord with a pound of spikenard and receives the Lord's approval (John 12:3). He is particularly interested that she wipes his feet with her hair, getting her own ointment back from him, "steeped in the character and virtue of His body." She then draws to herself not natural perfume but

---

28. This is another place where our modern translations differ a great deal from those in front of ancient Christians. Our precision in translation and knowledge of manuscript transmission have improved a great deal. Our creativity in interpretation has not.

the smell "of the very Word of God, and what she has put on her head is the fragrance of Christ" (160). John 12 records that the whole house is filled with the smell, just as the Holy Spirit has filled the entire world, and the believer's entire soul. In this loving gesture, Mary offers the gift of her faith and receives back the grace of the Holy Spirit, such that the believer smells like Jesus, such that he can praise her for doing a "good work for me" (Mark 14:6).[29]

That is far more embodied, far more erotic, than any way I was taught to read, to a degree that almost makes me nervous. Might it also then be truer?

In the word *drop* Origen sees something at first "small and insignificant," like the Son as God's unassuming way of saving the world. Origen points to prophetic texts like Daniel 2:34, speaking of a small stone cut from a mountain without hands, and Micah 2:11–12, referring to the "drop of this people" from which "Jacob shall surely be gathered." And he elaborates, "It befitted him who came to gather not Jacob only, but all the nations which, as the prophet says, were accounted as a drop in a bucket" (165). The drop in a bucket suggests a coming outpouring of many more such drops, and calls to mind Christ's kenosis: when he was "made Himself as a drop in His self-emptying of the form of God, and so to come and gather the drop of the gentiles and the drop of the remnant of Jacob alike." This leads Origen to Psalm 45: "Myrrh and a drop and cassia perfume Thy garments." The garments of the Word are his teaching of wisdom; myrrh suggests Christ's future death; and cassia, because it only grows in regions with much rain, suggests baptism. But the key meaning is that a drop suggests the self-emptying of the Word, and our joining with him as so many more drops in the bucket.

To read like this one needs a lexicon handy more than a dictionary. Words take their meaning from their biblical resonance, not from some essential definition provided elsewhere. The word *drop* means what it means across the breadth of scripture.

This is the place many interpreters will call Origen fanciful, and the charge is not wrong. Yet note the directions in which his imagination travels. He is searching for the Word. He finds the Word in linguistic connections to the New Testament (spikenard), in the shape of sensu-

---

29. Elsewhere Origen makes clear he does not run this Mary in John together with the sinful woman of the other gospels, though here he borrows the single verse from Mark.

ous discipleship (bent over Christ's feet, washing with our hair), and in the shape of kenosis itself (drop). He constructs this reading by roaming freely not only over the New Testament but over the Old as well. And now, subsequently, when we smell a powerful perfume, when we see a drop of anything, even when we notice someone's garments, when we touch our own or another's hair, we ought also to think of the self-emptying of God that saves us, turns us into his smell, covers us with his baptism, joins us to his own flesh and to that of all his people.

> Behold, He stood behind our wall, leaning against the windows,
> looking through the nets. (Song 2:9–10)

One of the striking features of the Song is the way the relationship between the lovers ebbs and flows. The two come together dramatically, and then the bride is left wondering where her beloved went and when she will see him again. At this point in the book, the pair have been together, and the bride is left longing for his presence once more. And here he is: having leapt the mountains in 2:8, he stands behind a wall, leans against a window, and peers through the nets. Origen is struck by this oscillation between divine presence and absence in the Song, and he notices that this oscillation matches the Christian experience of discipleship. Note the especially strong note of personal testimony in his first homily on the Song: "God is my witness that I have often perceived the Bridegroom drawing near me and being most intensely present with me; then suddenly He has withdrawn and I could not find Him, though I sought to do so" (280). Even when he appears, as he does here, the divine presence is not unmediated, but instead is interrupted by these barriers of wall, window, and net.

Origen finds several reasons for this intermittent nature of divine presence with us, but he concentrates on how the Bridegroom does not stay so that "she may long for Him the more" (232). The oscillation between presence and absence is meant to stir our longing for his presence once more, to make us search for him, since "He is found when He is sought for." Even when God is found again, it is not an unmediated presence. Rather, God is "neither wholly hidden, nor yet wholly in open view." This is fully appropriate for Origen's sacramental and God-soaked universe: God is present in words, in creation, in liturgy, supremely in Christ, but we have to be trained to see him, and then we have to grow in the virtue necessary to see him more.

But why a wall, a window, a net?

The wall suggests to Origen the stability of a house, signifying the church, the place where we are enclosed in the bulwarks of faith. It calls to mind the "stability of doctrines." These are necessary but not sufficient, for he "does not show Himself openly and wholly to her yet." He rather encourages her to come outside, "not to sit idle there," but to try and see him, not through a glass darkly but face-to-face. The window suggests to him the bodily sense, through which our soul looks out on the world. It can let in something dangerous, whether by lust or vanity, as Jeremiah warns, "Death is come up through your windows" (233, quoting Jer. 9:21). Or our windows can admit the glories of divine creation or the wisdom of the divine Word, such that the soul "perceives the Creator of all in the beauty of His creatures and marvels at His works and praises their Maker" (234).

Here Origen reverses his normal order and interprets with reference to the church only after interpreting with reference to the soul. Thinking ecclesially, Origen says Christ stood for a while "behind the wall of the house of the Old Testament," not yet showing himself to all people (235). Only later does he emerge from the house of the letter of the law and show himself to others, as he prophesied he would long ago. Here the demand on the bride to leave her house is matched by the description of the Bridegroom leaving his. God does not demand anything of us that God has not already done. In fact, God does not just ask us to do what God has done; God *enables* us to take that step. The nets are a reference to the predicament of the human race after the fall. Only the Son is not fallen, and so outside that snare, and only he is strong enough to destroy the net that encloses us. For his resurrection was not just for himself: "He also raised, together with Himself, those who were held by death" (238).

Origen's reading of the Bridegroom crouching behind a wall, a window, a net may or may not be wrong. But isn't it glorious? And further, shouldn't his filling of the content of a wall, a window, a net fill our understanding of those ordinary, everyday objects, so that the walls we see remind us of the stability of doctrine *and* the need not to sit idle but to set out, boldly, to meet Jesus. Give me the risky interpretation that draws us to love and follow Jesus over boring any day.

Hopefully by now these interpretive moves are becoming familiar: Origen uses verbal and imagistic and theological links to connect imagery in the Song with Jesus and the church. This is done not at a distance but with passionate proximity: Jesus wants to marry *us*, and to show *us* how a net or a window bears witness to this divine intent to wed. This linkage of powerful images in the Song to Jesus, and so to us, could continue almost indefinitely (if we had the whole of Origen's commentary, it doubtless would!). The images he runs through his imagination from elsewhere in the Song through Jesus to us and back include a shadow, a bed, a dove, a deer, a mustard seed, a fox, wintertime, and more. These created objects are only there to show the beauty of their Creator and to lure us into that beauty via Jesus. For that is what creation is for.

Reading Scripture with Origen as a Friend

Origen is the foundation stone for so much future allegory that critics of this tradition, both ancient and modern, have figured that the removal of this stone will undo a rotten house, and they have pulled hard. I have tried here to show why his exegesis makes sense within its own parameters and, further, why, understood aright, it is beautiful. If one's goal is a journey with the church, living and dead, into the unending mystery of the triune God, then Origen is an ideal companion. If the goal of reading this text is something else, then he will distract. One of the favorite epithets to hang on Origen is to speak of the need for more "sober" exegesis. Interpreters will often provide exegesis so sober that indeed few enjoy drinking it and the book remains closed for the church. As if foreseeing this, Origen exults, "Be you of one mind with the Bridegroom, like the Bride, and you will know that thoughts of this kind do inebriate and make the spirit glad" (271).

If you wish to read like, or even with, the third-century Alexandrian giant, here are some suggestions:

1. Read modern criticism. I know this sounds counterintuitive given my praise for ancient exegesis here, but it is not ancient criticism that is so inflexible as to exclude other approaches. The ancients read at multiple levels, after all. Origen worked desperately to find help with translation and manuscript transmission and sought wisdom from far beyond the bounds of the church—all disciplines in which we moderns simply have more information. Despite Origen's occasional disavowals, moderns' insistence that this Song celebrates

sensual human love can be assumed into allegorical interpretation, as I have tried to show here. Allegory includes the letter and then pushes deeper; it is literalist readers who insist on a single meaning that excludes competitors. So drink deeply of whatever helps you to love this text wisely and put their work to use. And remember the goal is to love God through love of the text.

2. Make connections. The Old Testament is wine: delirious, infatuating, and life-giving. And that which comes from the breasts of the Bridegroom is even better. Those who read the Song with Origen will never denigrate the Old Testament. It points forward; it is fulfilled but never left behind; it is wine. And those who read the Song with Origen will delight all the more in the New Testament, showing us as it does how to read the Old.

For Origen, all the energy and creativity of interpretation is dedicated to discerning how this word, phrase, sentence, or image bears witness to the God fleshed in Jesus who means to marry us. To see God wooing us even in the word that foretells his coming is to bring joy, delight, and even love. Once we have our spiritual senses honed to see him in all places, the difficulty is, having seen, to be transformed into one spotless enough to marry this One. The limitless energy necessary to discern Christ in all places (biblical interpretation) becomes a boundless energy to pursue love (holiness). Love rightly, yearn and long and desire properly, and you will see Jesus here.

3. Tell your congregation they are beautiful. Woo them with words as electric as these. If they do not blush occasionally, even regularly, as you preach, then you're not preaching from the Song. And if they do not passionately pursue the God here revealed, then you're not preaching *Jesus* from the Song. The final test for whether this way of reading is right and properly aligned with God's purposes will be whether the church becomes more faithful, more loving, more holy thereby. We might even say we can tell whether preaching the Song christologically is right if we see the church so intertwined with Jesus that they are one flesh; that when the Lord seems temporarily absent, it is only to reignite her desire, so that she (that is, we) pants after him, longing to find him once more.

For Further Study

Martens, Peter. *Origen and Scripture: The Contours of the Exegetical Life.* Oxford: Oxford University Press, 2014.

A very readable scholarly appraisal of Origen on the Bible.

Origen. *Origen: An Exhortation to Martyrdom, Prayer, and Selected Works.* Edited by Rowan Greer. Preface by Hans Urs von Balthasar. Mahwah, NJ: Paulist Press, 1979.

A taste of the breadth of Origen's work, including some briefer pieces that can be more accessible.

Origen. *On First Principles.* Edited and translated by John Behr. Oxford: Oxford University Press, 2018.

Translating Origen is a vexing business, and Behr is one of our most reliable interpreters of the early church. This book came out too late for me to consult it, but not too late for you to learn from it.

Trigg, Joseph W. *Origen.* The Early Church Fathers. London: Routledge, 1998.

A collection of some of his best work on the Bible, with each sermon or commentary helpfully contextualized.

3

Mary

Ponder and Treasure

If there's one key image that guides my reading of scripture, it comes from Origen, the great teacher from the late second- and early third-century church whom we discussed in the last chapter.[1] Origen compares interpreting the Bible to being a "spiritual herbalist." We might think of such a person as an herbal healer. She has to know every inch of the garden. She tends to it, pulls weeds, minds critters, knows when different herbs flourish and when they don't. And then she knows what every herb does in combination with every other herb. Pull this one up, grind it up in a pestle with that one, and—*poof*—it explodes. Don't do that. So take this one, grind it up with that other, combine it with a third, and it will heal this specific sort of ailment.

This spiritual herbalist is not a gardener for the sake of the produce. She is a healer. She seeks the good, the flourishing, the return to full health, of the patient. So she doesn't just know every inch of the garden and what every herb does in combination with every other. She also knows how to diagnose the patient. She can tell if a skin condition is a burn or an allergic reaction or just something to let heal on its own. She can tell when something is beyond her skill to heal and when the patient will be right as rain in no time. And—this is key—the better she can read a patient, the better she can read the garden, and vice versa. Paying in-depth attention to the one allows deeper attention to the other.

---

1. St. Basil of Caesaria and St. Gregory of Nazianzus, *Philocalia of Origen* 10.2 (p. 52). These teachings of Origen come from his later readers Basil and Gregory after Origen's own teaching had become suspect.

So it is, Origen suggests, with the interpreter of scripture. That one must know every scrap of the scriptures, every inch, every portion forward and backward. *And* the interpreter must know how to read the patient—that is, the church. The interpreter must know the specific contours of Ruth. And also of Exodus. Grind those up with a little Revelation and *bam*! No, don't do that; it will blow up. But take a little Ruth, grind it up in a pestle with a little Mark and a pinch of Paul, and it will heal this particular malady. But before that can even be begun, the healer has to pay deep attention to the patient. What's he suffering from? What sort of cure does this particular ailment need? Take a bit of the creative power of Genesis, combine the moral passion of the prophets and the preaching of Acts, and it will return this specific church to health in no time, just watch. "Expert anatomists can tell you for what use every part, even the least, was intended by Providence."[2] And they can do a great deal more than tell you. They take those herbs, mash them together, and place the mixture precisely where things hurt—to bring about healing, flourishing, the full life God intends for all creatures.

I love this image. It shows how we can tell that a good reading of scripture has taken place. Does the patient improve? No? Well, doctor, you didn't read the garden or the patient or both. Does the church return to the flush of pink in the cheeks, the spring of strength in the legs, the clarity of mind Jesus intends for all creation? Well done, doc. That's what you and your medicine are there for. The image works because it shows the Bible has a purpose, an end, a *telos* in Aristotle's terminology: the Bible is only there for the health of God's people and, through them, the thriving and flourishing of the whole world. If you read in a way that restores health, well done, do it again! If not, back to the garden, back to the anatomy lessons and diagnostic basics.

Expect to Be Surprised

This book is about the interpretation of the Bible, drawing especially on the wisdom of the ancient church. Christians throughout the ages have sought the wisdom of our earliest teachers, those who were closer in time and space to Jesus. They are heroes we have in common among most denominations, unlike later saints who are treasured by one or the

2. *Philocalia of Origen* 10.2 (p. 52).

other church but not by all. For the sake of this book, the church's earliest teachers are like the odd and strange aunts and uncles in an extended family. They're embarrassing at family gatherings. It's harder to figure out what to talk to them about than it is with someone whom you would choose voluntarily as a friend. And yet these unchosen cranks make you you. And if you can overcome that initial awkwardness, there is wisdom there, and even love. One of the first things we learn from our earliest teachers in the church is that the Bible has a purpose, a point, a goal, a *telos*. It wants to save us. Or rather God wants to save us, and the whole world that God created in the first place, and all who bear the gospel to us leave their fingerprints on it as they transmit goodness to us.

There are so many books about the Bible, and I am struck by how many of those books I read treat the Bible as a problem. How can we possibly ascribe any authority to this very old, very convoluted book from a long time ago and far far away? Or how do we seal off this book from any challenge that would dilute its authority and leave us without guidance? Either way the Bible is a sort of problem to wring our hands over. Yet Christians believe God is found in his bride Israel, his Son Jesus, his beloved church. God has held nothing back. If you want to know who God is, look *where* God is unendingly sharing the divine presence. The space between us and the Bible isn't a tragically empty vacuum. It is a resplendent party, full of angels and saints and not a few rogues, and there's a place for you and me. The host is Jesus alone.

Christianity is a mediated faith. It is always passed on *from* someone and *to* someone or it is not at all. St. Paul speaks of those who passed the faith on to him (1 Cor. 15:1, 3). We think of Paul as the bedrock layer of the house of the New Testament, but he insists he is not original. The gospel he *received* already had someone else's fingerprints on it. And this is nothing to lament. Christianity is the sort of gift you cannot receive without giving it away. Our fingerprints add to the many layers of those already there. And here is the most glorious thing of all—*God* has fingerprints. God is a Jew from first-century Palestine. We do not strive for a faith clean of prints. We rather notice the way that those who pass the faith on, and those to whom we pass it on, image Jesus to us in infinite variety. There is no Jesus without the church and no church without Jesus. Like members to a body with him as our head, we are one. And we rejoice together.

I am convinced that the Bible is a delight and that studying the Bible is about learning to see that delight. God has left it there for us so that we would learn to love God and neighbor. The Bible is a universe of wonder. I am convinced that much of what ails our churches could be healed if we saw the Bible this way—as an endless treasure house of delights. God has blessed us with an absolute cascade, an avalanche, of delights. And we stroll through like bored tourists, heads down, faces in our phones. Watch how the average minister reads the Bible in church. Does the reader actually expect anything to happen? Do those listening perceive him or her to think anything is alive in there?

As I write this, I am staying with an order of Dominican nuns in the wilderness of British Columbia. It is a beautiful monastery, Queen of Peace it is called. And they can't stop warning me about the bears. They have a warning on the website. Another on multiple brochures in my room. The sister who checked me in warned me about the bears: "Usually they just run away," she said. "But other times . . ." You'd think there'd been a rash of retreatants mauled by these mighty grizzlies, but no. The sisters are just being cautious, good hosts. I chuckled this off until I took a walk my first evening. I rounded the first corner and saw, not a hundred yards away, what looked at first like a dog, but no, it was a black bear, bounding away from me. So the legends are true.

What if we read the Bible with similar heightened awareness to what the sisters hope I will have here—on the lookout for something wild, dangerous, beautiful, thrilling? Or some One who might attack at any moment and leave us mauled, changed, a hip out of socket, limping away, forever wounded, and yet now strangely alive unlike anything previous?

And here's the even more amazing thing about God—God is not just above, beyond, better than. God is also less, lower, beneath. St. Augustine imagines standing on tiptoes, trying to catch a glimpse of a God who is unbound by time and space, who knows all, is all-powerful, and is entirely unbearably good. We can't imagine such a God. All our thoughts *are* bounded by time, space, weakness, our own sinfulness. But we can just brush up against the underside of such thoughts as we reach reach reach . . . and then we trip over the crucified slave who is washing our feet.[3]

3. Augustine, *Confessions*, 128.

Mary Reads the Bible

Think with me of Mary, a precocious young girl from a religion and century and part of the world without excellent job prospects for precocious young girls. I say "precocious" because she has studied her people's prayers. When an angel turns up with a cockamamie scheme to save the universe (Luke 1:26–38), Mary knows how to pray: "My soul magnifies the Lord," she exclaims (Luke 1:46–55). The prayer is an echo of Mary's ancient ancestor Hannah, another Israelite woman who miraculously becomes pregnant (1 Sam. 2:1–10). It seems that God is always granting life where there should be none. Mary knows the songs and stories of Israel. So when an angel turns up promising life to a girl with no husband, Mary knows not to respond like her relative Zechariah—with several excellent objections (Luke 1:8–20). Mary responds with some of the most faith-filled words in all the Bible, words that thrill down to this very day: "Sure." Or less prosaically, "Behold the handmaid of the Lord; be it unto me according to thy word." (Why do we still break into the King James for big-ticket verses?!) Mary stretches her mind and heart to imagine a God who looks with favor on the lowly, who does great things for unlikely people, who scatters the proud and lifts up the lowly (Luke 1:46–55), she stretches her thoughts so they can just brush the underside of such an unimaginable God, she reaches reaches reaches . . . and God becomes a fast-dividing zygote right underneath her ribs.

Mary and her husband-to-be, Joseph, have just had her first baby without yet being sexually intimate (try explaining *that* around your hometown). And shepherds turn up saying they'd seen legions and legions of angels singing and praising God for this oddly born child. She looks at her son, her savior, and savior of the world. He is in an animal trough (Luke 2:7). Wrapped in swaddling clothes. St. Ephrem the Syrian, a magnificent early church interpreter of our faith, says it is appropriate that Jesus is in a trough, a place for animals to feed. Because we, God's animals, will gather around and feed on him. And strangely, he will delight in this. Did not Isaiah anticipate that ox and ass would know their creator here, in a crib (Isa. 1:3)? Martin Luther compared the scriptures to those swaddling clothes. The Bible is like a baby blanket or diaper. By itself it's . . . not very appealing. Used and soiled, it's full of baby spit-up and other excrema. But wrapped around the Lord of the universe, that cloth is precious, glorious, beautiful. It holds the one who holds us all. So as Mary hears these shepherds' report, words from these working men who went to work that night with no idea their lives would be upended, words about the upending of the entire cosmos, she does something important: she "treasured all these words and pondered them in her heart" (Luke 2:19).

That's it. That's how you read the Bible. You treasure and ponder. You know the story well enough to break out in song—with thoroughly practiced improvisation.[4] And when the God of Israel works savingly anew, the way God has always done before and will do again, you treasure and ponder. You love the words. You pick over them one by one like words from a lover. You refuse to let them go but taste them over and over again, for each one has its particular spice. You smell them like a mother smells her child ("he smells like God," Anne Lamott said of her firstborn).[5] You taste the words ("they were like jewels in my mouth," Frank McCourt says of the first time he read Shakespeare).[6]

How often do you hear the person reading the Bible in church sound like they are "pondering and treasuring" the words, like Mary does?

Mary is our first tutor in reading the Bible. She shows us how to be tutored by the praises of Israel. She is not a scholar, as far as we know. That doesn't mean she's unintelligent, far from it, as her prayers and words attest. As I hinted above, Mary is steeped in Israel's prayers. She knows them intimately enough to improvise off them, and to pray in a way that is Israel-shaped. Her Magnificat, as the church has long called her prayer (for the first word in Latin, "let my soul magnify"), is not about her. It is not even about Jesus. It is about God—and God's character. God is one who sides with the lowly and then tilts the playing field so that the lowly are no longer lowly. Even more controversially, the prayer's tilting of the field makes it so that the lofty are no longer lofty (Luke 1:53). Mary is a master of prayer enough to improvise a prayer anew. My church's founder, John Wesley, said his Methodists had to be ready to "pray, preach, or die" at a moment's notice. Mary was ready to pray when an angel turned up talking about her upcoming miraculous, scandalous pregnancy. Mary shows us that the Old Testament is the womb of Christ. It is where God himself gestates among us and gets born. And this is the very strangest thing we Christians have to say about God—God is not only great, strong, almighty, all those things. Lots of religions believe those good things about God. God is also lowly, under

4. See Samuel Wells, *Improvisation: The Drama of Christian Ethics* (Grand Rapids: Brazos, 2004).

5. Lamott, *Operating Instructions*, 157.

6. McCourt, *Angela's Ashes*, 196.

Mary's ribs, at our feet. God in Christ has a face and an aorta and a Jewish mom. And that's about as strange as it gets. No wonder Mary ponders and treasures. You would too if God were making your feet swell and your back ache, giving you weird food cravings and making you "great with child."

Mary navigates between the common worries of both liberal and conservative readers of the Bible. Liberals want academic and skeptical seriousness. Conservatives want the Bible to be believed and trusted, not dissolved in the acids of our doubts. She is no skeptic, but she is . . . curious: "How can this be, since I am a virgin?" (Luke 1:34). She knows the stories of Israel. Matriarchs are miraculously pregnant all the time. Not normally without a husband, granted. But look at Sarah, Rebekah, Rachel, Hannah—God is the one who gives the barren woman children. In fact, God seems only to work through barren women. Here God takes how God has traditionally worked and magnifies it. Adds a twist. Not a barren woman but an unmarried one. Mary also trusts. Rowan Williams analogizes between Mary and other believers.[7] When any of us trusts, things get born. New life comes. Things that were not there before are now there, nearly miraculously. Mary trusts so much she gets pregnant. But it's not the Bible she trusts, quite. It's the God of the Bible, the living God of Israel, the only God there is. This is not a trust that protects, defends, shields off the Bible from change, God no. This is a trust that has her *enter into the story of the Bible itself*. She is an agent in the story. An actor in the play. A saint, the church calls her. Mother of saints perhaps. For her to ponder and treasure does not mean to preserve in amber, to kill the animal and stuff it for the wall. No, it means to become part of the story. If you believe in this God, you will not be the same for it. Mary studied Israel's story hard. It must have surprised her, as it did everybody, that the God of Israel would show his faithfulness anew this way. With a tiny rushing heartbeat right up underneath her own.

There is another time that Mary ponders and treasures. She and her husband are returning from pilgrimage in Jerusalem, where they have celebrated the Passover, where their son will celebrate another sort of Passover not many years hence. Traveling in a group, they are separated from the boy but think nothing of it. For a while. But soon they return to Jerusalem in a panic. This is any parent's worst fear, magnified in their case, for all the unbelievable things people have said about this child, the unimaginable way in which he has been born among us. Any par-

7. See his sermon "Waiting on God," in *Ray of Darkness*, 13–16.

ent would rather die than lose their child—how much more one who is the very Child of God? They find him in the temple, instructing the elders, amazing them, being amazed by them. And he sasses his mom![8] He asks why they wouldn't know or understand that he would be in his father's house. But he obeys, returns with them, goes home to Nazareth. And Mary ponders and treasures once more (Luke 2:41–51, esp. v. 51). Imagine the cocktail of amazement, fear, anger, delight, resolution—the myriad emotions she must have gone through. Only to find him anew. Right there in the temple that he never left. This is an image for us reading scripture. We may panic. We might be bored. But if we look hard enough, we will find Jesus right at its heart.

Mary's story does not end there. "A sword will pierce your own soul too," old Simeon promised as he blessed the child (Luke 2:35). Mary's role is not only to get Jesus born. That's the heart of it, but God is not done with her yet. She also appears at his crucifixion (John 19:25). She is there with the disciples at Pentecost (Acts 1:14). She forms a (small) part of St. Paul's telling of the gospel (Gal. 4:4). She appears, magnificently, in the book of Revelation, as a woman clothed with the sun, the moon under her feet, a crown of twelve stars, whose child is threatened by a great red dragon (Rev. 12:1–6). There is a reason Mary has haunted Christian imagination, causing rifts between Catholic and Protestant, summoning our attention and revulsion down to today. She is the first Christian.[9] The first to hear God's intention to take flesh and die and to say "hallelujah, sign me up." She is our model for a reader of scripture. She ponders and treasures. She stands amazed and joins up with God's world-redeeming work.

In Mary's lifelong yes and recurring act of "pondering and treasuring" is the story of salvation. Look at the image by Sister Grace Remington, a Trappistine from Our Lady of the Mississippi in Iowa who doodles as part of her prayer. Her sisters noticed this one and sent it out as a Christmas card one year, and the image went viral, as we say (a benevolent contagion, that). It is Mary comforting Eve. Notice Eve's misery—still clutching the fruit, snake coiled around her leg, her hair her only clothing, as in traditional portraits of Mary Magdalene. Mary

8. I take this way of putting it from Stephanie Allen, a layperson at Boone United Methodist Church, during a Bible study.

9. I take this language from the Baptist theologian Willie Jennings of Yale. Also in Baptist circles, Timothy George has made much the same argument; see his "Evangelicals and the Mother of God." See also Tim Perry, *Mary for Evangelicals*.

Mary Comforts Eve by Sister Grace Remington. Used with her permission.

offers no judgment, only grace. She directs Eve's hand to her swelling womb, to make clear that without *your* sin, sister, this grace would not have come. The two lock together in an embrace that shows both human misery-making and divine grace-making. Note that Mary need not even look as she crushes the snake's head—a fabulous touch by Sister Grace, to which every multitasking parent can relate. It is a reference to the *protoevangelium*, the first announcement of the gospel, that "he will strike your head, and you will strike his heel" (Gen. 3:15). I find that every busy mom intuitively understands this image: Snake? I got this, no need to glance down even . . . Mary, heedless of her own safety with bare feet, prepares the way for our coming salvation by trampling the serpent's head. Mary is an agent in this story, but she is also a model interpreter of it. Her embodied response to the God in her womb is a comingling of trust and surprise, uncertainty and hope.

Similarly, when we read the Bible, we expect the same. And this is very hard to do. We go looking there, knowing full well who we are searching for. And yet we prime ourselves, incite our expectation, tingle with anticipation to find him. Then we're surprised *how* we find him this time. But we do indeed. We go to scripture seeking the God of Israel, Mary's boy, the cascade of the Spirit. Reading the Bible, for Christians, is a matter of expecting to be surprised by Jesus again.[10]

Every Single Pelican

Let's look at two examples of the surprising way Jesus meets us in the scriptures in what might otherwise seem like stray details. These, too, are opportunities to ponder and treasure like Mary. They are places where we can learn to expect to be surprised by Jesus again.

One is in a bird. Psalm 102 is a lament psalm offered in a desolate Jerusalem so bereft of any people, let alone God's people, that it is now a favorite haunt of lonely birds. Owls. They nest in such desolate places and find a home (Ps. 102:6). Psalm 102 reads perfectly amidst national lament. Israel is a people whose heart has been torn out of its chest while

10. N. T. Wright has so often used "surprise" language in book titles that it would seem I am borrowing from him. As much as I have learned from him on scripture and theology, I was actually using this term before his string of books using the term came out. An argument for writing faster! See his *Surprised by Hope* and *Surprised by Scripture*.

still beating. It has lost its home, its temple, its raison d'etre as a nation, its God. Its great capital is a haunt for jackals and birds of prey that only come out at night.

St. Augustine, however, did not read "owls" in this text; he read "pelicans." But he doesn't know anything about pelicans. As a Christian in late fourth- and early fifth-century North Africa, he can only read this Bible in a poor Latin translation. He is constantly frustrated with the quality of translations available to him. But his purpose is not merely antiquarian. He is not trying to win trivia contests or pass exams or be proud of himself for knowing stuff most people don't. He is trying to interpret God's word for God's people. He preaches every day on the Psalms to people going to and from work. Most are illiterate.

Not knowing Greek or Hebrew enough to go look even if he could, Augustine writes to his friend Jerome. Jerome does know Greek (Augustine knows more of it than he lets on). More importantly, Jerome knows Hebrew. He learns it from rabbis and uses it to translate the entire Old Testament into the Vulgate, the Latin translation of the Bible that would guide the church in Europe for the next thousand years and more. Jerome explains about the bird in question in Psalm 102. They don't live in Augustine's part of North Africa. Mother pelicans, Jerome explains from Roman zoology textbooks, kill their young in the nest. Then they wound themselves, pour out their blood on their young, who then revive.

Augustine and Jerome are both hungry for things we take for granted. They long for better biblical manuscripts, access to languages. So they turn to Jewish religious leaders for help. They long for what our universities and seminaries and Bible colleges have in spades—historical criticism. Jerome lands on "pelican." Our contemporary interpreters figure this is an owl. We can be wrong. We can always be wrong, whoever "we" are. That's why we need the toughest-minded skeptical interpreters.

And Augustine doesn't believe it. "This report may be true or false; but if it is true . . ." In other words, Augustine knows he has to let the learning sit lightly. It may well be wrong. In which case he'll move on to something else. But for now he charges forward: "If it is true, observe how apt a symbol it is of him who gave us life by his own blood."[11] Christ is like the mother pelican, killing us, his young (Deut. 32:39). Then he wounds himself (herself?), pouring out his blood on us, who revive, born

11. *Expositions of the Psalms 99–120*, pp. 52–55.

again, covered in blood like at our first birth. Now every time we see a pelican, we think of and give thanks to the one who thought of the pelican in the first place (what was God thinking that day?!). We give thanks for all creation that is being redeemed through God's creative and sacrificial love. And now one piece of creation has been marked in our imagination for the God who makes it all and redeems it all in Christ. And the church has remembered. St. Thomas Aquinas prayed to Jesus as "our pelican divine." Medieval bestiaries described the legend about the pelican in devotional terms—they trained readers to read both the Bible and the creature, and to see the Lord of both in each.[12] One seminary at which I worked had a statue above each entryway with a mother pelican, wings out, protecting a nest, with tiny little beaks opening upward, expectant of food and love. When I asked my wife, Jaylynn, to marry me and could not get the words out, we looked and saw a flock of pelicans. Now that's either Jesus or a coincidence, in which case I wish you a boring life.[13]

Such symbols can, of course, be hijacked. The pelican became a sort of national symbol of the French monarchy, trying to contort Christian imagery into empire-supporting propaganda. The pelican on the Louisiana State license plate is a memory of French new-world colonialism and also a hat tip to the brown pelican in that state. No symbol, no word is safe, or sanitized, or useless for the powers and principalities. This is why we should read the Bible figurally. We have to combat that common human propensity to use our imagination for sin with God's desire to use the Bible to reshape human imagination for Jesus.

But look how thin a foundation this rests on, how tenuous a reading—an incorrect manuscript tradition, an incorrect biological observation, a fantastical animal story—in which we find ourselves. Those looking for scientific reason to discount this story do not have to look far. The reason Augustine likes it is precisely the reason a skeptic will throw acid all over it: it is delightful. Delight requires initial confusion, bewilderment, slowly giving way to recognition, anticipation, and then the thrill of breakthrough, discovery, and sheer, unmitigated joy.

And that's how to read the Bible.

12. Harrison, *Territories of Science and Religion*, 159–62.
13. I think I first heard this formulation from Barbara Brown Taylor.

Biblical Math

Another example. Just as tenuous and, I hope, just as delightful. John 21 tells the story of the resurrected Jesus restoring his disciples to fellowship, birthing the church, where, ever since, we rogues and betrayers and deniers and abandoners find ourselves restored to fellowship with the living God. Jesus stands before them, unrecognized (21:4). He asks if they have caught anything. No. He suggests the other side of the boat. They still don't catch on. Until the nets are full, and they are unable to haul them in. John recognizes it is the Lord. Peter, not the sharpest tack in the box, puts his clothes on. Before jumping into the water. He is a bit harried (21:7). Somebody counts up the total haul, and it comes out to a very specific number.

153.

I have had fishermen and fisherwomen tell me this would be an ordinary thing to do—to count the exact number of the miraculous draught of fishes. I believe them. We count things that matter to us, and somebody clearly counted here. But that does not exhaust the depths of mystery that the apostle John wishes to reveal to us. Numbers mean stuff in the Bible. Six is the number of creation. Seven of the Sabbath. Ten of the commandments. Twelve is the number of Israel's tribes. Seventy is the number of the nations. Christians add to these numbers—four is the number of the gospels, eight the day of resurrection. In other words, ancient Jews and Christians share a preconception that neither shares with us moderns—numbers mean stuff. This has to do with the way God has coaxed creation out of the chaos. There is a design and order to how God has created, a creativity and a beauty in the way things are. Think of the bumblebee in the flower. The suction cup on the octopus. And the astonishing miracle that is you or me. God is busy creating. And numbers show the proportion and design by which God has created. There is an elegance in mathematics, in science, in the order in the universe. Numbers mean stuff because they show forth the wisdom of God. They are the fingerprints of God on creation. So, why 153?

Well, Augustine opines, God is three in one as Trinity—Father, Son, and Spirit. God births the church to save us from ourselves on the fiftieth day after Easter, the day called Pentecost, when the Holy Spirit is poured out on all nations. And Pentecost is the third age of history: preceded by the age before the law and the age under the law, it is the age under grace.

So on the fiftieth day after Easter, the three-in-one God breathes (multiplies) a church into existence: 3 × 50, here in the third era of history, so you add 3 and get . . . 153. Biblical math. Don't build a bridge with it. But you can build a people of delight with it.

Not impressed?

OK, let's try this. Ten signifies the commandments with which God graces Israel. And seven is a historic number for the gifts of the Spirit described in Isaiah 11:2. The number in some more modern translations is actually only six—the Spirit of wisdom and understanding, of counsel and of might, of knowledge and the fear of the Lord. But this is a traditional place from which the church learns what sorts of gifts the Spirit pours out on us, having first poured them out on Jesus. Let's grant they could be seven in the original. So take that 10 for the commands, and that 7 for the gifts of the Spirit, and add up all the numbers from one to seventeen: 1 + 2 + . . . 17 and what do you get? 153.

Still not impressed?

Look what these playful math problems do. They try to tell again the story of the church. The church is the third age of history in which the triune God births a new people. The church is the people empowered by the Spirit to delight in God's life-giving law. If we don't like either reading, that's fine. Orthodoxy is not so brittle as heresy. If we object, faces turn to us and ask us to offer our own reading. Give us some sense of the pelican, some reading of the 153, that fills us with grace, insight, and delight.

Ancient and modern interpreters alike have struggled to do this. St. Jerome proposed that 153 could be the number of fish species in the world. And that would work—it would be a sign of the universal reach of God's kingdom, signified by the full net. It doesn't work. Folks already knew more than 153 species of fish in John's day. One Johannine commentator proposes this: "One of these days some ancient writing will come to light containing a comparable tradition to the varieties of fish attested by Jerome."[14] It is the ultimate gnostic hope. That the truth is tragically beyond our grasp, and maybe someday, some archaeologist will unearth some document that can unlock for us the mystery of the 153. The gnostics were ancient Christians who believed that only some superspiritual types could have access to the truth. The rest of us hoi polloi are just poor schlumps, out of luck. But

14. Beasley-Murray, *John*, 401–4.

the Christian church, in dismissing the gnostics, said that God is not so capricious as that. God generously grants God's saving presence in the scriptures to all of God's people. And the 153 is an example of that. Gnostics found whatever esoteric knowledge they wanted to find in scripture. Christians find one thing in scripture: Jesus. Not to find Jesus there is to neglect the one thing that is worth finding, the one who holds all things together. If the 153 is just a way of saying "a lot of fish," no one should be impressed—why count them? Record the number? Leave it in the Bible, pass it on through generations, and continue to read it in worship today? It has to tell us something. And that something has to delight.

From Enemies to Friends

History is not empty between us and the Bible. It is full of saints, mediating God's goodness to us. The words on the page of the Bible are not naked. They are clothed—with the lives of the saints that fill them out for us. Judaism has a name for the heresy of trying to read the Bible without the rabbis. They disallow it—no Jew has access to these words without its mediators. So, too, should we Christians. "Orthodoxy" means right belief or teaching, or right worship, or both. And it's how the church has come to speak of the proper teaching that passes on authentic Christian faith to us, that we transmit to others.

Orthodoxy is not just a set of correct answers. Thank God. Or I would have long since run afoul of it. So, too, would you. It is often presented that way both by admirers and worriers. And it is not so. To be a heretic—that is, to run afoul of orthodoxy—is not to think an incorrect thought. If that were so, we'd all be sunk immediately. No, to be a heretic is to *teach publicly* something that the church holds as incorrect. Dangerously so. In the ancient church, heresy was thought to kill souls. It was analogous to a public health hazard, an infectious disease outbreak. You don't treat that with kid gloves. You root it out. Sometimes, or oftentimes, we got confused and thought you rooted out people that way. It has made for some of our worst moments. I understand why some are therefore allergic to the notion of heresy. And yet, try to throw it out. Declare the idea of heresy a heresy. Go ahead. You can't. Anyone who thinks some ideas are right and some are wrong has a notion of orthodoxy and heresy. We can move the lines on heresy and orthodoxy, but we can't do away with such lines altogether. The distinction just means that some ideas are beautiful and worth keeping; others are detestable, do harm, and must be undone.

And here's the thing about heresy. It's fun. That is, it's illuminating. I think of it as an interesting mistake. At least some Christians at some point found this biblically and existentially revelatory—that the Son is less than the Father. Or there are two persons in the Son. Or the world is actually evil. Or there should be no Old Testament. These are all interesting false starts. And here's what we should do with heresy: bring up its plausibility. As Willie Jennings used to say at Duke, put your hand on the doorknob of heresy, but don't turn it.

For example, preaching at a vibrant Vancouver megachurch—in which some listeners had a rigid and high-walled view of God—I said that God *fears* prayer. I used the John Donne poem that calls prayer an "engine against the almighty," directed to do so by Eugene Peterson, whose evangelical bona fides I would have thought unassailable.[15] In prayer, God puts himself in our debt. Everything is reversed, and the almighty becomes our servant. This is as deeply paradoxical and odd as things get. But I pressed the point because I wanted to show how world-reversing prayer is. The point I wanted to make in the sermon is that the right sort of fear—the fear of the Lord—can drive out every other fear. But for this to be more than just folk wisdom, it has to be grounded in the incarnation, in the God who takes our flesh. I took the doorknob of heresy—it's hard indeed to find a verse that suggests God fears prayer. But I didn't turn it. That is, I didn't throw out the tradition. In fact, I honored it—I preached to make the word strange, because God becomes strange to us in Christ.

But God and the gospel don't simply stay strange. My point in this sermon was to tap into a place of my hearers' deepest fears (and from the negative reaction of a few, I think I may have succeeded!). Because that place of fear is one where God moves toward us, converting us, changing us anew into God's own image. I don't begrudge their objections. Again, we all have our orthodoxies. We just draw the lines in a way that excludes the people we care to exclude. And here's what God does in Christ. God puts himself on the side of the excluded. Wherever we draw the lines, God steps to the other side. God makes himself our enemy. God makes Jesus to be "sin," Paul says (2 Cor. 5:21), to make us into the "righteous-

15. See his *Reversed Thunder*.

ness of God"—that is, into what God actually is. In Christ there is a great cosmic trade. God takes all our God-abandonment, all our ruin, all our despair, and gives us instead God's own sonship, blessedness, glory, divinity. Now that's a good deal.

And now we're to make that plain in our preaching. We will make mistakes, but God is merciful. It's God we're talking about. We all have limited intellect. God asks us to submit to the rest of the community and not try heroically to go our own stubborn way. It is more fun to travel together. More beautiful. More Christlike. We might even call this traveling together "church." Indeed, in traveling together the church was born.

Jesus, after his resurrection, meets two of his bewildered disciples on the road. And he proceeds to flirt with them. Their manner is sad (Luke 24:17). His is playful. They ask if he's the only stranger unaware of the things happening in Jerusalem. "What things?" he asks, with the author and hearer of the Gospel of Luke fully aware who he is, but poor Cleopas and his companion are unaware. Jesus then proceeds to unpack, to interpret, Moses and the prophets as declaring the Messiah had to suffer before entering into his glory. It is a key theme of Luke, and arguably of all four gospels, that the surprise in the Jesus story is a crucified Messiah. Luke wants us all to see a glimpse of church on the road to Emmaus—Jesus walking along with us, perhaps incognito, showing us that if we want to see God, we have to look for the downtrodden, the crushed, those on crosses. He stays coy with them, intending to walk on, and relents to come eat with them only when they beg (an image for prayer if ever there was one). He takes bread, blesses it, breaks it, and gives it to them (24:30). Just as he had done at their final supper with him. Just as he had done at countless meals over the years. Just as he will do unendingly in his kingdom—but not yet. Jesus, someone said, eats his way through the gospels. Yet here he doesn't stay for dinner at Emmaus. He vanishes. There is no time to luxuriate in his presence. He is there and then not. "Were not our hearts burning within us while he was talking to us on the road, while he was opening the scriptures to us?" they ask one another (24:32). They go and tell the other disciples just who has been made known to them in the breaking of bread (24:35).

There is too much here to comment on fully, but I love Jesus's coyness with his disciples. He will not come out and tell them who he is. Instead he walks with them, teaches them, stays with them, presides over table for them. His identity dawns slowly, as a great surprise, and the moment they see him, he is gone again, leaving them with burning hearts and bewildered minds and a whole new way of reading the Bible, about which they go and tell others. There is no interpreting the Bible here without a whole-bodied experience. They walk. Their hearts are heavy. Here the Bible is fully fleshed, lived. It changes you. It's self-involving, other-involving, Jesus-involving, go-and-tell involving. This is not a search for mere head knowledge. There is nothing here that can be turned into a principle and taught without reference to Jesus. It is no good defending whether this actually happened in just this way—of course it did. We have a resurrected Savior or none at all. And good luck repeating it for others, defending it scientifically—it cannot be proven until Christ's return and the resurrection of all flesh, until which we trust and hope. This is a bewildering mash of a surprise. And it's how to read the Bible—expecting to be surprised by Jesus again.

And its climax is the Lord's Supper. Jesus presiding at table. Us as guests. Him as host. This is a strange meal indeed, in which Jesus is the host and also the guest and also the food. God will stop at nothing to get through to us, overwhelming us with symbols, piling them up one on another without carefully codifying whether and how they all make sense. One thing they are not is tragically empty, distant, cold. They are humming, hot-blooded, and full of life. A mystery, I like to say, is a physical place where God saves. Contrast a mystery with a puzzle.[16] A puzzle is something you figure out and you're done with—a crossword, sudoku, a Rubik's Cube. A mystery is more like the face of someone you love. The more you know, the more there is to be known, and the more you want to know. You can find the bottom of a puzzle pretty quickly—it's just a diversion. But a mystery has no bottom. You continue contemplating forever. A great danger, an idolatry even, is to turn any human face into a puzzle. Human beings are fathomless mysteries about whom there is always more to be contemplated and adored. How much more God, who makes each human being in the divine image? The God of the Bible always mediates his presence through objects: wine, water, food, the poor, the enemy, one another, creation, a face. Above all a face.

16. I take this distinction from Paul Claudel by way of Andrew Louth in his first chapter of *Discerning the Mystery*.

Note how they cannot recognize his face. This face is one they have contemplated and loved for years; one they now mourn as though the life of the entire world has died. Rowan Williams speaks of the contours of the face of the resurrected one slowly coming into focus. Remember this is the face of an enemy. These disciples have betrayed, abandoned, colluded, denied, turned in, and run. Some of the women disciples seem to have stayed by Jesus's side at the cross. All the boys have fled. They are his enemies in every imaginable sense. And now their enemy is among them. But he is not back for revenge.[17] He is back for the restoration of table fellowship, friendship, love, and a new sort of community based on those gifts that includes, potentially, all the world. The church is the beginning of God's new way of being human.

Now many a biblical text can appear before us as an enemy—one by which we are repulsed. Or they can appear before us as something boring. That is, worse than an enemy—something toward which we are simply unmoved, indifferent. The text can appear as one overly familiar. Or just plain lifeless. There are as many kinds of texts as there are human beings. And who we are as we confront a text on behalf of the community for which we read is just as varied. Then here's what happens. We see a stranger. He is unfamiliar but not hostile. He flirts with us. Stays coy. Won't identify who he is right off. But he does ask us why we are the way we are just now, with a little anger even (Luke 24:25–26). And he proceeds to explain to us, yet again, about this crucified Messiah, about glory that only comes through agony, about the whole of the scriptures testifying to just this. He seeks to walk on, but we don't let him. He sits down at table, takes, blesses, breaks, gives, and—wait, it's the Lord! And he is gone. But the flame in our hearts is not. And we continue walking to tell others of this risen Lord who still has a thing for the table.

For Further Study

Anderson, Gary A. *The Genesis of Perfection: Adam and Eve in Jewish and Christian Imagination*. Louisville: Westminster John Knox, 2002.

Anderson shows what ancient Christians thought they were doing as they noticed not only that Christ is Adam done right this time but also that Mary is Eve done right this time.

17. This theme comes from Williams, *Resurrection*.

Louth, Andrew. *Discerning the Mystery: An Essay on the Nature of Theology*. Oxford: Clarendon, 1980.

Louth is a patristics scholar who shows what ancient Christians thought they were doing as they read figurally: they were tuning their hearers' delight.

Williams, Rowan. *A Ray of Darkness*. Cambridge, MA: Cowley, 1995.

My desert island book. In sermons and addresses Williams shows how we cannot perceive all of God, not because God is tragically distant, but because God has come unbearably close.

4

Augustine

Suffused with Delight

I write this book as a lover of the church. There may have been any number of more efficient ways for God to save the world. And instead God chose the church through which to bless everyone else. The church is always Israel-shaped. Like Israel, we are not chosen for our own sake. God's blessings aren't *for* us. They're *through* us, *for* everybody else. So while I might prefer to be done with the church—while *God* might prefer to be done with the church—I can't, we can't, for it's the backward, stiff-necked batch of losers through which God has promised to work.

Not that actual church *people* know any of this, necessarily.

Ponder with me, gentle reader, all the terrible reasons folks come to church. Some come because someone more powerful makes them—say, a parent, or someone they're dating or want to date (power comes in lots of forms). Where I pastored in North Carolina, folks would come to church because it was good for business. I realized slowly that some folks only came to church when they could wear a suit (rare in our casual vacation town) and pass out bulletins, serve as ushers, or otherwise be seen. I remember a writer trying to decipher for puzzled Chicagoans why twenty-six thousand people per weekend would turn up at Willow Creek Church, the behemoth in the Windy City's suburbs. One interviewee seemed puzzled at her puzzlement: Where else would you want to be? he asked. The coffee is plentiful and free and cheerfully served. The show is *excellent*—drama and music and entertaining speeches. The musicians and speakers are pretty to look at. The childcare is free (think about that for a minute). Where else can you be treated in such a courtly, kingly manner in Chicagoland on a Sunday morning?

These reasons have little to do with a certain crucified and risen Jew from Nazareth.

Superficial rationales for church attendance point up one crucial question: What do we read the Bible *for*? The traveler who opens the Gideon's Bible in a hotel room to kill time between cable shows will have one set of problems; the Bible scholar at the university seeking tenure will have another; the leader of a Muslim or Jewish faith community seeking to familiarize her- or himself with the faith of the community's neighbors, yet another. These readers bring strikingly different skills and needs to their interpretive work. The hotel patron may need the most basic of introductions: this book has two halves, an Old and New Testament; the one looks forward to Jesus, the other looks back on him. The scholar needs to be able to read complex ancient languages like Hebrew, Aramaic, and Greek (and probably several more), and to be up on the scholarly literature enough to push it forward in a new direction for the sake of academic advancement. The imam or rabbi brings from their own religious community a set of hard-won interpretive skills, which will have analogies and points of equivocation with the skills required to read the Christian Bible well.

The Bible Is for a Specific People

Every blessing to each of these readers, but this book is written for another set altogether. Namely, those who find themselves regularly asking themselves, "What do we do *this* Sunday?" These are readers who have already decided Christianity is true, and even sought the church's blessing to go forward to preach and teach its truth to others. That church has helped educate them, placed its imprimatur and anointing on them, and sent them out to preach, teach, pastor souls, and lead that community in mission. The Bible is not only for preachers. God's gifts don't stay with their first recipients, ever. They are Israel-shaped, womb-shaped. They are also for laypeople who teach Sunday school, parents who teach children; anyone who teaches about God to another person must also interpret well. Both the interpreter and the listeners for whom she interprets have long since waded into the deep end of the pool. They have made promises to follow the God made known in Jesus through baptism, membership vows, confirmation, and more. They've passed on the coffee shop or the Sunday news, tempting though those are. They've braved their way through the awkward handshakes and complicated social interactions that constitute any human gathering. They're *there*, expecting to hear something that makes it worth their while to have shown up. Everything has been sung, said, and checked off up to the point where the leader stands to speak.

What now?

We've narrowed down our interpretive community quite a lot, from all-comers to the target audience for this book: those charged to teach the Bible in the church. But what sort of church? Some Christian traditions see preaching as a weekly reinstitution of the revival meeting. It is meant to lead listeners to conversion, and so will be followed by an altar call, or at least its half-hearted imitation among those previously converted who still feel the need for reconverting their insufficiently converted neighbors. Other communities, more sacramental in nature, will see preaching as a prelude and introduction to the rest of the liturgy. Its goal is to prepare God's people for the mysteries they are about to meet, perhaps by discussing the feast day appointed by the Christian calendar. Others expect comments on the "events of the day," loving a purported quote of Karl Barth: that we preach with the Bible in one hand and the newspaper in the other.[1] The danger of this, of course, is that we just give amateurish interpretation of the day's political goings-on with a patina of Bible superficially brushed on. Still others, of a thinkier evangelical sort, gather to hear Christian truth exposited in a way that engages other sorts of truth, not necessarily as a prelude to converting those present, but with an eye to equipping the saints to sort out truth from falsehood in contention with others during the rest of the week. The point is simply that the kinds of difficulty the Bible presents will vary with the kind of community on behalf of which one reads and the kind of event for which the preacher must prepare.

There is a commonality in all these Christian communities. At the risk of expounding on the blindingly obvious, what they all have in common is . . . Jesus. Any of the hypothetical secular interpreters above can read without reference to the crucified and risen Lord of the church. For them it does not matter whether the rabbi from first-century Nazareth has long since rotted in a tomb. Perhaps most importantly, such readers

---

1. Barth's most famous quote never sounds very Barthian, but apparently he did say something similar. See "Frequently Asked Questions," Center for Barth Studies, http://barth.ptsem.edu/about-cbs/faq.

have no need to see *themselves* as members of Christ's body, his hands and feet and fingers, with him as head. The difficulties they have may be enormous, but those interpretative complications will not be affected one whit if Jesus of Nazareth is now alive or dead.

The church gathers on the day Jesus rose. But that doesn't mean it's entirely happy about it. Again, at the risk of stating the blindingly obvious, Jesus rose a long time ago. Already in the New Testament itself there are signs of communities growing tired of waiting for his return (Acts 1:6; 2 Pet. 3:8). Yet this people still gathers week after week. The same folks will gather around the same book again, and again, and again. They want to hear something new. Or at least something old retold in a new way. If the preacher can feel tired of having to whip up something fresh when the customers have sampled the whole menu, parishioners might wonder why they continue to pass up the *Times* and free coffee refills.

Reading the Bible, like going to church, has a great deal to do with our desire. What do we really want? You can tell who a person is, most profoundly, by divining what exactly it is they most want. Donald Miller opines that the original *Star Wars* movie (renamed *Episode IV: A New Hope* for those of you with no memory of life without the prequels) is so compelling for this reason: you can tell exactly what every character wants.[2] Every ounce of effort is expended in acquiring that desire. Purity of heart is to will one thing, Kierkegaard said. The Bible exists only because God wants to use it to reorient our desire away from selfish things like material acquisition and career advancement and toward selfless things like love of God, the neighbor, and the poor.

Now, how do you teach the Bible in a way that participates in that divine reordering among people with no interest in being reordered? People who are there under some compulsion or other and are dead set against anything like an encounter with the true God, fleshed in Christ, breathed on the church in the power of the Holy Spirit?

I Can Tell They're Bored

In the early fifth century, Augustine of Hippo was the greatest Christian teacher alive. He may still be the greatest Christian teacher we've

2. Miller, *Million Miles*, 113.

ever had. (Hundreds of millions of Orthodox Christians will fight that assertion fiercely, but I'll stand by it.) And he receives a letter from a deacon in Carthage, a bigger city not far from his city of Hippo. Deogratias considers himself an excellent teacher. He likes teaching. He's good at it. Folks respond. He's good at rewiring desire from selfish to selfless; he can take folks who are there for money or the opposite sex or because they lost a bet or because they're sleeping one off and transform them into lovers of God and neighbor. Or so he says. His problem, he also says, is that *he's* bored when he teaches. He tries to teach, but he finds what he teaches trifling and lifeless. How, he wonders, can he teach what is boring to himself?

Augustine writes back a book called in his Latin *De catechizandis rudibus*, literally "On instructing the rude." This is usually translated more politely, something like the version I'm using, *Instructing Beginners in Faith*,[3] because Latin's *rudibus* doesn't quite mean what we think of as rude—uncouth, mean, unkind. It simply means ignorant, with no judgment implied. Someone who doesn't know something is rude. This is nearly the only book we have from the ancient church about how to teach those who want to become Christians. These are folks who simply don't know about Jesus, no judgment implied. And they want to know. They're a bit different than the audience I described above. They're a dream audience. And poor Deogratias is having trouble speaking to them in a way that he finds compelling.

Augustine's primary response is about desire.[4] There are three things going on in interpreting a text—the author and what he wishes to communicate, the words on the page in all their difficulty and glory, and the *desire of the reader*. We tend to think of interpreting a text as a matter of drawing out meaning, divining what was in the author's head. Those things are part of it. But another part, without which the other two are completely impotent, is the desire of the reader, what she loves and how profoundly. So, too, with the public teacher. Their passion is nearly the most important thing in whether and how we learn from them. Think back to your favorite professor in college or teacher in high school. What's the first thing you think of? Not likely their extensive knowledge. You may not even remember the content of what they taught

---

3. Augustine, *Instructing Beginners in Faith*. Hereafter, page references from this work will be given in parentheses in the text.

4. Williams, "Augustine's *De Doctrina*."

you. What you remember, I reckon, is their passion for the subject. The nerdy enthusiasm with which they approached their topic. The zeal with which they taught and passed on what they could. If teachers love what they teach, you notice and learn better. That's Augustine's primary response to Deogratias, presented gently but clearly: The primary thing that teaches is your passion, your love, your desire. If you adore what you're doing, they'll notice and come along. If you don't, well . . .

Augustine would surely take aim at the loveless state of much of our preaching—someone up front talking in a desultory way about a love that has long since turned to ash, and folks probably listening to this passionless exposition with even less affection. Never mind saying the sermon is false; it's too trifling to adjudge truth or a lie. You want to say to such a gathering: Hey, the God who made everything out of dirt and destroyed death with resurrection wants to love you into being a church on fire with the Holy Spirit. But if you did, they might just yawn again. As a listener, I find myself wanting to scream: Say something, anything, worth saying! Now! And if there's nothing urgent here, why are we bothering?!

Augustine's problem was different than ours. In his day, folks were streaming to church in unimaginable numbers. Christianity had gone from a persecuted Jewish sect to an empire-wide favored and even mandated religion in only the last few generations. So Augustine and many other priests and bishops felt they had to practice sussing out the truth of the motives that folks presented when they turned up for church. This is the opposite of the problem where I live in post-Christian Vancouver. Folks don't turn up for business, or to find someone to date, or for the entertainment. If someone turns up, they're more likely there for God. That's a gift.

Augustine is a doctor of desire. He knows how to work on people's longings—since that's where God works and he's seen God work on his. So he tells Deogratias (a bit confusingly, since Deogratias has said folks turn up *wanting* to be Christian and he's good at instructing them) to flatter his hearers. When they say why they're in church, they'll likely present something untrue. A façade. A religiously polite ruse. Fear not, Augustine says. Flatter them by treating it as though it were true. You say you're here to learn more about God (knowing that you lie, and you know I know, and I know you know, and none of us can say it)? Fantastic! Spectacular! That's the greatest thing about being alive—to know God. "Commend and praise that motive," Augustine advises, until the listener "actually enjoys being the kind of person he wishes to appear" (23).

The desire to become a different sort of person is precious. It rarely happens to us. But one way it can happen is if someone we admire sees in us a better sort of person than we presently are. And praises it, until it comes into being. This is finally what church is for. It is what reading the Bible is for: becoming a different sort of person. The sort of person the church calls a saint. That is, one resplendent with divine glory. One in whom and through whom the fire of the Holy Spirit burns. The point of the Bible isn't to learn what it says. The point of going to church isn't to be more religious. The point of both is to be made into nothing but love of God and neighbor.

Augustine knows Deogratias can't get someone there just with a few compliments. In fact, no one can get another person there. There is a deep mystery in who becomes the sort of person God wants all of us to be. We can't even guess, by examining folks' behavior in the judgy, gossipy way we all do, who's on their way to heaven and who has other reservations. All we can do is work on our own delight. And encourage others' delight. Teach with the sort of passion that marks the best teachers. "We are given a much more appreciative hearing," Augustine says, "when we ourselves enjoy performing our task. Then the texture of our speech is suffused with . . . delight" (8).

Delight is a social phenomenon. It is imitative. We delight in what we see others delighting in—especially those we admire. Augustine notices the way folks talk about a favorite actor. They won't rest until their listener comes and experiences that actor's work for themselves. Or a favorite gladiator (we might think of an athlete here). Augustine elsewhere recounts the social nature of desire by speaking for his friend Alypius.[5] He gave up watching gladiatorial contests when he became a Christian. But some old friends dragged him along. He resolved to listen but not be moved, closing his eyes. Then the sound awoke something. *Just* a peek maybe. And he saw the blood. And heard the roar of the crowd. And felt the surge of energy. And loved it. Longed for it. Gave himself over to it. How could he not? The crowd incited his desire until it became irresistible. This is a sort of perverse imitation of how things are supposed to be at church. We catch fire with the desire of the others there. "Before all else, Christ came so that people might learn how much God loves them, and might learn this so that they would catch fire with love" (19). All other projects of group enthusiasm are pale imitations of what the

5. See book 4 of *Confessions*, 90–110.

church is meant to be—a body of believers incandescent with Christ's love. This is why it's so hard to be church in Vancouver—there aren't a lot of fires to get consumed with. It's why Augustine has to suss out folks' actual desire for being part of the church—they may just be mindlessly swept up in the conflagration. But the nature of desire is the same. We notice others' desire. It shapes ours. This is why middle schoolers imitate their peers' fashion. It's why we pursue the entertainment, careers, marriages, and religions we have. Desire is what makes us human.

No wonder—God planted it in us to lure us back to God's self.

The Humble Christ Delights

But here's a problem. No matter how passionate a teacher in front of us is, we won't go along if they're teaching nonsense. Sure, they're really excited about the snake oil they're selling, but if it's snake oil, we'll step out, thanks very much. Their enthusiasm can be a cover for intellectual insecurity (as the professor's marginal notes say, "Argument weak: yell like crazy"). Folks ancient and modern get caught up in cults and sects and all manner of group ridiculousness all the time. We don't jump in headlong with such people. We avoid them. Pity them. However much passion, however hot the group conflagration, if what's being taught is not true, we'll be wise to steer clear.

This is where the content of Augustine's teaching comes in. The center of the Bible is Christ, who is, surprisingly, the "future humility of God," foretold in Israel's scripture (80). God, on Christian lights, isn't just high, lofty, far away, distant, unsullied with us. God, in Christian thought, is Jewish. Human. Not just great and holy but little and lowly. And since our neighbor's desire is the most important thing in shaping ours, *God becomes our neighbor*. In one of Eugene Peterson's truly inspired translations, "The Word became flesh, and moved into the neighborhood."[6] If it takes a neighbor's desire to set ours alight, then the one living and true God will become that flesh-and-blood neighbor. That is the high point, the climax, the heart, of the Christian Bible: the Word is made flesh to love us into being a new humanity.

Christ is the high point but not the beginning of the Bible, literally speaking. He comes in the middle. Or two-thirds of the way through,

---

6. His translation of John 1:14 in *The Message*.

really. What of all that real estate before him? I was taught to read the Bible by a fantastic youth pastor. He suggested we all read the Gospel of Mark and note the ways Jesus loves: he teaches, casts out demons, touches lepers, heals, spits on people's eyes, and makes them brand-new. Just act after act after act of tenderness and mercy. Count them all if you can. I started reading the Bible because I fell in love with Jesus. It revolutionized my life. It still does. Or rather, he does.

Our difficulty in teaching scripture, others' difficulty in learning it, are both related to our location in the middle of history, after the fall, before full redemption. There is no greater sign of our distance from that day that "eye hath not seen" than that "we like to discern the truth in an unusual way but grow weary of expressing it in the usual manner" (17). All is not lost. In fact, as ever with Augustine, God uses our sin to move us toward salvation. The theologian for whom the fall is a "happy fault," *felix culpa*, since redemption will be sweeter after the fall than it would have been without it, argues that God can make use of our hard-headedness in teaching and being taught. Scripture is chock-full of difficulty *by divine design.* Such "concealed oracles" work "to sharpen the desire for truth and to shake off the torpor" of those listening (33). If scripture's meaning were always plain, we would despise it. As it is, we have to work to discern its meaning. And because our distance from God is manifested as pride, God came in a humble form, "to the end that our swollen conceit . . . may be healed by an even greater antidote. For the misery of man's pride is great, but the commiseration of God's humility is greater" (24). God has designed scripture, intentionally, in a humble fashion, to humble us who are proud. He has hidden mysteries in there, or perhaps we should say *the* single mystery of the incarnation there, in places where we might not expect to find it, so we would have to hunt for it. Scripture is not transparent as our knowledge of God one day will be, so we have to work for knowledge by the sweat of our brow, as part of Adam's curse (Gen. 3:19). I remember complaining to a high school chemistry teacher about our awful textbook. She agreed it wasn't immediately clear. Then she shocked me: "Clarity is overrated in teaching." The authors wanted us students to work for their meaning. If they made reading too easy, we wouldn't realize how challenging chemistry is.

For Augustine, God has designed the way God teaches us with great care. Like the chemistry book, the Bible is intentionally unclear, for the sake of our instruction. The difficulty in reading drives us into community where we teach one another to read, understand, and live out the scriptures. So the Bible doesn't just recount history as a set of facts. It isn't just "one damn thing after another," in the sort of history we're all bored by. No, God teaches us who we are with intentionality. God wants us to be like the child at the Jewish Passover who asks, "How is tonight unlike any other night?" and hears the millennia-old story, "We were slaves in Egypt . . ." We. Not some other people a long time ago far far away, but us. Augustine compares the teacher of scripture to someone with treasures to display (14). She doesn't unpack them all at once. No, she veils them. And brings them out slowly. The reveal matters. The order. The joy with which the presenter presents. Scripture is designed to instruct our desire. Not to relay facts alone, but to make us different people.

For example, the story of creation: Could God not have created all instantly? God slowly creates and tells the story instead, so that we will learn and grow. It's not that God physically walks in the garden, or has a beard, or sits on a chair: these are images, for our benefit, meant to teach us something. Genesis records that God "rested." But God doesn't get tired or lie down or snore or wake up groggy. We do. God is using these images to show us something more profound. For Augustine this is a sign, a figure, a symbol—use whatever image you like. There are six ages of creation, from Genesis till now. The seventh is eternal rest for the saints in Christ. But that rest is not lazy, not Huck Finn's nightmare of lying around on clouds all day. No, the saints will contemplate all the good God did through them: forgiving sins, turning enemies to friends, restoring the world to rights. They'll remember that they lost the rest God gives in his commands. And then Christ came, with a humble glory that shushes angels. We "lost the rest" we had in "the Word's divinity, but regained it in his humanity" (71). God never stopped pursuing us, to the point of being clothed in our humanity and suffering death at our hands. That's a lot from the description of God resting! But God put it in the book for a reason: that we would notice its oddity, and probe deeper. God has a blessing for us here.

The implications are endless. We never stop learning eschatologically. Heaven, Jorge Luis Borges proposed, is like a kind of library (I know this sounds like hell for normal, less nerdy people, but bear with me). There is never a bottom to the growth we can undergo; the transfiguration is unending from one degree of glory to another. We also don't know all there is to know now. It is not as though Christ turns up and we suddenly have all the answers—far from it. In fact, in Christ, we see our degree of ignorance, foolishness, and fallenness all the more starkly. How could we ever pass judgment on anyone else? There is no human being or culture from whom we stand to learn nothing. Augustine is the great teacher of humility (*pace* much of his reputation). Delight is essential to humility. Insisting we know nothing, Socrates said, is the first step of wisdom. Every other step is like it.

"Long since, indeed from the beginning of the ages, this profound mystery has been unceasingly prefigured and foretold" (71). That's how to read the Old Testament: looking for traces of the one who will not rest until relationship with us and all creation is restored. This reading is not meant to prove anything to the skeptical. It is meant to delight the convinced, or those on the way to being convinced. It is meant to sit lightly—like a joke, or more, like a musical riff in an improvisational performance. A figural reading works on us who can't see. We look at the words with bewilderment. But then we start to discern a familiar figure. One who loves us. One coming toward us, to save. And we delight. "Look! He's here! Even here! I didn't expect to find him, and indeed, I didn't—he found me. Again! That's what he's always doing."

Now you may immediately feel the brakes coming on. Why read the Old Testament looking for Christ? Isn't that a foreign imposition on a text that knows nothing of him? Why not just be honest and read the New? This whole book is an answer to that set of questions. To clear away two misimpressions first: this is no more a foreign imposition than is Christianity itself. We think we gentiles have access to the God of Israel in Christ. That's outrageous! Unless it's true. And if it's true, we can read these texts in light of the one who writes us into the story. I can understand why Jews or nonbelievers might find this an imposition, but *Christ*ians ought not, lest we cut off our own salvation. Second, and more importantly, the New Testament reads the Old this way. When Jesus quotes the Psalms from his cross, or when the risen Jesus explains to dumbfounded disciples how the scriptures are all about his passion, or when Paul finds the church in the desert in Exodus, they are not just giving readings that would get them an F in most of our Bible courses (though there *is* that . . .).[7] They are teaching us how to read Israel's scripture. All of it, not just the portions they quote.

It is delightful to see what we love and did not expect to see. To be surprised by Jesus again. Or more personally—it is delightful to

7. Rushing past Mark 15:34; Luke 23:46; 1 Cor. 10:11.

see One whom we love when and where we didn't expect to. And it is in this context that we find one of Augustine's most famous lines of teaching: "In the Old Testament the New is concealed, and in the New the Old is revealed" (23; the Latinate forms of the words work in English too: the gospel is "latent" in the Old Testament and "patent" in the New). It's a handy formulation of the Christian distinction between the Old and New Testaments, and so shows up often in survey presentations of scripture and church history, as well as in scholarly discussions of Augustine's theology. What's less often noted is its relationship to this key Augustinian concern of how to delight oneself and one's audience, on the way to love's proper object of God and neighbor. Our delight is tickled as we *see* Christ concealed in the Old and revealed in the New.

To read the Bible with Jesus, we have to learn to *expect* to be surprised. And this is not easy. To go in *looking* for him would seem to dull the surprise! But look we must. He's shown us how. And we know it's him we'll find. We just don't know *how* he'll appear to us this time. We do not go to the Bible wondering which god we will find—we know in advance. We just don't know how *this* God, whom we have long ago met and long since loved, will meet us this time. In the Christian life, we have to learn to see double. There is the patent sense of things that happen, and then there is a deeper, more profound "gospel" sense of what they mean, divinely speaking. It is difficult enough to get the basic sense of stories right, like those in Genesis about Jacob. God chooses to work through a scoundrel like Jacob, and when we first read those efforts to glean a gospel sense of his story, they can seem odd, repugnant even. Augustine hopes we will press through that initial sense of being offended to see that perhaps these words can bear the weight of this interpretation placed on them, and make a sort of spiritual sense of words that did not seem before to have this meaning—that God chooses because God is faithful, not because we are good. The point of doing so is to learn delight anew. We are pleasantly surprised to find Jesus even here, above all places here, in the words of the very scripture that taught us about Jesus in the first place—and not in some holier people than us, but in people as flawed as us.

Jewels on a String

So, for example, Augustine points to all the ways God saves with wood (79). Those on Noah's ark are saved with wood. The people grumble at Moses, and he tosses wood into the bitter water at Marah and it becomes drinkable. This is, in one way, a surface reading, literally superficial. But what if surfaces are all we have? A people trying to be "crucified with Christ" think differently about wood (Gal. 2:19–20). And then we see glimpses of wood in the scriptures, in the world around us. All of these references to wood actually gesture toward and remind us of the wood by which God saves. This is proof of absolutely nothing. It's a wink. If we don't notice, so much the worse for us. But if we do, we're delighted and our love increases. If the image works to move us from puzzlement to enlightenment and finally to delight, it works. If not, another image is coming soon. Here we see another key to figural reading. It sits lightly. It is meant to flesh out details of the text in ways that show its christological resonance and increase our love for God and neighbor. If it fails to do that, fine, we'll keep reading, maybe the next one will increase love. And if this reading fails, God will supply another. The point is not to grasp for all time a single meaning, unseen by others. It is to open the text up, and our eyes up, to meaning that is now publicly available and can be shouted from the rooftops.

Augustine continues his gallop through biblical history. From Abraham to David we see the terror of Egypt, salvation through water, liturgical signs of the Passover (the marking of the doorposts is akin to the anointing of our foreheads in baptism, since our head is a sort of doorpost [83]). From the exile to Christ is a time of praying for our captors, building what we can for the common good while being ruled by enemies. And then Christ's own birth is one that marks a change—not in God but in us. God joins human nature, in what is not a divine degrading but a human ennobling.

> He knew hunger, he who provides food for all. He knew thirst, he through whom all drink is created and who, in a spiritual sense, is bread for those who are hungry and spring-water for those who are thirsty. He was exhausted by his travels on earth, he who made himself for us the way to heaven. In the presence of his revilers he became as one incapable of speech and hearing, he through whom the dumb spoke and the deaf heard. He was bound fast, he who freed

the infirm from their bonds. He was scourged, he who banished every scourge of pain from people's bodies. He was crucified, he who put an end to our crosses. He died, he who raised the dead to life. But he is also risen, never to die again, so that no one should learn from him to pay too little heed to death, as if there were never a life to come. (94)

For those unsure, this is what the church calls *preaching*. It's seeing ourselves in God's story and delighting in it. It *works* if one is liturgically situated. If not, it will seem like rhetorical sleight of hand. A trick. A lie. But if one's task is to bring this text to bear on the *same* community worshiping the same God today, its fundamental thrust will seem right, even if one may disagree with this or that interpretation. This is why leaders of other faith communities are more likely to have sympathy with this form of reading.[8] But Augustine sees Christian specifics in this sort of reading that go even deeper. In Christ, God brings about a great reversal that we Christians have ever to keep before our eyes lest we quickly forget. "It was not his wish to be made king by men, since he was out to show those whom pride had cut off from him the way of humility" (94). In Christ we discover God under a foolish sign. Will we not look under other biblical signs to find the God who always seems to be working in human lowliness?

Augustine suggests the teacher arrange these jewels on the string of history. There shouldn't be too many jewels lest we lose attention to each one. That is, we can't pile up too many historical incidents. And there has to be a string. Not a showy one—it's not designed to draw attention to itself but is there to draw attention to the jewels. The "golden thread," as he calls it, is the continuity of history, from the events in scripture to us gathered today (26). The teacher must show a continuity—subtly, not overwhelmingly, and certainly without forcing it. But with no string the jewels can't be seen.

And this showing creates a new "we." Augustine's advice to Deogratias is that he learn anew what he already knows as those in his charge learn it. His analogies are lively as ever: sometimes, when we show

---

8. Jon Levenson's masterful book *The Hebrew Bible, the Old Testament, and Historical Criticism* shows this is so on his account of Judaism, for example. Peter Ochs describes the way postliberal loosening of Protestantism's dogmatism about historical criticism opens up new conversations with Jews; see his *Another Reformation*.

guests around our city, we see things anew through their delighted eyes (46). Wow, you're right—I hadn't been noticing, but that's gorgeous. So, too, when we show people the treasures of the faith: we see them anew through their eyes. What is happening here is the church is becoming a new "we." I see with you. You see with me. We together delight in Christ. The knowledge that is Jesus and the love that is the Holy Spirit birth a new people called church.

Again, there is something erotic going on here. Augustine suggests the teacher show his treasures slowly, one at a time. The reveal matters. I can't help but think of the ups and downs of a courtship. Diving in bed all at once destroys the rhythm of the thing. There is an appropriately slow order to what we call falling in love. Augustine compares teaching to a sort of seduction. Even in a shameful lust, he says, fire burns hotter when it's mutual (18). Whether in shameful or chaste romance there is pursuit, feigned disinterest, efforts to surprise and get around defenses. Sometimes it all falls apart. At other times, to the great delight not only of the lovers but of the community surrounding them, love takes between two people. Promises follow. And fruit is born. And then pursuit has to begin all over again, even after marriage—in which case it begins again with the same person! In dating or in "shameful" seduction, it begins again with a new person. But the order of things is the same—because God designed it that way to seduce us in Christ.

As readers and teachers of the Bible, we get to play matchmaker between God and humanity. And that's why and how we read the Bible. If you weren't intimidated by the teaching task before, I hope you are now. There is immense hope, however. God desires for us to learn from one another in community. And as we do, we struggle together, and against one another; we harm one another and learn how to forgive. Teaching and learning make us into the sort of community God wants his church, and so all the world, to be. Augustine's words: "Love itself, which binds people together in the bond of unity, would have no means of pouring soul into soul, and, as it were, mingling them one with another, if persons never learnt anything from their fellow people."[9] So the difficulty Deogratias names—and anyone who teaches feels—is good and given by God, so that we would yearn to become the church God dreams about.

I'll leave you with one final, tangible example of interpretation. It's from the parable of the good Samaritan, a story so familiar we have in-

9. *On Christian Doctrine*, xiv, references made gender neutral.

surance laws with the title (Luke 10:25–37). First, we must defamiliarize it, or rather show that those teaching and listening are far less familiar with the story than we think. For there is enough there on a literal level to shock, offend, move, and inspire to holiness. It is not the religious professionals who help the wounded man, but the man's hated enemy. Jesus, in characteristic style, gives the star Sunday school pupil not a straight answer to his question "Who is my neighbor?" but a story that reverberates through time and accuses the best of us, pushing us toward far more radical hospitality.

Ancient Christians saw that reading. They also saw another as they ruminated on this text, prayed over it, committed it to memory, and tried to live it out. They noticed that the contours of the story match those of another, even bigger story. Its topography looks a lot like the map of the whole story of salvation history, or to shift the metaphor, its tune sounds like a movement in the larger symphony of the world's story that God conducts.

The man coming down the road is Adam. He is assaulted and left for dead, as all humanity is in the temptation by Satan and our common fall from grace. Our Jewish forebears, the patriarchs and prophets, came and went, but we remained in the ditch, left for dead. Then a Samaritan came. Jesus himself was accused of being part of this rival people to the Jews (John 8:48), and anyway, besides being human like us, he is also slightly unlike us, different, at odds with us, as one who is also divine. He picks us up, bandages our wounds with the salve of baptism, Eucharist ("pouring wine on them"), anointing, and the teaching of the church. He takes us to an inn (the church), he pays with two denarii (the Old and New Testament, or the twin commandment to love), and—this is key—he promises to return. "Now which of these was a neighbor to the man who fell?" It is God in Christ who is our savior, whose humanity makes him our neighbor, who tenderly cares for us and makes a promise to return and make all things right that now are not.

C. H. Dodd, a famous New Testament scholar, sees this as a sort of arch-misreading in church history. He wrote one of our greatest books on the parables to say why we should read differently.[10] That book still merits rereading, as a genuine classic with few peers. And yet, for those who worship Jesus in this Bible, in this creation, it is hard not to see his incarnation and saving work among us in the contours of this story. An-

10. Dodd, *Parables of the Kingdom*.

cient Christians, like our Jewish forebears, are willing to let a story mean multiple things—even if those meanings compete with one another. Dodd can be right and so can Augustine. And in the church, finally, who cares who is right? What matters is God's delighting of humanity back into right relationship with God, neighbor, creation. God is the one lifting us up on God's back, providing for us in the inn, promising to return and make all things new.

Does that reading not delight? Not to worry. Offer instead one that does. One that fascinates you, one that makes you long to know more, one that stirs you to love God and neighbor. It almost doesn't matter what the reading you offer is, not for now. The question is whether it moves you. Because if it does, it has a shot at moving them. It must also be true, of course. The key to interpretation, as Augustine once told Deogratias, is your delight as an interpreter. Your delight is what your listeners will notice. It is what will return you to the text for more. It is what has a chance to draw in your hearers. It is the tether God has left in your soul with which to draw you to God's self, and others through you.

Augustine pauses at one point in a sermon and says, "I am feeding you what I am feasting on myself."[11] There is always more on which to feast. And there is always more to distribute to others. The only way either stops is if the other does.

For Further Study

Augustine. *Confessions*. Translated by Sarah Ruden. New York: Modern Library, 2017.

> One could do worse than to read Augustine's own self-introduction, which is still enormously influential in the church and the broader culture. This is a beautiful new translation, though I work with an older one in this chapter.

Cameron, Michael. *Christ Meets Me Everywhere: Augustine's Early Figurative Exegesis*. Oxford: Oxford University Press, 2012.

> This is the most learned and accessible introduction among early church scholars to the way Augustine reads the Bible.

---

11. Sermon 339.3. I was directed here by William Harmless, *Augustine in His Own Words*, 156.

Smith, James K. A. *You Are What You Love: The Spiritual Power of Habit.* Grand Rapids: Brazos, 2016.

Augustine saw clearly that we are what we want. Jamie Smith draws out this observation in conversation with contemporary culture.

Williams, Rowan. *On Augustine.* London: Bloomsbury Continuum, 2016.

These learned and at times difficult essays engage and draw out Augustine's heart.

5

Learning Scripture in Nazareth

God Is Jewish, Catholic, and Pentecostal

I have two words in my job title that normal people (that is, people without seminary degrees) frown at. One is *homiletics*. The meaning is deceptively easy—it just means preaching. The Greek word for preaching was *homologeō*, and Catholics and some others still call what a minister does at church a "homily," so that goes down alright eventually. The other word is *hermeneutics*, the theory by which you interpret a text. The church invented hermeneutics as a field. We had to provide strictures with which to interpret the Bible, odd text that it is. Greeks before us had philosophy. Jews had law and traditions of commentary. All people have their stories. But we had this odd, bulky library of a "text," mostly written by Jews and now mostly lived out by gentile Christians, with a crucified rabbi as its binding, its hinge, its beginning and its end, as he is the beginning and the end of all things (Rev. 1:8). So very early on in the church's life our greatest thinkers wrote long and serious treatises about how to interpret the Bible.

This book is also about biblical hermeneutics: How *do* we interpret the Bible? I am convinced we have deep and wide wisdom in our church fathers and mothers who demonstrate how reading the Bible for the sake of the church's life together is meant to be delightful—to surprise us again and again. It is glorious, beautiful, life-altering, world-renewing, because it is a way of seeking Jesus, who promises to be found and then to leave us seeking him with even more joy. But by "delight" and "joy" I don't mean "fun" in some superficial sense. Worship, Annie Dillard opines, should be like approaching a live volcano—ushers should issue

81

signal flares and life preservers, they should lash us to our pews, lest the sleeping God awake and take offense.[1]

The dangerous joy possible in the community of Christ—the joy that is part of the process of becoming holier—shows how tenaciously committed Jesus is to his bride, the church, just as God is unrepentantly committed to his beloved Israel. Jesus is the only reason to bother with the church, miserable as it is. But if you seek him, that is where he is to be found, for better or worse. Flannery O'Connor said this about the church: "I think that the Church is the only thing that is going to make the terrible world we are coming to endurable; the only thing that makes the Church endurable is that it is somehow the body of Christ and that on this we are fed. It seems to be a fact that you have to suffer as much from the Church as for it but if you believe in the divinity of Christ, you have to cherish the world at the same time that you struggle to endure it."[2] I don't understand bothering with the church if there is no Jesus in it. I have known people who seek in the church a career, interpersonal glue for society, moral underpinnings, tradition, something. You can find all of those things without the pain of a local church, trust me. But for all its flaws, Jesus has promised himself to his church. He will be there. We are to meet him there. There is no other way. We are tempted to find him at the bar, in yoga class, behind our eyelids, and I get it—those are much easier ways, it seems. But Jesus is stubbornly, ferociously committed to his church. If we seek him, and we should, we best find the nearest bunch of compromised believers singing the sorriest music listening to the awfulest sermons we can. Because he'll be there. That's the batch of people through whom he is redeeming the world, impossible as that seems.

God Has Only Sinners to Work Through

This is another insight from Augustine that colors how I read scripture: God has only sinners to work through. You and me included. Because there are no "better" people available. We are tempted to think there are. That is why we leave congregations for ones that we think will suit us more, why we condemn other people but remain blind to our own

1. Dillard, *Teaching a Stone to Talk*, 40–41.
2. O'Connor, *Habit of Being*, 90

sin-marred visages. Every single one of our hearts is hopelessly "turned in on" itself, in Luther's and Calvin's language. We are commanded by God to love God and neighbor and use things. Instead, we seek to use God and neighbor and love things.[3] We are exactly backward—perhaps never more so than when we're convinced we're not.

Think with me of what this means. If human beings are presently as immoral as the inhabitants of Sodom and Gomorrah, of Egypt under Pharaoh and the Israelites under the judges, think how unbearably patient God must be. A God who is not unaware of any sin of ours or anyone else's is still letting creation run its course. A God more to our liking and designing would have stepped in and ended things long before now. Instead, God patiently bears with us. The Bible tells us that God has gotten fed up before—with the flood in the time of Noah (Gen. 6–9). The story shows that God is not blind or deaf to our misdoings. What God is, is unfathomably patient.

So don't be surprised if everyone you look out on in church as you preach is presently doing everything in their power to avoid the God of Jesus Christ, in all his patience. And yet—miracle of miracles—they're here! God has not abandoned us in our rebellion. God's Holy Spirit is working despite us to return us to God and love of neighbor. Sometimes Augustinians with the view of sin I give here sound resigned. Well, we're all sinners, especially when we're sure we're not, so all we can do is put limited strictures in place in the world to keep us from hurting one another more than we would otherwise. That is, sin becomes a recipe for despair. But sin is only half the story—and not even the most interesting half! The other is that God has not given up on creation. God has sown grace precisely where we have sown mischief. And God's grace is more powerful than our mischief. St. Paul, wondering aloud about the impact of human sin versus the impact of God's grace, has to say that the gift of Jesus is infinitely stronger than our sin (Rom. 5:15–19). Paul notes that whatever harm we do in Adam and Eve is immeasurably undone, overrun, realigned by God's grace in Jesus. Christ's cross has to be unimaginably more powerful than our sin.

And maybe that's why God is so patient—God is too good to leave us alone. And too good to force God's self on us. God will transfigure us and all creation into the creatures God intended from the beginning—or even greater than God intended at the beginning. You'll see. They'll see. Everyone will see.

---

3. It's an Augustinian distinction in his *On Christian Doctrine*.

A God Who Keeps Promises

The first question in biblical interpretation is, of course, about God. We're not inclined to see it that way—having been taught that the first questions are about what the author intended when he first wrote and what the original hearers might have heard. That is an important set of questions, not to be neglected, often throwing light on who God is. Yet the prior question is about who God is. The Bible exists at all only because God is summoning a people to bear witness to God's glory in the world. The church is that people, and the church has written, stewarded, interpreted, fought with, and loved the Bible for millennia, like Israel before us. The first question, then, for biblical interpretation is what God is saying *right now*. In other words, our preaching, teaching, and biblical interpretation should be drained of past-tense subjunctives: "this text could have meant," "this author might have been thinking of," "what might have been going through Jesus's mind . . ." No. We should speak in present tense. The living God speaks. Now.

And the first thing the living God says is "Go": "Now the LORD said to Abram, 'Go from your country and your kindred and your father's house to the land that I will show you'" (Gen. 12:1). With this command, God calls Abram with quite a task: "I will make of you a great nation, and I will bless you, and make your name great, so that you will be a blessing. I will bless those who bless you, and the one who curses you I will curse; and in you all the families of the earth shall be blessed" (Gen. 12:2–4). That's a lot of blessing! This is God's effort to reverse the damage we human beings have done in creation with our trespass in Genesis 3. God is working to repair what we ruin. And God is doing it in a very, very odd way: by choosing a people. Through what Jews and Christians call "election." By filling the earth with one family, who will be God's own people, God's flesh, God's Son in the world.[4]

Now, these verses have been badly misinterpreted, as have nearly all the verses in the Bible, but these in particular. Recently, in the United States, they have been taken as foreign-policy instructions regarding the nation-state of Israel. Zionism is its own meaty and worthwhile topic for

---

4. Michael Wyschogrod, in his "Incarnation and God's Indwelling in Israel," argues that whatever odd things Christians have done with the doctrine of the incarnation, it is God's idea, and Wyschogrod wants it back on behalf of his fellow Jews. The people Israel is God's flesh in the world. More below.

another author on another day.[5] But for now when we hear "Israel," we should not narrowly think of the country with the flag and army and troubling and troubled relationship with its neighbors. Israel is God's people in the world today; everyone who is heir to this promise to Abram is part of his family.

However, we can know there is a God of Israel only because there is a people called Israel now. It is amazing that today, some millennia after God's calling of a childless, landless man named Abram to have children like the stars of the sky and the sand at the sea, there are some thirteen million descendants of Abram on the planet, and billions more by faith in Christ. Could it be that God is actually a God who keeps promises? That God is . . . faithful? That's the real question, and answer, of Israel. The existence and blessing of this people says yes.

Walker Percy was a renowned novelist and philosopher from my native South, often overlooked today. He asked this marvelous set of questions:

Where are the Hittites?

Why does no one find it remarkable that in most world cities today there are Jews but no one single Hittite even though the Hittites had a great flourishing civilization while the Jews nearby were a weak and obscure people?

When one meets a Jew in New York or New Orleans or Paris or Melbourne, it is remarkable that no one considers the event remarkable. What are they doing here? But it is even more remarkable to wonder, if there are Jews here, why are there not Hittites here?

Where are the Hittites? Show me one Hittite in New York City.[6]

He is, of course, referring to the great oddity of the Jews' existence still on this planet. It didn't have to happen. Some of us gentiles have expended oceans of energy to see that it no longer happened. But Israel continues, praise God. My Jewish students often recoiled against this sort of sentiment—it can suggest a sort of fatalism by which Jews *had* to still be there, but Hitler or any of his predecessors could have "succeeded." Indeed, and my contention is that a world devoid of Jews would be a world devoid of God. It would mean God's promises had failed as surely

5. Good resources include Brueggemann, *Chosen*, and McDermott, *Israel Matters*.
6. Percy, *Message in a Bottle*, 6.

as if God had never sent Christ. We Christians depend for our salvation on the sturdiness of God's promises to the Jews. They're the trunk we're grafted into in Christ. If it falls, we all fall. And we have nothing more trustworthy than that to count on. Only the trustworthiness and blessing of God. Thankfully, there is nothing stronger than that.

When I was teaching the class on Jews and Christians about which I spoke in chapter 1, my students' slumped shoulders showed it's a difficult sort of "blessing" at best. They're proud of their Jewishness, even as they run the gamut of practice from Orthodox to nearly entirely secular. But they don't want to be bandied around like a football in gentiles' religious arguments. They don't want to speak of themselves in rhapsodic terms, as though God loves them more than anybody else—that way of thinking is dangerous. I found they want Israel known for standing up for the outcast, for human rights, for justice at home and around the world. They have their own rigorous arguments with which to speak of what Israel is and is not and haven't really invited me to weigh in (though I found the students I had in class curious enough to ask what I think and kind enough to disagree).

As a Christian, I have to maintain that something else is going on theologically with blessing and election—aware I do so with significant risks, named above. The Jews' very existence is a sign of God's faithfulness without which there would be no church, no Jesus, no God in the world. And that's the issue. Can this God be trusted? The reason God blesses Israel is that God promises to do so, and God *cannot* go back on God's promises. God will not. There is a people descended from Abram through whom God blesses the entire world. This is the unique way that God works—God goes through the particular to get to the universal, not the other way around. Scholars call it the "scandal of particularity." It's fine just to call it God's election of Israel.

And we Christians get in on this election of Israel through the odd way of Jesus grafting us into the tree of Israel (Rom. 9–11).[7] God is Jewish in that Jesus of Nazareth, God in our flesh, is Jewish. God is not, first off, our God. We gentiles are not God's people. The good news is not for us, not at first—Jesus comes for the "lost sheep of Israel" (Matt. 15:24). The Bible is not our book. None of this is for us. God has a people in the world—Israel. Not us. In an age filled with so much self-righteousness,

7. I'm aware of how much my frequent use of the word *odd* owes to Will Willimon. See, for example, his *How Odd of God*.

other-condemnation, religiously inspired hatred, this is a crucial message—God is not *ours*.

Here's what it means for biblical interpretation, the point of this book: never impugn Israel. Ever. Christians do this without even thinking about it and we must stop. A good check is to preach with an imagined "Jew in the pew." Even better, share your preaching with Jewish friends. Ones you know well enough to call you out when you malign Israel or anyone Israel cares about. Now notice this is fraught too! Do you really want to invite Jews to church? Do they want to come? Do you want to evangelize them? (No!) But might they be attracted to Jesus and ask about following him? I hope so. When I've attended synagogue, I've seen how beautiful Israel is and imagined myself following its laws. I'm filled with Israel envy. Look at all they have that we don't! A language, a history, a family. They know who they are and so are fiercely committed to justice in the world, practices that mark out a life of worship in every nook and cranny. But I'm committed to following the Jew Jesus. He calls a family of Jews and gentiles to be a strange offshoot of heirs to the promise to Abram.

The Jews make a claim on our preaching—that we should always look for the trustworthiness of God. This Israel-centered preaching also notices the shape of God's gifts. God is always the God of the particular. God chooses Israel first, through whom to bless the world. God chooses to be flesh in Christ in order then to save the church through him. God is always the God of the particular. God has eyelashes and a spleen and a Jewish mom. And that's about the most world-affirming description of God I can muster. That is, it's the most Jewish God I can muster. Our preaching must be world affirming, embodied, fleshed, sensuous, because the God with the belly button is all those things. Michael Wyschogrod argues that incarnation is a Jewish idea.[8] While it's thought to be a Christian idea, Wyschogrod insists, no, it's a Jewish idea. God is flesh in the world. The flesh of Israel. God lives at One Temple Way in Jerusalem. Sure, Christians have gone and done odd things with incarnation that most Jews reject. But the concept as such is Jewish. And Wyschogrod wants it back. So, too, for us Christians—to preach in a philo-Jewish manner we have to preach incarnationally, flesh-affirmingly, world-embracingly. All of God's gifts are Israel-shaped. They're not for us. They're *through* us for everyone else. And this is where my Jewish stu-

8. See note 4 above.

dents could not be more right. They don't want God's blessings for themselves. No, thank you. They want them only for other people—the vulnerable, the stranger, the refugee, those in danger. Because they've been in danger most of their lives as Israel. That's the strange "blessing" of being chosen by the God of Abraham. Now they see themselves in everyone in danger. So, too, should we Christians.

Jonathan Sacks, former chief rabbi of Great Britain, comments that God is for the world through being for the Jews: the exodus story shows that the only God there is intervenes in history . . . to free slaves. That's it. Not to prop up armies or dictators or empires of any sort, but to choose the crushed and elevate them to glory. And this should be the politics of a church that knows God is Jewish. Where are the crushed people with whom God is identifying now, whom God is raising to glory now, who need our friendship now? Jews know to help those in need. They see themselves there and remember when others did not help (a Canadian diplomat infamously said of Jews seeking refuge from the Holocaust that "none is too many"). So synagogues worldwide have worked to take in Syrian refugees. Syrians are not known for being overly affectionate toward Jews of late. That doesn't matter to the synagogues offering help. People are in trouble. Israel knows God is with them. That's God-in-our-flesh.

And in Christ we know that God is not only with Israel. God *is* Israel. Because God has a Jewish mom. The point of being Jewish, of being Christian, is to be a blessing to the world: "In you all the families of the earth shall be blessed" (Gen. 12:3). In Christ, through us, the God of Israel is making it so.

A Living Tradition, a Catholic God

As if that weren't odd enough, are you ready for this? God is also catholic.

You may already know that the word *catholic* means "according to the whole" or, more snappily, "universal." In the Apostles' Creed, the church affirms a faith in "the holy catholic church," by which we mean not simply the Roman Catholic Church but the whole church of Jesus Christ in the world. Whenever the church gathers in any place on the planet, however many or however few, there are always vastly more people in the room than you can see with your physical eyes. There are all the angels and saints, all of Israel before Christ, all the martyrs after Christ. The faith of Jesus Christ is *mediated* to us by others. Those long dead and those around the world who confess the same faith deliver it to us, and we in turn deliver it to others. That's what the "wholeness" of catholicity means. I can't be Christian without you who also claim Christ, however much you'd rather not claim me. G. K. Chesterton, the great English journalist and Catholic convert, pointed out that folks like to contrast tradition and democracy. But actually, he argued, tradition is the most democratic thing there is. With tradition, even dead people get to vote. Christians are those wandering around the graveyard counting votes, listening to more than just what Chesterton called "the arrogant oligarchy of those who happen to be walking around above ground."[9] Since God is catholic, the only way to hear what God says through the Bible now is to listen with the whole church, both long dead and living now, the church God promises to gather around the slain Lamb and the throne at the end of all things, leading the chorus of a renewed creation.

St. Paul counsels the Corinthian church at one point to "discern the body" when they eat the Lord's Supper (1 Cor. 11:29). This has often been taken to mean they should notice something about the sacrament. But in the context of the whole chapter, he's referring to an abuse in which the wealthier members of the church, who have leisure time, come earlier than the poorer workers and eat all the food, leaving not only no dinner for their harder-working brethren, but no Jesus. Paul isn't referring to the traits of the bread and wine as such. He's referring to our calling to recognize the face of Christ in one we've overlooked. To "wait for one another" (1 Cor. 11:33).[10] To recognize that I cannot approach and feast on Jesus without you, nor can you without me, and this is true whether or not you and I are alive just now, as we mortals judge these things. So to apply to today—we can't follow Jesus without fire-breathing Pentecostals. Without medieval women mystics burned at the stake for questionable orthodoxy. Without Roman Catholics. Without mainline liberals. Without the ancient church in the catacombs. Without the persecuted church today. Without the ones we'd least like to worship beside or with. That one, Jesus says, is me. Sit next to him or her. Get comfortable. You're going to be spending eternity together.

---

9. Chesterton, *Orthodoxy*, 22.

10. I first heard this verse used this way from Rowan Williams. I'm sure Will Willimon has influenced this paragraph as well. See also Gordon Smith's recent book *Evangelical, Sacramental, and Pentecostal*.

Now, what does this have to do with interpreting the Bible?

We tend to think of a tradition as a set of settled conclusions. This is true whether we're advocates of tradition or opposed to it: a tradition is a bunch of correct answers to submit to or rebel against. But a tradition is actually a running argument conducted by those who care about the goods that the tradition gives to humanity through time. The tradition of the church catholic is the good news of Jesus, raised from the dead, presented again ever anew in the lives of the saints, pointing toward a coming kingdom that will renew all things. If you care about that tradition, you're in—you have a voice. You must also do business with what others, living and dead, in the tradition have said. And your view can be corporately ruled against (we call these views "heresies"). But the tradition is never fixed, over, done. It is a living thing, constantly contributed to anew, trying to grow both in faithfulness and in creativity at the same time. The tradition lives in the lives of the saints—and God seems never to tire of blessing us with more of those. Herbert McCabe liked to say that we don't know what Christians will believe in the twenty-fourth century.[11] We *do* know they won't be Arians or Nestorians. That is, they won't think Jesus is a mere creature and not God, and they won't think Jesus is two different persons, one divine and one human. For a variety of reasons, some Christians in our history thought those things. The rest of the church over many decades realized that on the basis of the biblical witness those views had to be wrong, so we ruled them out. They are like roads with ropes across them: don't go that way, you'll die—but look at all these other ways you can go! Modern fantasies aside, ruling out heresies doesn't diminish freedom. It enhances it. There are an infinity of ways to be faithful. Heresy is a narrowing enterprise.[12]

Allow me to illustrate with a story again from our Jewish elder siblings in faith. The story is told of rabbis in an argument over what Moses wrote. The way rabbis argue is to cite previous rabbis, who read previous rabbis, who interpret scripture for the sake of the community's life together. Judaism has a heresy for those who try to read the Bible without the rabbis—only Karaites would try to attempt such a sacrilege. So as the rabbis argue, lucky for them, Moses turns up and proceeds to tell them he didn't mean that at all, he meant this other thing. They look at

11. Quoted in Owens, "Don't Talk Nonsense."

12. I take this view from Williams, *Why Study the Past?* See also Quash and Ward, *Heresies and How to Avoid Them.*

him, confused. "But wait, Moshe, did you read rabbi so and so, and rabbi so and so, and rabbi so and so?" The mediation of Moses, our limited access to him only through the tradition of the rabbis, is no tragic loss. It is, if anything, a gain. The form of Christian faith should be similar. We get at what God says by attending to the scriptures in light of this saint, that theologian, this movement, that event of faithfulness. There is no other way to get to the Bible, and so no other way of being in the presence of God.

To say that God is catholic is to say that it is a great gift to have a faith that is mediated through the tradition, the saints, the church. The space and time between us and the events of the Bible is no tragic lack. No one should wish they had seen the events of the Bible, miraculous though these were. Many who saw the exodus grumbled ten minutes later; most who saw Jesus's miracles shrugged and asked what was for lunch. The space between the Bible and us is not miserably empty; it is delightfully full—of countless stories of faithfulness and fraudulence, each illustrating who Jesus is to us. Tradition bears Jesus to us as physically as Mary bears the Lord in her body. When I think of why I believe, I think of three faithful grandparents, camp counselors who loved me and presented the gospel to me, preachers and sermons and friendships, oceans of hours of attention and love. Those are saints. They bear the gospel to me so I can bear it to others. Their lights do not compete with Christ's. His is brighter as it refracts through them. And God seems to delight in the good news of Jesus being born in the world this way. It is not some plan B, some accident, some surrogate for God's preferred manner of communication. Tradition is rather how God saves.

Protestants have long sought some fulcrum against tradition. There is good reason for this. Tradition can also obfuscate, abuse, hide. This is not surprising. The only sort of people available to bear the tradition are sinners, like us. We Protestants have so successfully shilled for this view that we have scrubbed the calendar and our prayers and our biblical interpretation clean of saints. There was a time when you would know what day it was by what saint's feast day was being celebrated (we still have odd remnants of this when marketers find it profitable). There was a time when you would solicit the prayers of certain saints for certain difficulties (not with prayers to them, but by seeking their prayers for you). And there was a time when interpreting the Bible was physically impossible without the views of previous saints. The words of the biblical text would be physically surrounded on the page with the words of the saints. We still have the form of this—our study Bibles busily reapply interpretive helps that we Protestants scrub away, so we have dispensationalist crystal-ball gazers or university-based historians or teenager advice columnists or whomever in the margins, helping us read. I suggest we also, or instead, include the stories and words of the saints once more. Fill the margins and the calendar and the sermons with these anew. It will take great discernment to choose which saint for which purpose— tradition is an ongoing argument, after all.

I'd like to use an Anglican to illustrate this view of God's catholicity. I asked Sam Wells, then dean of Duke Chapel, now a pastor at St. Martin-in-the-Fields in London, for the best novel about the Church of England. He replied quickly: *The Towers of Trebizond* by Rose Macauley. The premise is that a woman decides to evangelize the Muslims in the Middle East who have only ever heard the obscurantism of Eastern Orthodox popery. She is going to blast them with the reasonable, enlightened faith of the Church of England and they will convert en masse (lest we laugh too hard: this is no more foolish than the West's military adventures to this day). So she sets off on camel, mostly trying to distract herself from her own avoidance of God, clear to the reader, not clear to herself. A friend with whom she talks is a critic of faith. The narrator listens, and replies this way:

> From one point of view she was right about the church, which grew so far, almost at once, from anything which can have been intended, and became so blood-stained and persecuting and cruel and war-like and made small and trivial things so important, and tried to exclude everything not done in a certain way and by certain people, and stamped out heresies with such cruelty and rage. And this failure of the Christian Church, of every branch of it in every country, is one of the saddest things that has happened in all the world.

Welcome to any Church History 101 course—tradition as a bevy of errors harming and abusing. Throw acid on it and move on to living your life just fine tradition-free. She ponders and continues.

> But it is what happens when a magnificent idea has to be worked out by human beings who do not understand much of it but interpret it in their own way and think they are guided by God, whom they have not yet grasped. And yet they have grasped something, so that the

church has always had great magnificence and much courage, and people have died for it in agony, which is supposed to balance all the other people who have had to die in agony because they did not accept it, and it has flowered up in learning and culture and beauty and art, to set against its darkness and obscurantism and barbarity and nonsense, and it has produced saints and martyrs and kindness and goodness, though these have also occurred freely outside it, and it is a wonderful and most extraordinary pageant of contradictions, and I, at least, want to be inside it, though it is foolishness to most of my friends.[13]

That's the catholic tradition that our catholic God bears to us. Not a litany of unchecked successes. Nor a dismal promenade of unadulterated abuses. But people—sinners—whom God does not disdain to draw close to. In fact, drawing close to sinners is God's very purpose in the gospel, in all creation; it is what God is doing right now, the reason God is keeping the earth spinning on its axis.

Diverse People *Talk about Jesus*

Finally, God is Pentecostal. Before the Azusa Street revival in Los Angeles in 1906, there was no such thing as a Pentecostal. We are on our way now to a billion Pentecostals worldwide. That's a remarkable trend in a very short period of time. These are Christians who think the strange, outward expressions of faith in response to the poured-out Holy Spirit starting in Acts 2 were not just a onetime event. Rather, they are a sign of the Holy Spirit's ongoing self-outpouring on the way to renewing all creation.

I personally am no more Pentecostal than I am Jewish or Catholic, strictly speaking.[14] I do, however, argue here that *God* is Pentecostal, just as God is also Jewish and Catholic. That is, God is constantly pouring God's self out on all flesh so that we worship ecstatically, we speak

13. Macauley, *Towers of Trebizond*, 196–97. Wells notes his one mild dissent—he's not sure Christian faith is an "idea," however magnificent.

14. Depending on how you classify these things, the near on a billion Pentecostals are a branch (a big one!) on the Wesleyan family tree to which my people, the Methodists, also belong. That is, we wouldn't have Pentecostals without the Methodist revival, with its emphasis on the new birth, signs of the Spirit's work of sanctification in our lives, and work for the renewal of society.

in other tongues, we see signs and wonders, and we look avidly for the return of Jesus to make all things new. Mainline liberal Protestants like my tribe of Methodists have often been nervous about Pentecostals. Some denominations more explicitly repudiate such current-day signs and wonders. And there are many reasons to do precisely this. See above—God has only sinners to work through. Some Pentecostals are charlatans, not less than some mainline liberals and some atheists. But Pentecostals show us all this: Christian faith has to be weird. It has to be inexplicable. It cannot be domesticated or made safe or predictable, despite our bolted-down rows of pews, our tidied up veneer of respectability, our straight lines and dotted i's. God is wild, free, mischievous, beautiful—and God is sewing back together what we have pulled apart. This will look to us sinners like wild disorder. It is actually a sign that God has not given up on creation and is in fact using us to bring about the world God wants.

For example, Pentecostal Christians are vastly more ethnically diverse than mainline liberal Protestants in North America. One virtue that churches like mine have tried to promote for half a century is that of inclusivity. Synonyms are legion, but they include tolerance. Multiculturalism. We have pursued these goals with a variety of white-guilt-inducing postures, promotion of more diversity into the ranks of our leadership than exists in our pews, social justice initiatives at macro- and micro-levels, and so on. All good things. But notice this—the more we talk about "diversity," the less diverse we seem to become.[15]

By contrast, I don't hear Pentecostals talk about "diversity" all that much as though it were an end in itself, a virtue without remainder. I hear them talk a great deal about the Holy Spirit, about Jesus, about God, about the ways God is not done working in the world but is in fact living and active, drawing even you and me into God's wild and unpredictable ways of working. The more Pentecostals talk about Jesus, the more diverse *people* join them. So here's the Pentecostal rule for biblical interpretation: mainline liberal Protestants talk about "diversity"; diverse *people* talk about Jesus. So if you want diversity, talk about Jesus and see what kinds of unpredictable people turn up to worship him with you, speaking all kinds of languages we don't understand. But

---

15. A Pew study released in 2015 found my denomination, the United Methodist Church, more than 90 percent white—not a lot to show for our primary theological goal over the last half century. Lipka, "U.S. Religious Groups."

if you want more white liberals (or fewer, as statistics show . . .), keep on talking about "diversity." And then you can stay in charge of your decaying denomination.

Willie Jennings, teaching about the black church experience in America, notes the different ways African Americans received a gospel intended to keep them down. They would worship on their own, in brush arbors, at night, not just in the ways white churches on Sundays asked them to (in the balcony preferably). And their worship would be ecstatic, Spirit-filled, enthusiastic in the original sense. Part of what they were explicitly saying and doing is this: Our bodies are not yours. They are God's. And we will worship in ways that make you uncomfortable. Those in power like conformity, predictability, order. Those without are willing to move a little in response to the Spirit.

And this is precisely how Christianity has always worked. Andrew Walls is a great Scottish missiologist who started life as a church historian teaching in West Africa.[16] As he taught on the early church, he couldn't figure out why his students weren't coming alive in response, the way he had when first learning about such African intellectual giants as Cyprian, Origen, Tertullian, and Augustine. Then he realized, oh, wait, these students *are* the African early church. They are *already* alive. They didn't need to import the ferment, the excitement, the freshness of the early church. They already had it to spare. Walls began to study how the gospel moves from one culture to another—first Jewish, then Pentecostally to all nations, from the once Christian Middle East to the then Christian continent of Europe to the now fervent parts of the world such as Africa, Asia, and Latin America. Christianity seems to be the sort of thing that dies in the middle and renews itself on the edges—giving over dignity to its receiving culture as new people understand the gospel in their own terms. And in the process of giving it over, those giving it are themselves changed. They have to learn a new language. They have to eat new foods and learn new customs. This exchange creates ferment, liveliness, new life, beauty. Like Pentecost. We also see here new life, new outbreaks of Pentecost, the gospel transmitted. Walls's present-day example is in his hometown of Aberdeen, Scotland, where, he says, most of the great downtown cathedrals in that

---

16. See his *Missionary Movement in Christian History* and *Cross-Cultural Process in Christian History*. Maybe if Walls had better book titles, Philip Jenkins would not have had to popularize his work with *The Next Christendom*.

beautiful city are closed, converted, changed into nightclubs. But one has gone another way. It is now an African immigrant church asking itself how it can reach out to a city full of lonely older white people.[17] The largest congregation in Europe, in Kiev, is pastored by a Nigerian immigrant pastor. That's the odd, Pentecostal way the Holy Spirit works: we look in this direction and see only decline. But then the Holy Spirit sneaks up behind us and mischievously breathes new life where we were sure there were only graves.

I have had the privilege of teaching a seminarian here in Vancouver named Joachim Chisanga. He and his family responded to God's call to go (Gen. 12:1) from their native Zambia to plant a church in neighboring Botswana. He did, the church thrived, and he and his wife, Nancy, raised their four children in that prosperous southern African country. Until a new government program asked Botswana institutions to be sure there were not Botswana citizens being denied jobs held by foreigners. "Localization," it was called, in the administrative doublespeak with which governments mask outrages. Joachim's pastoral job was advertised, no applicants came forward; nevertheless, his visa was not renewed, and he was forced to go home. The church closed. And he applied to our seminary across the world to find time to figure out his next steps. His wife has joined him, and they are working on visas for their children (Gen. 12 again). He is close to landing a pastoral but not parish job that would leave Sundays free to "work for the Lord." He misses worship in his native southern Africa—more expressive, more free, more Pentecostal. Yet he thrived at our quite-liberal seminary with gay, lesbian, and trans colleagues. He found it a home, a haven, a family, a layer of kindnesses over against the exclusion he'd recently suffered. And he influenced them in turn. His church here has been a Filipino Pentecostal congregation, for God is busily refreshing Christianity in western Canada with Asian immigrants, among others. Joachim is just one of millions of people on the planet on the move for reasons both benign and tragic. And God is not above using our sinful machinations to bless God's world. Canada is proud of its receptivity to immigrants, though not so much of its Christian heritage anymore. This place may find itself surprised that in remembering that one aspect of its once-Christian tradition—welcoming the stranger—it rediscovers the rest.

17. See my interview with Walls: Byassee, "Andrew Walls."

This is how God works—counterintuitively. Yet God also works in accordance with his promises—faithfully. In the language of the African American church, God doesn't always come when you want him, but he's always on time. God does not cede his promises to Israel in order to be faithful to the world in Christ. No, God works through them. God is still Jewish and always will be. God does not move on from his faithfulness in Christ to reach beyond the church—no, God *is* Jesus and vice versa. And the good news of this Jewish, Catholic God has reached the heart of Africa where many of its sons and daughters are on the move, reminding people who once knew but have forgotten that God is also Pentecostal.

I hope you have noticed the Trinitarian pattern to this chapter as I have argued that God is always Jewish, Catholic, and Pentecostal, roughly corresponding to the three persons of the one Godhead—Father, Son, and Spirit. God keeps divine promises. God fills history and sacraments and tradition with God's own redeeming presence. And God is untamable, charismatic, free, delightful. This is the God for whom we look in the Bible as we read for the sake of the church. And we do so knowing this—God will get the world God wants. God is bringing the kingdom about which Jesus preached and which the Holy Spirit now sows in our midst. There is not a thing we can do to stop it. We can pitch in, which makes us fully human. We can work to hinder it, which dehumanizes us and others. But we cannot undo it. We cannot even hurry it—God keeps God's own timetables. We can only bear witness, work toward it, tell others about it, rejoice at signs of its arrival, lament signs of its distance, and long for it. But make no mistake. God will do it. Because God keeps God's promises—in the most delightful ways possible.

For Further Study

Bossy, John. *Christianity in the West 1400–1700*. Oxford: Oxford University Press, 1985.

The author's aim is to critique the Reformation's polemic that Catholicism was dying at the end of the Middle Ages. In showing this was not so, Bossy also gives us a glimpse of the vibrancy of Catholic life, filled with saints living and dead.

Sacks, Jonathan. *Not in God's Name: Confronting Religious Violence.* New York: Schocken Books, 2015.

The former chief rabbi of Great Britain is a beautiful reader of the Bible who here models how to engage other faiths with charity, even delight.

Walls, Andrew. *The Missionary Movement in Christian History: Studies in the Transmission of Faith.* Maryknoll, NY: Orbis Books, 1996.

Truly great books deserve better titles. What sounds like a boring mission report is actually a description of how God works in history—Pentecostally.

6

Gregory the Great

Tracker of Hidden Mysteries

There are few easier ways to get an academically trained professor or pastor's hackles up than to suggest that we should read the Bible figurally. Centuries of determined opposition to this ancient Christian practice of reading, rooted in the Reformers' concern about evading the Word, the Enlightenment's concern about obfuscation, and modernity's worry about turning back the clock of progress, all bubble up into a boil. Contemporary theologians' concern with "Platonism," which is taken to deride bodies, history, and the surface of things (a dubious reading even of Plato, let alone of most of the church fathers), and much more valid concerns about losing the Jewishness of the Bible's roots both add to the reflexive antagonism. Each of these streams of thought has its great saints and its valid concerns. But why exactly the depth of antagonism to allegory?

My sense is that the deeper and rarely spoken worry is that allegory looks like a lie. A text that is patently about one thing is, it seems, twisted to mean another. And that is as valid a concern as there could be. But here's another concern: look at the vacuous state of our preaching. This is not a new concern. It's hard to imagine a religious community gathered around the spoken word that has not bickered about the quality of that word. The point is not to long for a golden age that never was. No, this concern is rooted in humanity's common plight since the fall. We preachers are to stand and give a word that sets people free, that tells the truth, that converts all of us from one degree of glory to another. And yet we often don't do it. We evade. We tell cute little stories. We insult people's intelligence with pious trivialities and drivel. In short, we talk about something other than the Word of God, fleshed in Israel and in Jesus, who saves by the power of the Spirit in the church.

And that's the most valid concern there could be with any act of biblical interpretation: that it fails to tell the truth we meet in Jesus in a way that drags us down the road with him to Emmaus and then out into all the world to preach and baptize and serve. Figural reading is designed to keep us from avoiding Jesus. Those who derived this way of reading from the Bible, from church history, and from their own spiritual lives knew a great deal about the human experience. We're constantly trying to walk away from our commitments to God and to one another. Preaching can be a gift from God to call us back to God and neighbor. But even those of us bold or foolhardy enough to stand over the Bible and talk about it to others often, in that very act, avoid the God who judges and saves us.

Immoderately Christological Interpretation

Figural reading, by contrast, keeps the triune God before our eyes in every act of exegesis. It demands that we take these words with absolute seriousness. If it comes off as a trick, if listeners feel fooled, it doesn't work—they'll stop listening and the preached word loses its power. But if the preacher can show how even these words, perhaps words that are unpromising on their face, bear witness to the incarnation and to the hard road God has made for us in the flesh of Jesus (that is, discipleship), then listeners' faces will turn from puzzlement, to surprised appreciation, to joy and wonder. And for a moment, instead of going our own way in sulking self-loathing as our forebears slinked from the garden, we will take halting steps into the garden of God's delights in scripture and taste the sweet fruit of contemplation and grow spiritually strong.

Gregory the Great (540–604) would seem an unpromising companion with whom to learn about biblical interpretation, at least for a Protestant audience, since a more proper nomenclature would call him "Pope St. Gregory." A student asked me once whether he called himself "great"! (He was called "great" by his successors in the Middle Ages.) Far from intentional self-promotion, the crucial place of humility in the Christian life pops up as much as any other precept in his teaching, to the dangerous degree that he will speak of God allowing his people to sin so as to avoid the greater danger of pride. Gregory is sometimes spoken of as the first medieval pope, and his theology was crucial for such fixtures later lambasted by the Reformers as monasticism, masses for the dead, veneration of relics, and papal involvement in civic affairs (Gregory can be defended on each of these scores, but not here). Most importantly, Gregory is known, and as often today scorned as he once was praised, for his elaborate biblical exegesis. He wrote an almost endless commentary on Job focusing especially on the moral interpretation of that text, meant for monks, that even those who are otherwise Gregory's friends are fond of lambasting. One great historian of mysticism derides that text this way: "It would be a complete mistake to estimate the *Morals* as a commentary on Job. . . . They should be read without any thought of Job, and without any attention to the constant allegorizing."[1] Even Robert Wilken, perhaps Gregory's most articulate contemporary expositor and defender, writes this of a bit of Joban exegesis: "Even the sympathetic reader is likely to respond: 'Really?'"[2] Modern contempt of Gregory is all the more glaring in contrast to medieval appreciation of him. For our forebears, Gregory was "the first among the masters." He was "the venerable and most approved doctor in the catholic faith," the "most gentle doctor," the "great mirror and tree trunk of God's church," the "outstanding homilest," and, my own favorite, "the sharpest tracker of hidden mysteries." Medieval interpreters took to calling him "our Gregory," a riff on the ancient practice of referring to "our Virgil."[3]

The very shrillness of the modern protest suggests something important is going on in Gregory. He may not always be right, but he will always be interesting. When listening to Gregory, the line between truth and insanity may be thin indeed. But for a people who worship a once-dead Jew, such thinness may be fully appropriate.

What's it like to read the Bible in the company of this particular church father?

It's extravagant. Luxurious. It just goes on and on. Long past when even the most patient fans of Gregory's might wish, he's still piling up meaning upon meaning. Gregory has a deep delight in the gospel and, congruently, a deep delight in the words of scripture, and one can imagine the monks listening to his expositions, finding his delight contagious as they learn how to seek Jesus and our life in him. Gregory's work is like

1. This from Butler, *Benedictine Monachism*, 113, quoted in Schreiner, *Where Shall Wisdom Be Found?*, 22.

2. Wilken, "Interpreting Job Allegorically," 215.

3. Terms of endearment come from de Lubac, *Medieval Exegesis*, 2:118.

a Victorian home that just keeps rambling—another turret here, another window garnish there, an extra wraparound porch if you like. Once I was at a worship service in rural Uganda that continued for hour after hour. I asked an American who'd spent more time there when we were likely to take a break. "In Uganda," she said, reversing the Western adage, "more is more." So it is with Gregory's exegesis. For him the scriptures bristle with mysteries. His task as an exegete is to point these out to eager hearers so their delight in the Word can be increased—not to mind the time. Why would one ever want to moderate that?

Gregory has an equally keen interest in the human personality, and his most frequently read and translated work, the *Pastoral Rule*, gives advice for spiritual directors for how to offer wisdom and correction to as many different kinds of people as can be imagined. Recall the image from Origen of the interpreter of the Bible as an organic healer, the botanist, who grinds up the right medicine after attending to the patient carefully. Gregory describes the work of the biblical interpreter on behalf of the community in similar terms. The reader of the Bible has to ascertain not only what the text in front of her means. She also has to tell exactly what the patient—the individual or congregation in front of her—needs. One has to grow into a deep place of spiritual wisdom to make such a judgment. One has always to read both the Bible and the people, since the real work of exegesis, of "drawing out," is to draw one's hearers away from sin and into grace. In Gregory's own example, Job's comforters often speak words that are true, abstractly speaking. But their words are untrue in their application to Job. The comforters have failed to faithfully ascertain the health of their patient (Job, as one who suffers righteously in the image of Christ, is actually quite healthy). So Gregory: "In anything which is said the occasion, the time and the person have to be considered: whether the truth gives strength to the words which are said, whether a fitting time demands it, and whether the nature of the person does not stand in the way of the truth of what is said and the fittingness of the time."[4]

It is morally demanding to read the Bible in Gregory's company. He has an endless fascination with ascetic renunciation: our problem is that we desire the wrong things, and the solution is growing in the disciplines required to want the right things in the right way. Gregory

---

4. Moorhead, *Gregory the Great*, 136, quoting Gregory's *Moralia in Job* 39.64. This selection of his work in translation is a joy to read and is not difficult to procure.

received this tradition of ascetic renunciation from the desert mothers and fathers before him, and he passed it on to the Middle Ages in the form of the seven deadly sins, a list he helped formulate. In fact, this emphasis on moral progress as the point of reading the Bible is one reason some theologically conscientious interpreters avoid Gregory. He sounds like Pelagius, the ancient heretic who encouraged folks to work hard and earn their salvation. The point of reading the Bible seems to be moral improvement—a goal Augustine showed to be a fool's errand. Gregory thinks God wants us to resist evil and has granted us the ability to do so. Yet this does not have to lead to a grim moralism; it can simply mean that through the incarnation God has healed fallen human nature enough that we can make moral progress. Here Gregory is in sync with some modern theologians and ethicists who attempt to reclaim the tradition of the virtues. For St. Athanasius before him, if you want to understand the minds of the saints, you must live the lives of the saints (the switch to the plural is awkward in English—those who steep in the Bible use the word "y'all" where modern individualists prefer "you"!). The point of reading the Bible for Gregory is to become holy. Indeed, the point of being alive for Gregory is to become holy—that is, shot through, radiant, with love of God and neighbor.

A final preliminary: there is a deep but often unnoticed parallel between Gregory's biblical exegesis and his other most famous work, the *Dialogues*. In this text Gregory sought to show his readers that sixth-century Italy was not bereft of saints. Monks and others had heard stories of the desert fathers and mothers, and as it ever seems, the miraculous was not so prevalent in their day. Gregory attacks this position with unrelenting but gentle ferocity. He tells us story after story of holy men and women in Italy who did combat with the devil, miraculously cured illnesses, averted natural disaster for monasteries and villages, divined the secret sins of people's hearts, and more. This text is one that Gregorian critics often point to: it seems rather credulous to so easily assent to Gregory's stories of sinners struck dead or children rising from the dead. Yet Gregory is after something important and worthy of emulation. The saints are not gone. God has not confined the miraculous to the past. No: the world is full of holiness. You have only to look.

To learn to see God at work in our day in remarkable ways through modern-day saints is in deep parallel with learning to see God at work in every detail of the scriptures. Whatever our own position, it's a good bet that those inclined to see God still remarkably at work and God re-splendently present in the Bible will be one and the same congregation.

Reading to Restore Contemplation

What I'd like to do in the rest of this chapter is to imagine what it's like to read the Bible with Gregory the Great, to invite him into our study to read both the text and the people with whom we're preaching. To treat Gregory as a friend would not mean to defer to him on all points, like his sycophantic imaginary dialogue partner in the *Dialogues*, Peter. It would mean to disagree with him at times and to have him disagree with us. My goal is to introduce him to you here and us to him, in hopes that as friends we may all grow in love for God's word and in wisdom for how to speak well from it for our ministry today.

When Gregory turns to scripture, he does so on behalf of the church. This may be so blazingly obvious as not to merit mention—he was only the pope, speaking to monks in early medieval Europe. There weren't yet universities for which one could read in order to commodify ideas. Yet Gregory's particular way of putting it early in his commentary on Ezekiel is poignant: "I know that I have understood very many things in holy scripture when in the company of my brothers which I was not able to understand by myself." All teachers have this experience—the best way to learn something is to be on the hook to teach it to others. An interpreter *sees things* when she goes to scripture on behalf of the church that she wouldn't have seen reading on her own. Gregory is not denying the importance of individual reading, prayer, and contemplation, far from it. When reading in private, the mind, "conscious of its failings, when it considers what it has heard, strikes itself with the dart of grief and pierces itself with the sword of remorse, so that all it can do is weep and wash the stains with streams of tears."[5] (Did I mention Gregory can write a little?) The point is this: scripture can only be read in and for the sake of the gathered Christian community. Individual reading leads back to communal worship and learning, where a new *we* is created. In reading scripture, the line between "we" and "they" gets blurred, smudged, for in reading scripture we all become part of the body of Christ, where we, they, and I are all intermingled, both in space now and through time.

5. Moorhead, *Gregory the Great*, 51, translating his commentary on Ezekiel, 2.2.1.

For Gregory, the goal of all human existence is contemplation of God. One scholar translates "contemplation" as "attentive regard," paying the right sort of loving attention to God, as Adam did when he "habitually enjoyed converse with God and in purity of heart and loftiness of vision mingled with holy, angelic spirits."[6] Unfortunately for us, as heirs of Adam's fall, we are now incapable of that depth of attentive regard. We are, in a memorable image, like children born to a mother in prison. We may hear from her of "the sun, the moon, and the stars, the mountains and the fields, birds flying in the air and horses running in the fields," but having ever lived in a dungeon, we may "doubt whether the things [we] heard [our] mother describe actually existed."[7] One day, at the beatific vision, the contemplation intended for us creatures will be restored in full. In the meantime, the church is a place of training for that vision by learning to see God and creation aright through the reading of scripture. But contemplation does not mean a bloodless form of reading. For Gregory, to contemplate God is to put ourselves in the position of Mary Magdalene at the tomb after the resurrection. The men leave, but she stays behind, weeping (John 20:11). She has already seen that the tomb is empty, yet she stoops down to look again and sees the angels. Why did she remain and look again? "It is not enough for a lover to have looked once, because the force of love intensifies the effort of the search."[8] Mary looks again. And that's why she sees.

God has not left us alone after Adam. God has come among us, incarnate, and risen, leaving us looking for him. Occasionally, like the lover in the Song of Songs, we find him briefly, but then he is gone again, and we are left to search anew, our desire inflamed. This is what Gregory is doing as he finds Jesus throughout the pages of the Bible: he is doing the work, as one scholar puts it, of a "doctor of desire."[9] He is training our desire aright to find Christ where we hadn't expected to find him: in an empty tomb or in the most unlikely corner of the Old Testament. We'd better look hard: as soon as we find him, he'll be gone. We had better look again.

For example, in commenting on John 1:27, when John the Baptist insists he is unworthy to untie the thong of Christ's sandal, Gregory first

6. McGinn, "Contemplation in Gregory the Great," 147.
7. Gregory the Great, *Dialogues*, 189–90.
8. Gregory the Great, *Forty Gospel Homilies*, 188–89.
9. Leclercq, *Love of Learning*, 31.

notes the comparison in status between the two and John's insistence on Christ's superiority—plain and literal enough. One of the misunderstandings rampant about allegory is that it effaces the letter of scripture. But ancient Christians did not imagine that scripture had only one meaning. For them to exposit one meaning is not a choice for one over another, for scripture can have an enormous variety of meanings, depending on the words on the page, the needs of the listening audience, and what God wants to say to God's people. In fact, Gregory can worry at times that rushing past the literal or "historical" meaning of a text can "keep the light of truth concealed"—for example, if a text mandates giving to the poor and we would rather not. Allegory is a matter of reading both the letter and more deeply than the plain level—not in a way that elides the theological claims of history but in a way that deepens them. And the key fact of history is the incarnation. Allegory is "christological literalism," a taking of the words with utmost seriousness in light of Jesus Christ.[10] And so Gregory does here, with that sandal thong: sandals are made from the skins of dead animals. When "our Lord came in the flesh[,] he appeared as if shod in sandals because he assumed in his divinity the dead flesh of our corrupt condition." The Lord's sandal is a sign of God's incarnation. How exactly do we understand the joining of these two natures in one man? As John makes plain, we cannot: "In no way can we discover how the Word took on a body, how the supreme life-giving Spirit came to life in his mother's womb, how he who has no beginning both is and is conceived. The sandal strap is the bond of a mystery."[11] The gospel is not that Jesus wears sandals that John feels unworthy to untie. The gospel is that God wears skin, and no one can understand that—we can only adore.

All that from the thong of a sandal! It is commonplace for modernist interpreters of the fathers to damn them with faint praise at this point with a reference to their "ingenuity" or "fancifulness." In my favorite dismissive trope, critics will often express their preference for more "sober" exegesis. Yet notice how this non-sober exegesis works: a familiar passage and a striking visual image—God wears shoes—are linked to the inscrutable mystery that saves us. We profess the truth of the incarnation, and it remains to us, in another favorite Gregorian image from the gospels, only to weep, to kiss those sandaled feet, and to wipe them

10. Byassee, *Praise Seeking Understanding*, 215–16.
11. Gregory the Great, *Forty Gospel Homilies*, 24–25.

with our hair. Notice what this reading is not interested in: divining the meaning that the text may have had in John the evangelist's or John the Baptist's head. Such projection is never easy even when we have access to the speaker, let alone when their words have been remembered, written, redacted, and canonized. It is also beside the point. These words are situated in the scriptures the church takes to bear witness to the triune God. The point is not what *was* in a human mind; it's what *is* now in God's mind for the church's benefit. And notice further that from now on, each time that reading comes up again, it is marked with an asterisk, a red thread tied around the finger to remember: this, too, points to the incarnation, as does all of scripture, if we read it aright. Something that at first would seem to have no saving value (feet and sandals, "just" a figure of speech) turns out also to witness to the mystery that saves us, and we move from uncertainty to surprise to delight, and our love for God and our inclination to follow God's commands are increased.

Or at least that is how it is supposed to work.

A Preacher's Art

Gregory is one of the architects of what would come to be called the *quadriga*, the fourfold layered meaning of scripture beloved in the Middle Ages. Yet Gregory himself doesn't usually speak of a text as having four levels. He speaks rather of three: the literal or historical or plain reading, the allegorical or theological or mystical, and the tropological—having to do with morality.[12] Medieval interpreters saw these levels not as properties somehow locatable within a book. They are rather nimble approaches to reading, practices rather than properties, elucidated as levels to remind interpreters to read in a variety of ways: with attention to Jesus and the morals of the church and, later than Gregory, with regard to future hope. Gregory's hermeneutical apparatus is nothing so grand. He simply traipses along with the scripture, line by line, pointing out how each bit relates to Christ and then to the church. As

12. I am intentionally obscure when naming levels of texts. It seems to me that debates over biblical hermeneutics are often conducted at the level of terminology: if only we can get our terms clear, everything will be fine. This is philosophically shoddy and theologically untenable. Debates about biblical interpretation can only be solved with actual exegesis, not with technical descriptions of what one will eventually do when one gets around to offering a reading.

ever, he provides an analogy: the letter of the text is like the foundation of a house, the typological sense is like its walls, and finally, "by the grace of moral instruction," the exterior of the house is painted in appropriate colors.[13] And in case this sounds altogether too static, scripture is a living thing for Gregory. Scripture actually grows *with* the reader, adapting itself to our further needs as we grow in wisdom, keeping us humble by its inexhaustibility.[14] Scripture is a vast field of growth, a topography of grace, with easy places for those who are not advanced and rigorous ones for those who are. We'll never exhaust its depths.

Gregory's attention to the depths of scripture is one of the primary gifts he gives to biblical interpretation in the church of our time. No one any longer should disdain the gifts of historical criticism. At its best, it cracks open for us the letter of scripture and demands from us habits of attention that the church desperately needs. My primary objection to it is that it doesn't demand *enough* attention to the letter of scripture. For the letter, read rightly, leads to the Spirit, who bears witness to Jesus. For example, Gregory follows his patristic predecessors in seeing in Ezekiel's vision of the chariot an image for the Bible. Ezekiel 1:16 reads that "their appearance and operation was like that of a wheel in the middle of a wheel." For Gregory, the wheel within the wheel is an image for the Old Testament and the New, for the latter "makes clear what the Old Testament indicated." Then he piles on a series of types that run through the two testaments: Adam sleeping and Christ dead, Isaac carrying wood for his sacrifice and Christ bearing his cross, and so on, until he lands on the mercy seat. This place of atonement in the tabernacle is covered with two gold cherubim facing each other, overshadowing the seat that God will overshadow and from which God will judge the Israelites (Exod. 25:17–20). And to whom can this image point but the mediator between God and humanity (1 Tim. 2:5)? What can the cherubim indicate but the fullness of knowledge? They are made of gold as a sign of pure truth. Their wings cover the mercy seat because we "are protected from the failings which threaten us by the strengthening teaching of sacred scripture." And the two cherubim face each other "because neither Testament disagrees from the other in any respect." They indicate Christ slightly differently, to be sure, the one showing him more openly and the other more obscurely; the one a "prophecy," the other "an exposition of the

13. Gregory the Great, *Morals on the Book of Job* 7.
14. Moorhead, *Gregory the Great*, 21.

Old." Yet the cherubim face each other with the mediator in between them: "The cherubim would have turned their faces away from each other, if one Testament denied what the other promised."[15]

Now defeat that argument, if you can: if the testaments disagreed with one another, surely the cherubim would face away from one another. We must recover this way of arguing biblically. Here at a place in Exodus where the mystery is thickest, in instructions to Israel so precious they were cherished and savored for millennia, where the union between God and humanity for the sake of covenant and mercy took physical form, how can we not see the Savior whom we believe to be the fulfillment of that union? It would take an act of dexterous exegetical gymnastics indeed to insist Christians must turn away.

In case such a reading from Exodus seems a stretch, we can try a sermon preached on one of Jesus's resurrection narratives. Gregory preached on Luke 24 and John 21 a few days after Easter. Among those in attendance would have been some of the newly baptized, whose postbaptismal catechesis would include coming to see all creation in light of the Christ who had just worked to save them. In such a liturgical context it would take unnatural contortions *not* to preach christologically. The texts of those gospels show plainly enough that Jesus is raised, and bodily so. But what more is present? Scripture stops to tell us what the risen Jesus ate. In John he makes a breakfast of broiled fish and offers the disciples bread (John 21:9); in Luke *he* eats what *they* have available—broiled fish (Luke 24:42) and, according to manuscripts used in the patristic era but redacted on most text-critical accounts, honeycomb. Why these particular menu items? We could be tempted to give an answer using the word *just*: the gospels are *just* showing that the risen Christ really ate. Or we could open to a more maximal answer that refuses the *just*. Scripture chooses its words with care. Few people place strictures on their food like the Jews. And no attention had been paid earlier in the gospels to how fish is cooked. Now it is. What does it mean?

"What are we to believe the broiled fish indicates, if not that 'Mediator between God and humanity' who suffered?"[16] This is Gregory's standard mode of introduction: interrogative and christological. Allegorical exegesis, Wilken often points out, is reading in reverse of how we mod-

---

15. Moorhead, *Gregory the Great*, 55–56, citing his commentary on Ezekiel, 1.6.15.
16. Moorhead, *Gregory the Great*, 72.

erns normally read.[17] We read to discover what the author means to say. In reading the Bible we already know what the Author always says: the Word who is Christ. For the church fathers, the "game" of reading turns out to be the reverse of our norm: here we try to discern how *these* words refer to this already-known meaning. So how do broiled fish, bread, and honeycomb refer to Jesus?

"It was he who condescended to lie hidden in the waters of the human race, allowed himself to be caught by the snare of our death, and at the time of his passion was broiled, as it were, in his affliction." Divine self-emptying (kenosis) among us, submission to suffering, and transformation into something edible are all signaled in one brief sentence. But the story does not end there, for he "showed himself to us as a honeycomb in his resurrection." Gregory continues: "Or perhaps he . . . wished to express the two natures of his person through a honeycomb," with the wax signifying our flesh and the honey his divinity (possessives get messy in incarnational thought: perhaps it is *God's* flesh and *our* divinity now). Notice Gregory is incarnationally heavy but exegetically light. He searches out doctrine in its fullness (kenosis, passion, resurrection, two natures) but switches quickly and without compunction from one interpretation to another: "Or perhaps." Gregory continues to move from God in himself (*in se*) to God for us (*pro nobis*): "He who could be broiled like a fish in his human nature strengthens us with bread in his divine nature," he writes, referencing John 6:51, in which Jesus compares himself to bread from heaven. This is another standard move: bringing in a witness from elsewhere in the Bible to support his allegorical interpretation. It is not just in Gregory's imagination that bread refers to Jesus. It is in *the Bible's* imagination that bread refers to Jesus. And so in the church's, in all creation. Bread is no longer just bread, not ever. And the final incarnational and soteriological move: "See how suitable it is for us to imitate this. For the Redeemer draws attention to what he has done in such a way as to make a smooth path for us, his followers, to imitate. For look, our Lord wished to associate honeycomb with broiled fish in what he ate because the people who do not withdraw from the love of interior sweetness when they experience tribulations for God here below are the ones he receives to eternal quiet

17. I heard this from Wilken during a seminar on Augustine's Psalms exegesis at the University of Virginia in the fall of 2001. David Steinmetz deepens the image in his essay "Miss Marple Reads the Bible."

in his body."[18] Gregory has finished his kenotic move from God toward us by showing the way made for us in Jesus's divine flesh: "to make a smooth path for us." So the lesson about enduring trials with internal equanimity is driven home in God's flesh and bone. Gregory has narrated the entirety of salvation history via three physical objects: fish, bread, and honeycomb. And in so doing he has made full sense of the difficulties through which God's people, listening to him preach, now proceed. What were formerly mere textual difficulties are now steps left in God's flesh for us to climb upward, heartened by the sweetness of the honey of the Word.

Allegory aims to keep still what must be kept still (the truth of Christian teaching in the creed, the words on the page) so as to let move that which must move (the creativity of interpretation, the extravagant kenosis of God in Christ, our turn from wretchedness to righteousness). It is a preacher's art. It moves through levels of interpretation fluidly, from literal to doctrinal to moral, because that's how *God* moves *us*: from words on the page refracted through Christian teaching to our very bodies, practices, and desires. A direct line runs through divine action toward the human heart, and the preacher tries to show the congregation that this is so, so they will act accordingly. As Gregory himself pleads, "Let us place the footsteps of our holy longing on the road towards God every day."[19]

The Christology of Job

Gregory's approach to interpretation is an effort to "overwhelm."[20] And the examples suggested here perhaps do not give sufficient evidence of that overwhelming quality. The christological readings just keep coming, like wave upon wave. Gregory compares the scriptures to the sea, with waves ever crashing in ways that differ, yet remain the same. In his

18. Moorhead, *Gregory the Great*, 73.

19. Moorhead, *Gregory the Great*, 73, quoting gospel homily 24.6.

20. "The divine teaching by things is directed at the whole man, intellect and feeling, and he should respond to it with warmth and eagerness and spontaneity because he is struck by its brilliance, and not because he has thought out his response and decided it is reasonable. He is intended to be overwhelmed." Evans, *Thought of Gregory the Great*, 53. Of course, if such readings were *un*reasonable, they would fail to overwhelm, and rightly could be dismissed as ridiculous.

own practice, his heaping up of images shows this better than anyone could explain it. In one place he says the word *waters* can mean any of six different things—the Holy Spirit, holy knowledge, evil knowledge, tribulation, the passage of peoples, and the minds of those who follow the faith. The word *mountain* could have any one of five meanings: the incarnate Lord, the church, the covenant, the apostate angel, or a heretic.[21] We instantly see that these simple, physical, visually arresting terms have a depth of biblical resonance that allows the preacher to choose from a stunning variety of possibilities, like a painter with an overfull palette. The point of all this profusion of possibilities is not chaos. It is harmony. Allegory is a heightening of the letter, not its evisceration. It is what Robert Wilken calls a "mystery" of "excess." Gregory compares the listening parishioners to strings on an instrument (an image used elsewhere in our tradition for the verses of the Bible). Those gathered are stretched out to hear the preacher's words, and he plucks them to make melody.[22]

In one way, allegory is about Christian interpretation of the Old Testament.[23] The New Testament is patently about Jesus—in what way would it need "updating" by being read christologically? It already *is* christological. Yet in another way, in tune with Gregory's intention to overwhelm, all scripture must be read allegorically. It must all be pressed from letter to allegory to our own souls. So while the Gospels and Epistles purport to be about Jesus and the church, the book of Job does not. And just so Gregory enters it with relish, enthusing over interpreting books that others have mostly avoided. He plunges in after a request from the monks with whom he lives as a papal emissary in imperial Constantinople. And he does so at length, with a work fifty times longer than the quite long biblical book it comments on. Readers like Gregory chew the scriptures for a living, they are like cattle chewing cud, seeking to suck every ounce of wisdom from the text. Gregory comments like one of them, patiently taking his time, and reads Job christologically.

This latter move is naturally the most controversial. We might even call it beyond controversy—there is almost no one today who argues in favor of a christological reading of Job. Yet there are good reasons at

21. Moorhead, *Gregory the Great*, 22, citing *Moralia* 19.6.9 and 33.1.2.
22. Evans, *Thought of Gregory the Great*, 83.
23. See, for example, Wilken's "Face of God for Now."

least to entertain a christological interpretation of Job's lament.[24] One, the book has a sort of atemporal, ahistorical character to it. The theophanies at its beginning and end are history-like but do not purport to be unadorned history. The text is full of jagged edges, impenetrable bits, simile, metaphor, and allusion. If it is simply a set of transcripts of speeches, it is dull indeed—but of course it is not. To read a text like this christologically is to lend it a new context: in addition to reading literally, historically, linguistically, with sensitivity to the words and history depicted, we also read in the context of a community of the baptized making progress from Jesus's flesh to his divinity. With even the slightest attention to who the "we" is interpreting, a christological reading becomes far less absurd. Gregory himself was often ill (Bernard McGinn, the great historian of mysticism, speaks of Gregory's illness as one of the great events in the history of spirituality).[25] To ask *a pope* not to interpret a long biblical book about innocent lament over suffering and divine response in some way other than christological would be asking rather a lot indeed. So too for any of the baptized.

We must also say that Gregory will not satisfy in all places. His christological reading tends to push him to overlook Job's own lashing out against God, or at least to minimize it. His quite unapologetic moralizing for the sake of monks' spiritual lives leads him to glide over some of the literal text's great themes, including its attention to wisdom and its puzzlement over the treatment of God's faithful. I present here some of Gregory's reading of Job as a sort of proposal to the church. If he can again propel lives of faithful prayer through deeper attention to the letter and spirit of Job, then he should again be studied, translated, and emulated. For Gregory, the life of a saint can be a "living reading."[26] The saints never point to themselves—their lives are readings of scripture that point to Jesus. Gregory puts it this way: "The good things which we know of the lives of holy people are nothing if they are not true, and worth very little if they do not contain a mystery."[27]

For Gregory, that mystery we seek in all reading is Christ. Job, as an innocent sufferer tempted by the devil, counseled wrongly by fam-

---

24. For an outstanding recent approach to Job not itself interested in Christology, see Hankins, *Book of Job*.

25. McGinn, "Contemplation in Gregory the Great."

26. Moorhead, *Gregory the Great*, 23, referring to *Moralia* 24.8.16.

27. Moorhead, *Gregory the Great*, 155, citing *Moralia* 20.48.

ily and friends, then answered in the whirlwind, is a prophet, or even the voice of Jesus himself, speaking sometimes in his head, sometimes in his members. Susan Schreiner describes Gregory's hermeneutic this way: "The sufferings of a 'simple and upright' man positively begged Job's story to signify the passion of Christ and the persecution of the church."[28] As Gregory himself puts it, "Because Christ and the church, that is the head and the body, is one person, we have often said that blessed Job figuratively stands sometimes for the head and sometimes the body. Therefore, with the truth of the history having been preserved, let us interpret what is written in an allegorical way." What does Job look like, read this way? Let's look at a few texts.[29]

> "If I am asleep, I shall say: When shall I get up? And I shall await the evening again . . . and I shall be filled with sorrows until the darkness. My flesh is clothed in rottenness and clods of dust. My skin is dried out and wizened." (Job 7:4–5)

Gregory was often ill. Even worse, he thought, he had to take up the duties of bishop of Rome when he would have rather prayed in solitude. His physical trials with illness and his spiritual ones with having leadership foisted on him allow him to read Job with particular intensity.[30] For Gregory's Job, affliction is a spiritual gift.[31] It leads to proper compunction for our sins and humility in the face of any spiritual achievement. In Gregory's language, lifted from Paul, affliction turns our attention from the outer person to the inner, since the former is being punished, the latter renewed (2 Cor. 4:16). Gregory compares those who want to pursue the spiritual life without difficulty to those who want to wear a victor's crown without even running the race. Affliction leads to genuine freedom. Such outer pain turns us inward, where we contemplate God's goodness despite, or in the midst of, difficulty. We come to see adversity as a sort of spiritual home in which we can grow and flourish. For Gregory, the saints worry most in prosperity. It is not our natural state. Job is the ideal companion on

28. Schreiner, *Where Shall Wisdom Be Found?*, 32.

29. The texts that follow are taken from Moorhead's translations in *Gregory the Great*.

30. Leclercq, *Love of Learning*, 25–29.

31. I am indebted to Schreiner, *Where Shall Wisdom Be Found?*, 29–31, for this entire paragraph.

a journey to regain the unending contemplation of God's "uncircum-scribed and unending light," lost in Adam, restored in Christ, fitfully entered into in our present state, to be hoped for in full eschatologi-cally. Gregory comments on Job 7:4 ("If I am asleep, I shall say: When shall I get up? And I shall await the evening again") by noting human inconstancy. Though the first person, Adam, was "created for this pur-pose," to "lift himself up to the citadel of contemplation," we who sin in him continually fall back down asleep, for we are "always subject to change by the motion of alternating desire."[32] But sleep means more than inconstancy. It also is a Pauline word for sin, from which Christ raises us (Rom. 13:11; Eph. 5:14). So we should wish for adversity so as to be prodded into awakeness.

The reference to rotting flesh signifies humanity's fall: "corruption" and the "murk of wretched thoughts" from recollection of our vices. An unsurprising reading, yet Gregory immediately shifts from moralizing for an individual hearer to interpreting these words in a churchly sense: "There are many who are my members through faith, but they are not healthy and clean in what they do." Here the body of Christ speaks of the individual experience of trying to be holy within a church that can never fully be. Wizened skin refers to a body of people "unwilling to be stretched out through patience towards things of the future."[33] I can think here only of a mainline church that has let the moisture in its skin evaporate, the skin itself to become brittle, without a hope that powers the church in ministry.

Now notice here: these readings are made to edify spiritually, and they do so quite literally as well. Each word is pored over for detail about the spiritual life. Note, too, just how bodily this reading is: flesh and skin and resting and waking are all bodily motifs. Allegory, whatever else it means here, is not a flight from the body, neither my own skin nor the "skin" of the community gathered. Allegory is a way God makes space for us in his scripture. Here that is shaped less by christological concerns than by the spiritual life of Gregory and his hearers.

"I know that my Redeemer lives, and at the last day I shall rise from the earth. And again I shall be enclosed within my skin." (Job 19:25–26)

---

32. Moorhead, *Gregory the Great*, 129, on *Moralia* 8.10.19.
33. Moorhead, *Gregory the Great*, 132.

I would say that modern scholars debate the historical Jewish and Christian reading of this famous passage as a reference to bodily resurrection, except that they do not. It is taken nearly universally to be a reference to anything other than something doctrinally dear to the communities of people, Jew and Christian, in historic continuity with those who wrote, preserved, treasured, and canonized this scripture. Two contemporary homiletical commentaries, written by scholars with impeccable academic credentials, differ on this point. One makes a slight gesture of support toward the possibility of a resurrectional reading.[34] The other brings it up only to dismiss it.[35] One way to mark the difference between Gregory and most contemporary exegetes is that he *begins* with christological interpretation presupposed and leaves himself time to see where the words go from there. Most moderns either dismiss christological moves altogether or only gesture at them piously at the end of their otherwise non-christological exposition, with no time or space left to intepret the words in Christ's light.

For Gregory, this passage is a reference not only to Jesus's resurrection but also to ours. For Matthew points out that in the wake of Easter many saints also rose, showing us that resurrection is not a onetime event but the future destiny of humanity (Matt. 27:52–53). Gregory is sympathetic with those who look at bones and ash and shake their head at the idea of a resurrection of the dead. But he feels he has the overwhelming evidence in his favor: "For what does the world imitate in its elements every day if not our resurrection?"[36] Day gives forth to night and back again. Seasons pass and we see "a kind of resurrection" as "leaves burst forth as if from withered wood." But resurrection is finally a wager on God. "Why should we be surprised if the one who forms great trees from very fine seeds should again, when he wishes, shape very fine dust which was reduced into its elements away from our sight into a human being?"[37] This

34. "It is our contention that the so-called modern consensus is mistaken and that the ancient view is substantially correct." Janzen, *Job*, 136.

35. Newsom's actual language is significant: although a christological and resurrectional reading is "rarely advanced in scholarship today, the issue still draws a disproportionate amount of attention to these verses. To understand this passage in terms of its original context and significance, one must set aside the later history of its appropriation in Christianity." Newsom, "Job," 477. In other words, if previous modern interpreters had the unfortunate bother of undoing fulsomely Christian exegesis, due to the unfortunate influence of Handel's *Messiah*, she is going to take the next step beyond such inconvenience and ignore those resonances altogether.

36. Moorhead, *Gregory the Great*, 61, on *Moralia* 14.55.70.

37. Moorhead, *Gregory the Great*, 62.

is a common patristic argument for resurrection, which I call "thickening the mystery." You have trouble believing in the resurrection, do you? Well, we already believe God created the whole of creation from nothing. Which is harder—creation *ex nihilo* or resurrection from remains? Here resurrection, the heartbeat of Christian faith, is foreshadowed in the Old Testament, and Christian teaching about the trustworthiness of resurrection is shown to have roots as long as Israel's. Here allegory is a resurrectional art. Those trained to see life breaking forth from death will be ready to see Jesus break forth from the letter of scripture, not least where that letter points to the resurrection of the righteous.

> The LORD blessed the end of Job more than his beginning. And he came to have fourteen thousand sheep and six thousand camels, and a thousand yoke of oxen, and a thousand she-asses; and he had seven sons and three daughters. . . . After these things Job lived for a hundred and forty years; and he saw his children and his children's children until the fourth generation; and he died in old age, full of days. (Job 42:10–15)

Any interpreter has to struggle with the "happy ending" of Job—does it ruin the rumination that has come before? Lost children cannot simply be replaced like lost property. Modernist evasions of these problems can come from saying this was a later appendage onto an earlier pristine text. Gregory has no such solution available. So he turns elsewhere.

"Because Christ and the church, that is the head and the body, is one person, we have often said that blessed Job figuratively stands sometimes for the head and sometimes the body," Gregory reminds his readers. He fixes first on the "twice as much" that Job receives back here in the book's conclusion. The Lord will receive back twice as much, Gregory writes, when he receives back the Jews who are his chosen in addition to the full number of the gentiles (citing Rom. 11:25). Or, he suggests, the double return could be a reference to the eschatological reunion of body and soul in the resurrection. He returns to the former reading as the stronger one based on the brothers and sisters who "had known [Christ] before." Christians have often been at our worst in predicting the conversion of the Jews. Gregory elsewhere can speak of Christians and Jews as the two breasts of the one body of the church, in a suggestive image.[38] Gregory

---

38. Cited in Evans, *Thought of Gregory the Great*, 137, referring to *Moralia* 24.8.17. For

has some anti-Jewish rhetoric here for which Christians should still re-pent: the Jews "knew" him before "when they despised him in his pas-sion." Yet for our purposes the *manner* of their conversion is important: the Jews convert when they "put aside the observance of the superficial letter, they are so to speak fed in the holy church with the best part of mystical utterance, as if it were nourishing food."[39] For Gregory there is an obvious and unbreakable link between discerning the divine nature of Christ and discerning the mystical teaching of scripture. We Christians today may confess that divine nature, but rarely do we see allegory as its natural outcome. Even more rarely do we preach Christology. We are then like Gregory's rhetorical Jews, who read the text but fail to see Jesus mysteriously and troublingly present in it.

A reader can almost physically, audibly hear Gregory's interest pick up at the numbers in Job 42:12. The seven sons and three daughters sug-gest the restoration of the children who died previously, and Gregory takes the restoration one step further: the mention of "twice what he had before" suggests Job receives back his prior children plus ten more. Then the animals: they "designate the accumulated totality of the faithful." Did not the psalmist say, in one and the same breath, "we are his people, the sheep of his pasture" (Ps. 95:7)? First, those camels: sometimes a camel is the Lord, and sometimes the pride of the gentiles. A camel low-ers himself to receive burdens from others; so, too, our Lord "voluntarily came down from his lofty power." Gregory cites John 10 on this ("I have the power of laying down my life"), and the evocative "eye of the needle" passage (Matt. 19:24). I cannot count the number of times in my pastoral life I have heard the ridiculous story of the "eye of the needle" as a gate in Jerusalem through which one could pass, though with difficulty—a total evisceration of the story in addition to an urban legend. Gregory is not tempted: "A camel passed through the eye of the needle, when our Redeemer entered through the narrow straights of his passion."[40] His suffering was like a needle, pricking him, showing how even the unlikely might enter heaven. For we proud people would not bend our necks if he did not first. Gregory tightens this turn from Christology to discipleship with a glance at Rebekah in Genesis. In a passage I had never noticed, but

---

more on Gregory and the Jew as a rhetorical trope, see Markus, "The Jew as a Hermeneutic Device."

39. Moorhead, *Gregory the Great*, 137–38.
40. Moorhead, *Gregory the Great*, 146.

will never now fail to notice: when she saw Isaac, she got down from her camel and covered herself with a veil (Gen. 24:64–65). She represents the gentiles in our proud vices who must come down, blush, and turn away, after which we remember Paul's question: "For what fruit did you have then in those things of which you are now ashamed?" (Rom. 6:21).

Not only is the entire gospel told through the lens of the camel, with biblical supports throughout, it is also done christologically and then, if you like, anthropologically, as hearers are encouraged to follow the difficult but good road Jesus has left for us in his flesh. Not only that, but otherwise dark corners of the scripture are illumined such that we cannot now go back to them unillumined. The reading may not be right. We may, communally, judge it to be wrong, but we should have to judge it, and we should notice at once how simultaneously literal, beautiful, and historical it is.

After similarly playfully serious readings of the other animals, Gregory turns to the numbers of animals. (1) Gregory notes that one thousand is a perfect number: the number ten made three-dimensional, a cube standing securely on its base. Yet as readers of scripture "we transcend all these things as we make progress in the depth of scripture." Geometry is not enough. (2) Ten is a perfect *biblical* number because of the commandments: "every sin being held in check by no more than ten expressions." (3) Jesus's workers in the vineyard are paid with a denarius, a coin consisting in ten, which opens a spectrum between obedience to the law and grace. (4) More elaborately now: human beings are made up of three spiritual qualities (the mind, soul, and strength with which we love the Lord; Deut. 6:5) and four physical ones (hot and cold, moist and dry). We are paid a denarius because these seven are joined with God's three: "contemplation of the divine Trinity." (5) Seven virtues are our toil in this life (traditionally outlined in Isa. 11:2–3), (6a) with the threefold Trinity as our reward, or (6b) when faith, hope, and love are joined to these seven virtues.[41]

Those six-plus readings come fast and furious, playful and serious, biblical and experiential. They tell the whole gospel anew even as they hold themselves lightly. If these readings do not satisfy, Gregory would turn to us, ready to be edified with a reading from us. If we had none, or if we replied that the numbers are meaningless, he would be baffled. What is scripture there for if not to increase our delight in and wisdom about the God who is saving us?

---

41. Moorhead, *Gregory the Great*, 149.

Reading While Overwhelmed

What can biblical interpreters learn from Gregory's exegesis? First, that it can be fulsome. We can pile up meaning upon meaning on the text of scripture without worrying that it will buckle under the weight. To answer Hans Frei's old question, the literal sense of scripture will stretch and will not break.[42] We can do this if we offer readings with a light spirit, rigorous attention to the words, and a desire to have our readings conform to christological shape for the blessing of our hearers. Doing this time after time will show hearers that scripture does not mean simply *one* thing, in pinched-off, dour math-teacher scrupulosity, as if one answer is fully correct and all others equally wrong. Rather, God's scripture means everything God means it to mean to God's people now and through time. A profusion of readings shows what we do with scripture is delight. The image for biblical interpretation is not a far-off target, a strong bow in hand, hoping we may hit the bull's-eye. No, scripture is a cascade, a waterfall, a profusion of God's gracious and abundant truth. We may not understand it, but that is because God is so overwhelmingly present, not because God is so aloof and far off.

Second, we should notice both the overall patterns *and* the minute details in the Bible. Gregory's reading of Job *works* because he sees it as a reference to a spiritual battle waged on Job by Satan with God's allowance and forbearance through it. It also works because he digs into the meaning of the number one thousand, the nature of the camel, and every line of forty-two chapters. There is a kenotic arc to Job, as there is a kenotic arc to human life. In Job, the dream- or fantasy-like opening and conclusion explain, in a way, the laments in the heart of the book. So, too, with the Christian life for Gregory: between creation and final redemption there is an infinity of little pathways that God's people cross. Job, read both at macro- and micro-levels, read both christologically and in the particularity of each of our souls, offers wisdom for all.

Third, Job is a particular tonic for what ails the church today. Job is not happy. Gregory's reading of Job is not happy. It might be wise. I speak not of our age's fascination with and captivity to the prosperity gospel. I speak more broadly of the way Christianity specifically and religion generally are instrumentalized to give us a better life. Gregory's Job shows us something different: this life is one of profound, illness-

42. Frei, "Literal Reading."

producing, family-losing, livelihood-annihilating sorrow. And this is not because Job has sinned (never mind the words of his friends); it is because God chastises those whom God chooses. There is here wisdom not only for drawing sustenance from every line of scripture but also for drawing meaning from every line in the face of God's saints, worn by tears and toil as they are, and so aptly reflecting the face of the man of sorrows. And, surprisingly enough, to interpret this way, via this much sorrow, is really the way to cross-shaped resurrectional joy.

For Further Study

Gregory the Great. *The Book of Pastoral Rule: St. Gregory the Great.* Translated by George Demacopoulos. Crestwood, NY: St. Vladimir's Seminary Press, 2007.

It is striking how often Gregory's pastoral counsel leaps off the page and into the present—a fine guide for preachers still today.

Leclercq, Jean, OSB. *The Love of Learning and the Desire for God: A Study of Monastic Culture.* New York: Fordham University Press, 2003.

Father Leclercq introduces us not just to the life of the monastery but to the ancient and medieval ways of thinking about God as our deepest desire.

Moorhead, John. *Gregory the Great.* The Early Church Fathers. London: Routledge, 2005.

This book has a fine introduction to Gregory's life and includes samples of his sermons and commentary on Job.

7

The Institution
of the Old Testament

No Death, No Resurrection

In this book I try to lay bare the strange and wondrous ways ancient Christians read the Bible, and to imagine how we might learn to do something analogous in our day. This is a project of creative retrieval: we can't say exactly what our forebears said, for even the very same words said now will be heard differently.[1] Nor can we start from scratch. We have to say something analogous—faithful by being different. How precisely do we do that?

Nicholas Lash's analogy is helpful for me here.[2] He describes the way a medieval person might take a brown garment, tie it around the waist with a rope, and go around preaching. That person was putting on the dress of a poor person. He or she was trying to recover the practices of Jesus living among the poor, experiencing poverty personally, and so showing God's heart for the poor. This move of creative retrieval showed the world something about God that had been lost. It spawned great religious orders, inspired faith across a continent and beyond, and affects us in the church and the world today. But replicating it precisely is impossible. You could tie the same robe around your middle with the same rope and go and preach around the same city and the signal would not be "radical solidarity with God's beloved poor"; it would be "religious professional with a master's degree putting on a performance." The latter is no bad thing to do—some of us spend our lives doing precisely

---

1. I take the language of "creative retrieval" from David Ford in *The Future of Christian Theology*. It is similar to Greg Jones's language of "traditioned innovation," unpacked at www.faithandleadership.com.

2. Lash, "What Authority Has Our Past?," in *Theology on the Way to Emmaus*, 55.

that! But it's not the same thing. To say something like the same thing, we actually have to change. But how to do so in a way that's faithful?

More Weathered Than Ever

From where I sit, it seems as though every institution I care about is coming unraveled. The United States is ruled by a public embarrassment of a person, intent on wreaking havoc for personal gain, supported by fellow know-nothings who mindlessly thrill to his every tweet. We have had bad leaders before, and will again, and this is no surprise—politics is how we arbitrate public disputes. But this one is especially intent on shredding institutions. They are frustrating. They work badly. Anyone who has bumped into a government agency of any kind cannot but agree. And yet the answer is not to throw acid on them, cathartic as that may be briefly. It is, instead, to improve them. Dismantle the ones that don't work and rebuild new ones. What Trump and his supporters seem not to realize is that institutions maintain goods through time that make us more human (this was, until recently, a "conservative" thing to say).[3] Frustration with the federal judiciary or law-enforcement organizations or election processes or whatever is understandable. Taking a sledge-hammer to them is not. Conservative political philosophy, it has colloquially been said, asks before demolishing a fence why it was put there in the first place. That form of conservatism is long gone in this day of the new barbarians. Today US leadership vents outrage, spews venom, reeks entitlement, and lurches from crisis to disaster precisely because it pleases the audience and draws great ratings and leaves its opponents distracted and demoralized by their inability to defeat the clown. Meanwhile, the systems put in place to humanize our life together are not suffering mere neglect. They are suffering assault.

The state from which I come, North Carolina, was a sort of harbinger for things to come with Brexit and Trump. Before Trump came to power, North Carolina was ruled entirely by one political party bent on bending the laws of the state to its permanent rule. Election laws were changed and congressional districts racially gerrymandered. A

---

3. I am borrowing Hugh Heclo's argument that institutions are the most humane thing there are. Just try living in a place without them (we Americans may soon find out!). See Heclo, *On Thinking Institutionally*.

ridiculous fight over bathroom laws ensued. When a governor of the other party came to power, that office's levers of power were stripped, his ability to gain traction intentionally undone. North Carolina, long a bastion for enlightened government in an otherwise more backward south, became a laughingstock. All because a politically middle-of-the-road state was suddenly and barely ruled by one party vastly out of step with the majority of its citizens. Uninterested in keeping voters' trust, this party sought to change the laws to stay in power. It is failing. Some of the most interesting political and religious movements going have come out of reaction against this demagoguery. Moral Mondays and the NAACP leader William Barber are showing us the civil rights–era dream of an African American church leading a movement of freedom for all people is not dead. It is needed more now than ever.[4]

But other institutions we once trusted, ecclesial institutions, are fraying fast also. My denomination, the United Methodist Church, is fast pulling itself apart over the politics of inclusion. We have long been a mainline liberal denomination, for which any policy that can be identified as more "inclusive" will necessarily win the day, as if that were the lone content of the gospel of Jesus Christ. But this matter has been stopped over gay and lesbian people. Declining conferences (what we call dioceses) and churches shriek that LGBTQ people ought to be placed in leadership immediately or we are no better than Jim Crow–era racists. But faster-growing conferences in the southern states and faster-growing denominations outside the United States are more traditionally inclined on this and other issues. They tend to see homosexuality as a behavior, not an essential marker of identity. And they despise seeing their money go to a denomination whose leadership either quietly or loudly insists on gay and lesbian leadership. To move "left" on this question means to have a more white, more American, and less ecumenical body. So like the Anglicans and other mainline denominations in the United States before us, we Methodists seem bent on going the way of dissolution. And the very breadth of commitment of Wesley's Connection—the one that says you don't have to choose between being evangelical and inclusive—will be shattered.

And no superiority please, dear Canada. The mainline and evangelical wings of the church have been pulled apart much harder and longer here than further south of the forty-ninth parallel. The United Church of

---

4. See William Barber's book with Jonathan Wilson-Hartgrove, *The Third Reconstruction*.

Canada has a very small and interesting evangelical constituency, but it is far from the center of gravity of the denomination. Evangelical church leaders with whom I speak in Canada don't know the first thing about liberal denominations like the United Church. And regular Canadians don't know the first thing about either. The church that is supposed to be the agent through which Christ is renewing all creation is having trouble finding renewal itself.

What do these crises have in common? In each, institutions meant to humanize us are instead busily degrading us and others. They each involve the media. What draws ratings is conflict, outrage. So you depict your opponent as morally loathsome, people tune in, they take umbrage and support your position at the ballot box or with checks, and you "win" that way. Institutions designed to guard and pass on a common good are thereby turned into levers of power for personal and in-group profit.

Each of these institutions has survived greater challenges before. That's why they are institutions—they are "weathered presences."[5] This is not their first go-round. Yet it is significant they are each under duress at the same moment and for some of the same reasons. Each is confused about what it exists for. Participants are bent on the short-term gain of vilifying opponents and oblivious to the long-term corrosion to the institution caused by sowing cynicism and outrage. And each in its own way pits liberals against traditionalists, progressives against conservatives. The labels are clumsy at best, ridiculous at worst, but they're used, and still have some minor usefulness. Liberals seek inclusivity. Traditionalists prefer to guard the way some things have been. Each needs the other—without umbrage at the other, neither would exist.

Less sensationally now—institutions grace our lives. Last Sunday my family and I spent time in worship, as Christians do on the day of resurrection. My pastor-wife helped lead; we sang and prayed and gave and were blessed to go into the world; we ate and fed the needy and befriended the stranger and evangelized those who don't know. Then we spent time together as a family, walking and eating and resting. Then we had friends over and caught up, ate some more, prayed, and sent them on their way rejoicing, though sad to see them go. Imagine life without these institutions: church, family, friendship, and the subsidiary institutions that make them possible and keep them healthy—school, hospital, government. They humanize us and others. To use the language of the Orthodox tradition, they

5. It is Heclo's perfect image. Heclo, *On Thinking Institutionally*, 127.

also divinize us. They are unbearably beautiful. And we don't even think about them directly unless they're under duress. God grant us more and more faithful humanizing and divinizing institutions.

Institutions grace our lives because they are all participants in the body of Christ. Insofar as a school educates well, a hospital heals, a relationship ennobles, a parish worships, a government honors and protects people (especially the most vulnerable)—these institutions do what they're designed for in God's economy and reflect the body of God's Son. Institutions are collective efforts for good. I have no idea how this Augustinian view of institutions should apply to the United States, to Canada, to North Carolina, or to the United Methodist Church. Augustine is convinced the church is, as the cliché goes, a hospital for sinners, not a mausoleum for saints. Anytime anyone thinks they can leave and start a better church, Augustine scoffs: you'll only be taking yourself and your problems with you! There is no uncompromised church then, only a batch of people on whom Christ is shedding his mercy and grace. Similarly, there are only sinners available to populate, lead, criticize, condemn, and leave those institutions to start "better" ones. And they shouldn't do it. They should stay. Receive mercy for the sins they have no way not to commit. And learn to look on one another with the gentleness of a fellow sinner, one who is absolutely lost without the grace of Christ.

And you know what's amazing? God does not give up on us. God is still willing to draw people to himself through these institutions. God is remarkably unfussy and undiscriminating about the means by which God will restore all things. I wish God had higher standards. But then we'd all be in trouble.

Preaching in a "Weathered Presence"

But something is wrong with how the church has been preparing people to preach the gospel in the space of these "weathered presences"—a problem particular to the seminary. Do we assume that somehow the conversation between scholars trickles down to the way we each train future ministers at our institutions, who then preach to their congregations differently? If that filtering-down model ever worked, it certainly does not now. Our keener students may wade into the nuances of our conversations, but how they minister to Christ's people will not likely be changed much by mastering such nuances. Differences that to us scholars seem worth yelling about would draw a shrug at best at the parish level. Meanwhile another pipeline is broken. We've long had an implicit "relay race" model of biblical interpretation—the biblical scholar tells us what the text once meant, hands off to theologians or historians, who pass the baton to practical scholars, who then teach future ordinands how to preach.[6] The problem is, as Lash argues, the baton never actually gets passed. The biblical scholars don't want to give it up. And why should they? There could always be more debate, discovery, knowledge about the Bible. So what actually gets passed down the academic chain, or reaches any hearer not paid to be interested in it? Nothing. The first runner starts with the baton but just keeps circling the track, never handing it off. Meanwhile other academics keep giving papers and publishing books, talking to one another and imagining we're serving the church. What does the average pastor reach for when she has to preach? Not our work, but something much more accessible and easily applicable. Can you blame them? We're not talking to them, so they listen to someone who is. The American Academy of Religion is not opposed to Joel Osteen—on the contrary, it has made him possible.

Meanwhile, pity the poor preacher. They're doing their best, praying, longing to serve God and God's people. They can't very easily talk about the political matters toward which I gesture above. If a church is faithful, it will have folks across the political spectrum represented. They didn't come to be harangued about how they vote.[7] They came to hear something about God. So the preacher will oblige best they can. If more liberal, they will preach something from the Synoptic Gospels about Jesus being inclusive. If more evangelical, something from Paul with a bit more doctrine and a leaning toward conversion might come up. Either

6. It's Lash's image in "What Might Martyrdom Mean?," in *Theology on the Way to Emmaus*, 79.

7. A friend here in Canada explains that her family stopped going to the United Church parish near their house when the minister couldn't quit talking about Ronald Reagan and nuclear missiles. They quietly vanished. They already disdained Reagan, so they didn't disagree with the politics. They just didn't turn up at church to hear American politics fulminated against. One can imagine the seminary training of that preacher—the gospel is always already political; whatever current conservative outrage is an analogue to the racism that birthed the civil rights movement, not to speak out is to imitate the quietists through history whom we now loathe . . . There is a reason in the mainline we keep circling back to slavery, civil rights, South African apartheid, and the rights of indigenous peoples. Those issues flatter us as being on the "right" side. *We* weren't at the time, but never mind.

way the Old Testament is often avoided. In a politically charged world, the Old Testament is already fighting territory. Preachers figure we have enough of that as is. So you stick to what's comfortable, familiar, safe.

The argument of this book is that we should do no such thing. We should preach Israel's scripture. Those stories and songs of the Old Testament are unfamiliar indeed. So we should make them familiar. There is no way to know the biblical God otherwise. The church must reimmerse ourselves in the saga of Israel. Nothing less will do amidst a world coming apart. My sense is that part of our antipathy for institutions, named above, comes from our antipathy for the Old Testament, which is chock-full of God-bearing institutions.

And then we must read Israel's scripture with reference to Jesus. We do not go to Israel's scripture for antiquarian knowledge, to bone up on trivia, to know more stuff. We go there to be forged into the body of Christ, to be made God's people in the world, to become disciples who can help our institutions weather the storms of our current moment well. Most churches attending to the Old Testament are made up of mostly gentiles. Our gentile way into Israel is via Jesus, who grafts us into a story not our own. Without Jesus, this is not our book, our story, our gospel, our God. But in Jesus we, too, get to relate to the God of Israel. The way to read Israel's story is through the one who makes it accessible to us. What's happening right now is Jesus is teaching the church how to read his Bible. We should hear what he says and obey—that's what it means to be a disciple.

To recapture why engaging and preaching the Old Testament are necessary for institutions in a world being torn apart, I draw on two important and recent books on theology and the Old Testament: Brent Strawn's *The Old Testament Is Dying* and Hans Boersma's *Scripture as Real Presence*. Each is an excellent work by a brilliant scholar worth considering in depth and detail.

Imagination Scriptural and Sacramental

In Strawn's fantastic book, *The Old Testament Is Dying*, he argues that the Old Testament is like a language that has no young people learning it, and fewer and fewer people using it for daily life, and so will be extinct in nearly no time at all. As a Bible professor, Strawn finds this analogy apt for the Old Testament in the church and points out the wisdom we gleaned from engaging Marcion in chapter 1: the New Testament cannot be far behind if the Old goes. Strawn's book is a sobering appraisal of the language of the Bible in our churches: its health is not strong. Few native speakers are left. We must turn all our efforts to reviving this language, using it anew, teaching it to our children. A pastor with no knowledge of the scriptures is like a pilot with no knowledge of the instruments. And Christians who have fallen out of love with Israel's scripture are Christians from whom our Jewish neighbors have a good deal to fear indeed.

Strawn's remedy is in the Bible itself. The book of Deuteronomy is about the immersion of a people in the teachings of the Bible. It has—no, it *is*—what we need for reacquaintance with, renewal in, recaptivation by God's law, God's teaching, God's Torah. And its primary teaching method, like any good language teacher, is repetition. We are to talk about the stories of the Bible with our children, to talk about them on the road, to mark our bodies with them, to perform them in our public life together, to become the different sort of people in the world that the God of Israel asks his people to be (Deut. 6:4–9). Only then can the world be blessed through our difference. And only then can we be the people God longs for us to be, as God's delight, God's chosen portion, God's bride. Strawn has wonderful suggestions for how to do this. We must sing the text. We must perform it anew—not simply repeat it, but re-present it creatively in our corporate life together. Languages that are living adapt as users do new things with them—yet they are also rooted in repetition, whereby they stay identifiably the same language. Here I find Strawn entirely correct: we must read the Old Testament, Israel's story, and we must perform that story in our corporate and family lives together.

Strawn demonstrates for us what a *scriptural imagination* looks like. Our mind, our body, our relationships are all inspired and governed and explained by scriptural patterns. We know the Bible's stories, we see its themes repeating throughout history and creation, we use them to communicate with one another, and we delight in them. This is a very different approach to the Bible than has predominated since the Enlightenment, which has often left the Bible cut up in ribbons on the floor, looking for "real" history. This is, instead, letting the Bible be legendary and delighting in it. Our culture has spent billions producing and consuming grand legends like *Star Wars* and *The Lord of the Rings* and *Harry Potter*.[8] People

8. I've heard this same point made by Quinn Caldwell, United Church of Christ

are dying for stories. The church has the greatest one—the one without which those others would not exist. But we stow it away, apologize for it, blame it for the ills its followers have done, try to protect people from it. Strawn shows we can do something more radical than these things: we can steep in it, sing it, delight in it, learn to teach and be taught by it again.

But I'm left wondering: After all of Strawn's and others' good spade-work on the Old Testament, can we read it *as Old Testament*? Strawn resists letting Christ into the story of the Old Testament too much. The Old Testament must, as is often said, be read "in its own right," with "its own voice."[9] There are good reasons for this insistence, and Strawn asks for an approach that features "bothness," to listen to how each testament bears witness to the God we worship. I want to ask, Can we see how the Old Testament does, indeed, bear witness to Christ, making explicit what it often leaves implicit? Strawn provides much of the rationale with which to read in a way that shows the patterns of Christ, but he himself does not do so. He faults the New Atheists and others who read scripture flatly, ruling out figural interpretation of any kind. He draws on church tradition with which to defend the integrity of the Old Testament. He focuses on the Song of Moses in Deuteronomy 32 and gives a lovely reading of the way Israel learns the language while singing the song. The song recounts God's favor to Israel, God's saving works that delivered Israel, after which they unfortunately grew fat, disinterested. Then the song switches to the second person: "*You* grew fat, bloated, and gorged" (Deut. 32:15). But then by the end of the song, Israel has elbowed its way back into God's favor once more, speaking in the first-person plural again: "Their rock is not like our Rock" (32:31). The entire story of Israel is one of divine blessing, human rebellion, and divine restoration. That's the story from Genesis to Deuteronomy, here sung in capsule form. It is then later re-presented in the Maccabees, as loyal Jews are martyred and die with this song on their lips. The book of Revelation re-presents it once more, mixed with the Song of Miriam by the sea, as the saints around the throne once again hymn our God (Rev. 15). Strawn's example is perfect. Only those practiced in Deuteronomy's song can sing the Lamb's praises at the end of the world.

I'm left wondering, however, about any other options for re-presenting Deuteronomy, performing it in our corporate life together,

---

minister in Syracuse, New York. His unpublished paper was shown to me by Anthony B. Robinson.

9. Stephen Fowl is highly critical of such metaphors in his *Engaging Scripture*.

singing it with fidelity to what's ancient and also with attention to what the God of Israel has done anew. Jesus himself learned Israel's song, and presented it in his flesh, and invited even us, who were no people, to be his body. Jesus is often presented in the New Testament as the prophet like Moses toward which Deuteronomy looks forward. His Sermon on the Mount casts him as a Moses-like teacher, presenting five blocks of teaching like Moses's five books to his newly constituted Israel, the twelve disciples. John's Gospel presents Jesus as the one of whom Moses and the law spoke. In a breathtaking rereading of Deuteronomy in particular, St. Paul reads Deuteronomy's assurance that God is not far away as a sign of Jesus's saving work among us: "Surely, this commandment that I am commanding you today is not too hard for you, nor is it too far away. It is not in heaven, that you should say, 'Who will go up to heaven for us . . . ?' Neither is it beyond the sea, that you should say, 'Who will cross to the other side . . . ?' No, the word is very near you; it is in your mouth and in your heart for you to observe" (Deut. 30:11–14). Paul cites the passage and interprets: to say that the word needs ascent into heaven is "to bring Christ down," or that it's in the abyss is to express a need "to bring Christ up from the dead" (Rom. 10:6–7). The promise that the word is near, on our lips and in our hearts, is a reference to "the word of faith that we proclaim," for "if you confess with your lips that Jesus is Lord and believe in your heart that God raised him from the dead, you will be saved" (Rom. 10:8–9). Deuteronomy's exquisite promise of the Lord's tender nearness is, in Paul, transfigured into a promise that Jesus is raised and salvation is here, now, for us and all. All we have to do is speak.

This is precisely the sort of reading of the Old Testament that I was taught not to do in seminary.[10] But Paul does it. And he does it teaching the church how to read Israel's Bible. The church is not a people who naturally have access to Israel's covenant. We are grafted in by Christ's grace to a people, a story, not naturally our own. We do not make a point of following all of Deuteronomy's laws, but Paul's arguments link the God of Israel to Christ's resurrection and drawing of the gentiles at the end of the world. Our way to re-present Deuteronomy's story is in the life of the church, broken open to us in Christ.

---

10. To be fair, Richard Hays's *Echoes of Scripture in the Letters of Paul* is a landmark book for the reclamation of figural reading of the Old Testament. He argues that Paul's hermeneutic is ecclesiocentric more than Christocentric.

Strawn has his own reasonable arguments against this. He brings up reading the Old Testament the way the New does as a false hope, a poisonous way forward. His worry is that we would pidginize the Old Testament—that is, reduce its rich and variegated language into something stunted, like the languages traders between foreign cultures concoct with which to conduct simple business. He wants no supersession of the Old Testament—that is, no sense that it is left behind, in need of correction, insufficient in itself, the "old cliched and tired ways of relating the testaments" as if the Old Testament "somehow *needs or requires a New Testament alongside it.*"[11] Reading the Old Testament cannot be "overly Christocentric," as if Old Testament history "somehow comes to a covenantal 'climax' in the New Testament and the New Testament alone."[12] Strawn does give back with his left hand what he takes away with his right—he does draw on New Testament scripture at times, and he does say the church reads the New alongside the Old. But he tends to bring up the New Testament only at the end of sections, like a sort of pious doxology, not to read the Old in its light.

Something is lost here: the New Testament's *way* of reading the Old. Paul's weird and counterintuitive approach to Deuteronomy is just one example. What if, instead of mentioning the New Testament in homiletic or doxological asides or concluding words, we bring up its readings early, and debate them, immerse ourselves in them, see what sort of new connections are made thereby? Otherwise we run the risk of saying that we can re-present, re-perform Deuteronomy, but Jesus cannot. Paul cannot. The church cannot.

Jesus is our way into Israel's scripture. He is the one teaching us about himself from this text. Jesus is no supersessionist—he loves his fellow people Israel (see Rom. 9–11 here). And our way to love it is through him. You cannot be overly christological. You can be wrongly christological, or stupidly, insensitively, in a way that makes for poor readings of the Bible. But the covenant indeed comes to a climax in Jesus, who is Savior of the world, Messiah of Israel, God's own Son, our Lord. And that confession cannot be muted in order to listen to the Old Testament's "own voice." For he is its own voice. There is no other way for Christians to approach this text.

11. Strawn, *Old Testament Is Dying*, 226, 224.
12. Strawn, *Old Testament Is Dying*, 228.

Bringing Up Jesus at the Beginning

Strawn shows us we must read Israel's scripture. Hans Boersma shows the second contention of this chapter: that we must read it with reference to Jesus. This is, naturally, the more contentious of the two contentions. Boersma is an evangelical drawing on deep Catholic resources. His primary argument in *Scripture as Real Presence* is that scripture is sacramental: it renders Christ really present to us. The Christ who meets us in scripture does more than divulge information to us. He confronts us, saves us, and transforms us on his way to transforming the entire cosmos into the world God wants.

In Boersma's terms, our *procedure* for interpreting the Bible is not neutral or godless. It is, like everything else in creation, a reflection of Christ's lordship, whether most of its practitioners realize this or not. Boersma's way of putting this has to do with metaphysics—the way reality is. And reality itself is sacramental—participant in the deeper reality of God. Christ is not smuggled into the Old Testament but rather discovered there—just as he is not smuggled into our view of creation but rather found there, to the church's delight. The surface is never all there is. Boersma confronts the common claim by historical critics that the Song of Songs is "just" an erotic poem. We can see the plausibility of the surface case: God is not mentioned, and the two are not explicitly said to be married or even necessarily Jewish. So a quasi-intellectual "argument" develops that the book got into the canon by some mistake and amounts to soft-core porn. Didn't the rabbis and church fathers develop elaborate procedures to keep it out of the hands of minors?

In a beautiful chapter called "Nuptial Reading," Boersma shunts aside these distractions without difficulty. No church father is alarmed at the sensual material in this book, nor is any Jewish interpreter. The one patristic source so literalist as to think the book is merely about sex is the only one who agreed it shouldn't be in the canon![13] But our ecclesial forebears were not Victorian prudes. They were aware that we have bodies and that those bodies are endlessly good. So we can agree without difficulty that the book is about sex. The subsequent question is this: What is sex about? For Boersma, drawing on Platonically inflected Catholic Christianity, sex means more than sex. For the rabbis, sex is only there as a reflection of God's stormy love affair with Israel. For the

13. Boersma, *Scripture as Real Presence*, 187.

church fathers, likewise, sex shows us the deepest truths about Christ's passion for the church: it bears fruit, it veils mysteries, and those mysteries are delightful, and deadly serious—they contain threats precisely because they birth new life, surrounded as it always is in this world by death. Sex is never just sex. It shows what it means to be human—and how good God is. Elizabeth Clark, a great patristics scholar but not herself a Christian, observes that Origen's reading of the Song of Songs, replete with references to Christ and church, takes its bearings from Paul's interpretation of Romans 9–11.[14] All Origen is doing is reading Israel's scripture in a Pauline-tutored, christological manner. We do this not to do violence to the text or to ignore its graphic nature. We do it because this is the deepest reality there is: the Lord Jesus longs to marry his bride, the church. That is, all of us. The Song teaches us to burn with the same desire he has for us.

This is precisely the moment when those of us taught by historical critics demur, mock, roll eyes. Why do we do this? Historical criticism's greatness lies in its patient unfolding of human knowledge through time. Those writing the Song did not know the names "Christ" or "church."

Yet we must also ask about what we know now and would not wish to unknow. We know more through time than our forebears knew at the time. We Christians confess that Jesus is Son of God, Savior of the world, the deepest truth not only about the scriptures but about all human beings and creation itself. And then we see details we could not have seen before—greater knowledge of Jesus than we would have had otherwise. "Let him kiss me with the kisses of his mouth," the Canticle opens, and Origen sees this as the longing of Israel for a messiah. He then pivots back into Israel's history for previous songs of longing sung by the bridegroom's friends, the prophets: Miriam's song by the sea, Moses's song before death, the song of Deborah and Barak, and more (Exod. 15; Deut. 32; Judg. 5). To burn with passion for the bridegroom is to long to *know* (with all that verb's biblical connotation), to plunge back into Israel's scripture with new eyes. It is, in short, a way to relearn to love the language of the Old Testament, for which Strawn longs.

---

14. "When read with an historian's eye, Origen's *Commentary on the Canticle of Canticles* resembles nothing so much as Rom. 9–11, in which Paul's argument for the union of Jew and gentile in Christianity reaches its climax." Clark, "Uses of the Song of Songs," 390, quoted in Boersma, *Scripture as Real Presence*, 205.

Boersma's book contends that Christ is the treasure in the field of which Jesus's parable speaks, drawing on Christ's image in a way we first saw with Origen.[15] Christ is always already hidden in Israel's scripture. When we interpret christologically, we are not bringing something foreign to the text. He is already there, in the fullness of his mystery. The Greek word for treasure, both Strawn and Boersma point out, is *thēsauros*. To draw out the right word is to select just the right treasure from the Bible's storehouse of memory for what the gathered people need just now. The preacher's responsibility could not be more weighty. Thankfully she has to invent nothing from scratch. Jesus is already there, revealing greater depths of who he is for the world's blessing. And we get to take part in the strange and beautiful way that he's saving the world.

If Strawn shows us a scriptural imagination, Boersma shows us a *sacramental imagination*. God is always working through created things to bring salvation. God's saving work is always mediated—wonderfully so—through scripture and saints and sacraments and creation and one another. There is nothing that is not made "in Christ," and so nothing that cannot show Christ if one knows how to look (see here all of Col. 1). A sacramental universe is one that is shot through with meaning as God constantly works through creation's mediation to bring about the world God wants.

Institutional Resurrection

What do we do with the sorts of institutions mentioned above that seem so catastrophically to be failing us?

In N. T. Wright's theology of Israel, he offers an analogy. There is a fire raging. The fire truck is on its way. But unfortunately the fire truck itself has fallen into a ditch. Someone or something must get it out of the ditch to go and fight the fire. The truck is Israel. It is the family through which God means to bless and repair the world. God's coming in Jesus is designed to get the truck out so it can go and fight the fire.[16] The rescuing people itself needs rescue. That is what God brings with the redeeming work of Christ. It's not a bad analogy to institutions. They are meant to

15. Boersma, *Scripture as Real Presence*, 17.
16. Wright, *Paul and the Faithfulness of God*, 504.

humanize us, to divinize, to participate in Christ's kingdom. And they're all broken. They all need saving. The answer is not to leave them in the ditch. It is to be part of their return to doing the saving work for which they are designed, and for which God refuses to leave them behind.

Augustine's understanding of humanity is helpful here. He is the first one we know to use the phrase "original sin," and so is often pilloried for it. He teaches that all of us from Adam are alienated from God and neighbor and working out that alienation for the rest of our lives. I see plenty of evidence that he's right: in my own heart, in the church and institutions I love and lamented above, in the world. But brokenness is not the last word. Every tear in the fabric is one that Christ is presently repairing on his way to mending the whole world. Not only that, but the mended version will be more beautiful than the original. This is Augustine's teaching of the "happy fault," *felix culpa*, that God can even use our faults and flaws and harm of others to bring blessing, and so God will weave them all into his final tapestry of creation. What we mean for evil, God means for good (Gen. 50:20). This is a dangerous teaching—couldn't it lead to folks feeling excused for the harm they do? If our hearers don't ask a version of this question, we are not preaching the gospel of grace (see Paul's response in Rom. 6). Yes, it is dangerous. Preached rightly, grace is always a scandal. And it's how God works. Adam and Eve's fall is only *there* to be forgiven in Christ's much more overwhelming grace.

In his monumental book *The City of God*, about the history of God's people from beginning to end, Augustine speaks of two cities throughout history. One is the city of God, coherent by its twin love for God and humanity, joined as limbs to a body, with Christ as head, and so linked corporally to all the other saints. The other is the earthly city, bound for destruction, coherent by its lust for power. Call it "the city of dirt," if you like. The two are intertwined throughout history and will remain so until sorted out by Christ at the judgment. Try to disentangle them and you waste your time or hurt someone. This scriptural imagination allows Augustine to tell the story of Rome, recently sacked by Goths in the year 410, for which disaster pagan Romans were blaming the Christians ("if it rains, blame the Christians," Jerome joked). In response, Augustine argues that Christians did not undo the Roman Republic. A republic, by definition, exists to do "public things"; it sees that each person is given his or her due. But Rome never gave to God what was due to God. Instead it worshiped demons—who delight in the lust for power. Occasionally,

Augustine can use Rome's own rhetoric of decline against it: to say there was a time when Rome was better suggests "the world" can be better or worse (and that better is, uh, well, better). You can't really criticize something well that you don't love, at least implicitly. And Augustine has a lot of good criticism of Rome.

Augustine has left many a reader with a chastened view of politics. With his theology of original sin and his debunking of public triumphalism, Augustine teaches us to be humble, especially when we're sure we're right and someone else is wrong. He also teaches us to be humble because Christ meets us in humility. We should never be surprised when folks misbehave. God only has sinners to work with. Here's what will surprise: Christ is constantly raising up saints, even among people as ordinary as us. Sometimes the degraded structures of repair in our world are themselves repaired, and repairing. The church pays diligent attention to Christ's work of birthing holiness in a world as sordid as ours—we point it out, we encourage others toward it. But we're not surprised when kings are awful. Nearly all the kings in the Bible are awful. We thrill when God raises up prophets to say as much and priests to conduct traffic between heaven and earth, to forgive our sins and tell us about the things of God. And often the priests in the Bible faithfully mediate heaven and earth.

And God's chief prophet, priest, and even king is none other than Christ, who is the origin, climax, and end of history. Whatever crisis we face will vanish. Jerome wept uncontrollably when Rome fell. Augustine shrugged. The city about which we care most profoundly is the city of God. The nation-state as we know it may falter. The church as we know it and the institutions that serve it are no less fallible. And so there will be more works of mercy required of God's people. And more holiness-raising by Jesus. My contemporary politics include observations about the present order of things, which I'm happy to discuss (notions of taxation, public largesse, international order). But that's not the gospel. Folks can disagree with me about those things and still stand with me on what really matters. The gospel is that Christ is renewing all things. There is work to do to take part in that. And it's humanizing, holiness-making work, made possible by a scriptural imagination and a sacramental imagination.

When we see the brokenness in the world around us, we will not pontificate or denounce. We know ourselves all too well as sinners to do that. We will lament, pray, look on with compassion. And we will get busy picking up the wreckage. Not building some other foolproof building elsewhere—no, it would just fall too. Jesus promised that every treasured institution will be thrown down, and then resurrected, in his body. The church exists to show us this—that Jesus is Lord, that these institutions, like every person, will one day bow the knee, that in the meantime all should serve him as best they can and seek mercy for when we fail, as we will often. The only sort of institution we can ever have in this age is a broken one, currently being repaired, one day to be as resplendent as his resurrection body.

We don't read the Bible, then, to condemn, to declare ourselves right and others wrong. We read it to repent, to praise God, to be gentled into being the saints God intends every creature to be. We read it to develop a scriptural imagination and a sacramental imagination. We read it to follow the Jew Jesus, who learned the Bible intimately on his mother's knee, and who now teaches it to us intimately as we learn to bend ours. We do so as a broken and breaking institution, graciously joined to Christ in his death and resurrection, through which God is restoring all things.

For Further Study

Hays, Richard. *Echoes of Scripture in the Letters of Paul*. New Haven: Yale University Press, 1989.

This is a crucial book for the beginning of a reappraisal of the New Testament's christological reading of the Old as not simply supersessionist.

Heclo, Hugh. *On Thinking Institutionally*. Oxford: Oxford University Press, 2011.

A lament for the loss of institutions in our culture that sketches a rationale for their goodness.

Lash, Nicholas. *Theology on the Way to Emmaus*. London: SCM, 1986.

These essays imagine a reading of scripture that is constantly refreshed by the tradition of the church and embodied in the church's life together.

8

Four Senses

Reading the Bible with the Early Church

How do we read the Bible? That question gets to the heart of this book, and indeed it gets to the heart of Christianity. As an academic, my instincts are to equivocate, nuance, qualify. But we finally have to answer—a church is waiting—how do we read the Bible?

We read it listening for God's voice. And then we tell others what God says. Anything less is false humility.[1]

These people are gathered to hear a word from the living God. And the interpreter of the Bible is the one charged to give it. I say that with trepidation. We are all aware of the harm that can be done by those claiming to speak for God. We have tried to put appropriate safeguards in place against such abuse. But the greatest abuse might be this: pretending to read the Bible without asking the God question. And not in the past-tense subjunctive mood ("the writers of this text may have thought . . .") but in the present indicative: "God says . . ." Any reading of the Bible that stops short of saying what God says now is a waste of time and a tragic abdication of the interpreter's calling and responsibility.

Pay special attention to when the Bible reads the Bible. And pay greater attention still to when Jesus reads the Bible in the Bible. All of the holy scriptures point to him—Israel's scriptures point forward to him, the New Testament points back to him, the gospels portray him. Any reading of the Bible that neglects Jesus, the Lord of the Bible, has also been a diversion, a wasted opportunity, a shirking of God's intention for humanity.

---

1. John Milbank indicts modern theology generally for its "false humility" (*Theology and Social Theory*, 1). There is something to what he says.

After one of his miracles in the Gospel of John, Jesus defends his actions and his identity with an appeal to scripture: "You search the scriptures because you think that in them you have eternal life" (5:39). His hearers are right to do this. All of his hearers, down to the present day. We search the scriptures for the life "that really is life" (1 Tim. 6:19). He continues, "And it is they that testify on my behalf." Like a witness in a courtroom, Israel's scripture bears witness that Jesus is who he says he is—the one who works in full cooperation with his Father, who will judge all people, who will raise the dead (John 5:19, 22, 27). Jesus continues, "If you believed Moses, you would believe me, for he wrote about me" (5:46). Throughout this chapter of John, Jesus insists that Israel's scripture points forward to him, that those who search it for life should hear its voice testifying to his lordship. Now, this is, of course, written amidst controversy—its polemical edge is clear even in a cursory reading of John 5. Jesus tells his hearers to search the scriptures and to find him there. We, the church, should pay heed. Not simply for fear of what might happen if we do not, as Jesus's warning tone implies. But so that we may delight in finding him, as John insists elsewhere (10:10).

The ancient church developed an elaborate fourfold method for reading the Bible. They searched for scripture's literal meaning, and then often also for three sorts of figural meanings, allegorical, moral, and anagogical, as we have seen previously in this book. This chapter will work to creatively reappropriate a fourfold approach to the biblical text. But we should note that these are not four different properties in texts. Texts don't *have* a moral sense the way a person has brown eyes or a short temper. These are flexible approaches to reading a text for the sake of a community. And some won't work in some instances. Origen insisted some texts have no literal sense worthy of the name; many fruitless hours could be spent trying to assign an allegorical sense to a text that should be spent otherwise. These approaches to texts are quite fluid. Nicholas of Lyra distinguished two kinds of allegory: one the author of scripture may have been aware of, one he likely was not. The point is clear—these are not airtight compartments. They are gifts of different sorts to enable the church to do different things with the Bible as the situation demands. Furthermore, the literal sense of the scriptures is the foundation, the most important, the one without which the others fail. This is the great gift of the Protestant Reformation to which I belong—an insistence that we read the Bible literally, lovingly, obediently, and that the text of scripture norms everything else we say about God. The first and most difficult duty of biblical interpretation is just to read the text and tell others what it says. And that's difficult enough for a lifetime of reading.

A Complicated Letter

The first thing to do with the Bible is to read it—patiently and exactingly. This is no simple task, of course. Most disputes in the church and not a few in the world have been over how to read the Bible. But before we problematize, we read and listen for God's voice, and as church we do what God says. This is hard to do—like everything else that is worth doing. Our everyday English usage already tramples on the word *literally*: "I literally died," we heedlessly (and quite illiterally) say after a close scrape. Liberal Christians—my tribe—often speak of taking the Bible "seriously but not literally," thereby granting themselves a reprieve from more troubling miraculous and moral portions of the Bible. But the letter of the Bible is no onerous burden from which to seek refuge. It is God speaking to us. And this is a miracle—a God who speaks, who even delights in expressing affection, who longs for flourishing for the creatures God has made. We read this text first as a summons from One who loves us. And we read it attentive to those with whom we read. For as the horticulturalist image from Origen suggests, no reading happens in a vacuum. We read the text and the needs of the people simultaneously. The church's worship is another literal reading. That we gather in Easter for feasting, in Lent for fasting, at a wedding for rejoicing, a funeral for mourning—these also shade our attention to the letter. One theologian describes this sense of scripture as the "letteral"—we pay attention to the way the words are on the page, and in our lives.[2]

As a teacher and practitioner of preaching, I am thinking here first of reading the Bible for the task of preaching. There are as many other reasons to read the Bible as one could imagine, but this is a central task of the church, and so not a bad place to begin. The first way to read the Bible literally is to read it as a story—that is, to make as clear as we can the story presently being told. I don't just mean in the passage at hand, but also how the passage at hand relates to the grand story being told in the entire Bible. Sometimes, a wise friend points out, you have

2. It's Graham Ward's phrase from his *"Allegoria."*

to take out the cover of the box that the puzzle came in and see where the confusing piece fits into the whole.[3] The Apostles' Creed is one such large-scale rendering of the story of the Bible—the God of Israel saves the world through Jesus. Before the church had creeds, we had what historians call the *regula fidei*, the rule of faith, a creed-like synopsis of the whole of scripture. Arguably, there is no Christianity without such a rule.[4] This large-scale story means we have to relate what we're reading at the moment to that grand story of the creating, saving, and restoring work of God. A story from the Pentateuch is about God's election and liberation of Israel and creation of the world. A story from the Epistles is about the apostles' work to form a church in Jesus's image. A story from the Prophets is about God's passionate demand for justice, first among God's people and then in the whole world. A story from Revelation is about the world God is surely bringing and that God dreams about in the meantime. If above I insisted that we read the Bible to see what God says, present tense, here I insist just as strongly—every biblical text has to be shown in its relationship to the overarching story of the Bible.

Of course, some portions of the Bible seem to tell no story at all. The Proverbs offer fortune cookie–like advice on life. The Epistles offer searing moral demands. The law in the Torah sets out details for a society that seeks justice for the least. Further examples abound. Yet these nonnarrative texts are themselves intelligible only in the context of the narrative of God's coming to dwell with his people. It is a preacher's responsibility to show the patterns of how this smaller text relates to the overall text of scripture.

A few things I do not mean by reading the passage literally: This is not the place for historical criticism alone. We must attend to what historians tell us about the text—to its jagged edges, its linguistic conundrums, its geographical particularity or even confusion, the ways it has come down to us with the seams showing from multiple stitchings-together by editors. But historical data alone do not make for a literal reading. They are anticipatory of a literal reading. A reading is itself an interpretation. It is a focusing. It announces, "This is what God says here," in light of all the historical and other approaches to the text that have gone into background research.

---

3. I take this from pastor Craig O'Brien of Origin Church on the campus of the University of British Columbia here in Vancouver.

4. Rowan Williams argues this in his "Doctrinal Criticism?"

A literal sense is far from simple. For the Bible often argues with itself. Origen was surely not the first to notice that light and dark are separated before sun and moon are created—surely Genesis is *trying* to show us to take the letter very seriously, so seriously we also read on other levels. Joshua often pronounces some enemy of Israel vanquished. The next chapter that enemy is back, marshaling again for battle. What's it saying—literally? That the editor was clumsy? Psalm 50 describes God as one who has no need of sacrifice. "Do I drink the blood of goats?" the Lord asks. That is, God quibbles with the very system of sacrifice that God himself has instituted! There is nothing bad about sacrifice—indeed, God asks it of us. While Christians speak of Christ as the final sacrifice, informed by the book of Hebrews, we still speak of worship as a sacrifice of praise, of our gifts to God as a sort of dim reflection of Christ's own sacrifice. No, God does not get thirsty, does not require blood, does not lack money, even as God does ask the Israelites and the church to make offerings. As has long been noted, sacrifice is not *for* God—it is for the ones offering, to shape them, us, into being the sorts of faithful people that God wants. Simply to offer a literal reading of scripture is no simple thing. Just try reading the Sermon on the Mount's denunciation of all violence—and then try practicing it as a community.

The ultimate literal "reader" is our Lord Jesus, who did far more than read Israel's scripture. He presented it over again in his flesh. After Jesus's prophetic demonstration in the temple, when a rationale is demanded of him, he describes it as his Father's house (John 2:16). He is asked for some sign that might demonstrate his authority to reinterpret the temple this way, and he offers his coming death and resurrection—as a tearing down and rebuilding of the temple. For Christians, the Lord's temple is Jesus's body, teaching, crucified, risen, and returning. John goes on to say the disciples remembered these things after his resurrection (2:22). They found the psalm text, "Zeal for your house will consume me," and continued to read the rest of Psalm 69 in his resurrection light (2:17). They see there also Psalm 69:21 and remember Jesus announcing his thirst from his cross (Matt. 27:48; Mark 15:36; Luke 23:36; John 19:29—a rare case of all four gospels in full harmony). Jesus *is* the literal sense of scripture. These small portions he quotes stand in for the whole, in a surprising literal reading by which he presents all of Israel's scripture over again in his life: the betrayal agonized over by the psalmist, the deliverance that comes at the end of so many psalms, mercy even for his tormenters, and the renewal of the entire cosmos for which God chose Israel in the first place.

Additionally, a literal reading is not inhibited by doctrine, for the creeds are based on literal readings of the text. This is no diminishment of freedom—on the contrary, all freedom comes within restraints, blessedly so. It is a sort of hermeneutical spiral, as commentators often note—hopefully a blessed cycle rather than a vicious one! No artist is ever without constraints of material, time, theme, and no text is without the constraints of doctrinal formation. Doctrine can be challenged by texts, and blessedly often has been—the last century or two has seen new attention to Jesus's earthly life, almost entirely neglected by the historic creeds, and to God's faithfulness to his promises to Israel, even more neglected historically. In fact, the doctrines of the church inform and form our literal readings. They safeguard the mystery.[5]

A literal reading of scripture is also much more profound than anything else we might offer in teaching from the Bible. So much biblical interpretation does something else. Sermons offer pious sentimentality ("Jesus is almost as inclusive as I am . . ."). They are a chance for the preacher to disburden his or her soul. They seek to entertain. They offer advice for life. Stop it. Just read the text. Literally. Say how it relates to the story of God and God's people. Do so guided by Christian doctrine. And do so in a way that delights those hearing into deeper discipleship. Show us Jesus through this text. Don't leave us bored. That may be the ultimate unforgivable sin.[6] The God of the universe wants to save the world through an unmarried pregnant teenager from the sticks . . . and we hearers are left looking at our phones for solace from boredom?!

In a literal reading, we should look for the weird. Accentuate the odd. Show people the text's depths until they squirm. If a text is morally objectionable, make that plain. Don't avoid it or apologize for it or work around it or hide it. Don't hold it at arm's length. Show it. Often my fellow liberal readers and I have run from and effectively hidden problematic texts from the church. I understand why—these are hard to interpret and difficult to stomach for those who have gathered for a word of encouragement on Sunday morning. The thing is, they know those

5. I draw here on Jonathan Rogers channeling Flannery O'Connor's language in *Terrible Speed of Mercy*, 9.

6. Fred Craddock often said a version of this—that being boring in preaching is the worst homiletical sin.

texts are in the Bible somewhere. They'll find them. And when they do, if we haven't preached on them, we've given them no tools with which to interpret those difficult texts.

Then we have to take a step beyond showing the literal text in all its grit and glory. We have to love it. And show the hearers we love it. This is such a simple observation I hesitate to make it: those who teach the Bible well love it. They rejoice in it. They dance with it like a bride, as Jews do once a year at their festival of Simchat Torah. They wrap it around their arms, bind it on their foreheads, mark their gates and doors with it, talking about it with children at home and away, filling their mental and physical and familial space with God's delightful words (Deut. 6:4–9). I especially love this Deuteronomy text, for it may once have been figural—surround yourself with God's law, it says. Yet Jews for centuries have practiced it quite literally—wrapping the law around their arms, binding it on their foreheads. Is it literal to do physically what a text may have once meant figurally? Of course, the command may once have been literal, before taking on inevitable figural depths. The lines blur and smudge. But Israel's practice embodies what scripture proposes—and with delight.

A final example for now. Jesus is jousting with the Pharisees once more in his wordy way in the Gospel of John. His listeners object—isn't he making himself equal to God? One thing Jews know is they will die before they blaspheme, just watch. And Jesus says, sure, I'm saying I'm a god. "Is it not written in your law, 'I said, you are gods'? If those to whom the word of God came were called 'gods'—and the scripture cannot be annulled—can you say that the one whom the Father has sanctified and sent into the world is blaspheming because I said, 'I am God's Son'?" (John 10:34–36). In the psalm to which Jesus refers, the eighty-second, a scene is set like a heavenly throne room. God has a sort of council, a divine coterie, and God addresses his courtiers: "I say 'You are gods, children of the Most High, all of you; nevertheless you shall die like mortals, and fall like any prince'" (Ps. 82:6–7). Jesus seizes on this to say that the very Bible that teaches Israel that there is no God but God also grants the status of "god" pretty widely—why cannot he, God's own Son, claim it? Christians might go on and add that all those adopted in baptism can also call ourselves daughters and sons in the Son. And this is no threat to divine unity—God's greatness is such that God has no rival, not among God's angels (one traditional interpretation of the court in Psalm 82) nor among us lesser creatures. What is God is always and altogether God—the Father, the Son, and the Spirit—and God endlessly pours out the divine life on and in us so that we can become more godly forever and yet never threaten God's unique divinity. In John 10, an odd text is read in an odd way by an exceedingly odd Savior and dished up for an odd people becoming odder. That is, holier.

One can almost gauge the faithfulness of a preacher's work, and so of a congregation's life together, by the comfort and depth with which they delight in the Old Testament. I say "almost" only because fundamentalist communities can take the Old Testament in dangerous directions. But of course any text can be taken in a dangerous direction by anyone for a myriad of reasons. No text or interpretation is inherently safe. The Old Testament represents some 80 percent of our Bible, millennia of our history, a variety of genres not present in the New, and it is not immediately transparent to what we already wanted to say. It is always already weird. And it is always already delightful. It represents God's multi-century love affair with God's people on the way to God saving the whole world. The Old Testament is full of stories that no sensible people would tell on itself. Nations tidy up their histories, show themselves in their best light. Not Israel. Israel tells story after story of its own recalcitrance, stiff-neckedness, unwillingness to be who God wants. This yields the tragic fruit of the church often pointing a finger at Israel and saying, "You! You're the problem!" when of course the point of the text is for us to blame ourselves.[7] To place ourselves in the position of Israel, and to tell story after story of all the clever ways we have avoided God's summons. Because the more deeply we tell the stories of our unfaithfulness, the more patently we see God's grace. Look how patient God is to choose and love and restore a people like us. And through us, the whole world.

Allegory: Who to Trust?

When mainline liberal Christians like me turn to later Pastoral Epistles, we might remember, vaguely, warnings in seminary that Paul probably didn't write the stuff that claims Paul wrote it. Then we see the hierarchy and misogyny in these lists of ethical codes, and we turn back to

7. My colleague Rabbi Dr. Laura Duhan Kaplan points out that al-Qaeda propaganda often quotes Western news outlets' criticism of Western societies. The *New York Times* means to criticize to improve a culture; the West's sworn enemies take that criticism as a rationale to destroy it.

the synoptic Gospels to find a Jesus there much more to our liking (or so we think). So we miss passages like Ephesians 5, in which the writer recommends a mutual outpouring between husband and wife that reflects Christ's self-outpouring for the church: "This is a great mystery, and I am applying it to Christ and the church" (5:32). Marriage, with all its delights and dilemmas, only exists at all to show us something about God: that God will not be God without us. And humanity's relationship with God, with all its unutterable beauty and all its unbearable trauma, is discernible throughout creation. For Paul, all creation testifies to the self-outpouring of a Creator who loves not at a distance but at the most intimate. Those who interpret the Bible do so on behalf of a people whom the Lord intends to marry, and on behalf of the God set on the marrying.

Do you see what we miss by neglecting our own Bible? And as for the passages we'd rather skip for their teachings on gender, the church has resources for reading those as well. "Adam was not deceived, but the woman was deceived," and therefore women should learn, not teach (1 Tim. 2:11–14). Gary Anderson's book *The Genesis of Perfection* describes how the church fathers read this passage.[8] Eve was deceived, sure—a moderate offense. Adam was *not* deceived—that is, he knew exactly what he was doing. His offense is the greater. Read the text again, and see whether it is indeed patient of such an interpretation. Close reading of the letter is no opponent of what we care about most. It is its very precondition.

Anderson is one among many interpreters of the Bible drawing on the deep wells of ancient Christian wisdom in ways that hold things together that we often tear apart. For example, it is commonplace in biblical studies to point out that Genesis 1–3 describes nothing like a "fall" that has been so important in later Christian theology. Another commonplace is that Genesis itself argues against the Christian doctrine of *creatio ex nihilo*, that God brings the universe out of nothing: there is, patently, a formless void and a wind—chaos, but not nothing (Gen. 1:1–2). In other words, relatively ignorant of the church's depth of teaching, we glance at the Bible in a sort of flat, wooden way and quickly shake our heads at the misreadings the church has long perpetuated.

Actually, Christians were not ignoring or willfully misreading the Bible as they constructed doctrine. They just tended to read the Bible differently. They read it figurally, tracing out its logic into areas the Bible

8. See chap. 5, "Is Eve the Problem?," in *Genesis of Perfection*, 99–118.

itself didn't make explicit or fully flesh out. And crucially, the church assumes the Old Testament is authoritative when it is deferred to, not just when it is referred to.[9] Having built up doctrines on the basis of scripture, Old Testament and New alike, the church reads the Bible anew in their light. So, for example, creation *ex nihilo* isn't really about origins—it's a way of trusting that God is providentially guiding the cosmos, that God always has more resources than we can presently see, and that the world is marked not by tragic lack but by God's generosity. Such a doctrine is built from many places in scripture, and then shapes the life of a community that reads scripture anew in its light. Perhaps, Anderson suggests, creation "without opposition" is a better way to put it, quoting the Jewish biblical scholar Jon Levenson.[10] The fall is not obviously present in Genesis 3, read unfiltered. But then no one ever reads anything unfiltered. Paul elevates the doctrine for a reason—Jew and gentile alike receive Christ's benefits in redemption, and so Jew and gentile alike must have been in dire trouble. Israel had ways to speak of the immediacy of human rebellion—the pyre in the tabernacle is no sooner lit than it is profaned (Lev. 10). God no sooner gives the law than the people have already created golden calves and risen up to "play" (the way frat boys "play"; see Exod. 32). Paul could be wrong, but what he is doing is not ridiculous, and it is not non-Jewish: he is seeing the pattern by which God always works presented anew.

Allegory is simply the offer of another reading than the letter. It is not first, for Christians, the effort to touch up something embarrassing, to tidy up a flaw in a text or muzzle its distinctive voice. It is, rather, to read the letter so deeply that we see something "more" present than is obvious on a first pass. When Paul tells the Corinthians he is passing on what he first received, that Christ died "according to the scriptures," he is not just signing up to a remote creed, as we sometimes do. He is showing the challenge of the earliest church, "to pore over the old texts afresh" in light of the crucified and raised firstborn son.[11] So Jesus "does not supplant" the firstborn son that is Israel (Exod. 4:22). Rather, his identity is "deepened by attending to the plain sense of Israel's scriptural witness." And subsequently we, the church, have "traced and retraced" "nearly

9. It is Christopher Seitz's lovely phrase in *Word without End*, 222.

10. Anderson, *Christian Doctrine and the Old Testament*, 45, quoting Levenson, *Creation and the Persistence of Evil*, 122.

11. Anderson, *Christian Doctrine and the Old Testament*, 77.

every square inch" of the Bible as we attempt to "map out the identity of God's beloved Son."[12] Contrary to what we sometimes say or show, the church has no power to cast off Israel's scripture, however difficult we may find it at times—to do so is just to cast off ourselves and our God. Rather, having seen God's face in Jesus, we return to the scriptures that birthed him, Mary-like, alert for signs of his presence there that we could not have seen in advance but cannot now unsee. And we delight.

I have written extensively about allegory elsewhere and see its dangers, of some of which the church has long been aware. How do we not just use it to make the Bible say whatever we already think, however unfaithful? There are rules in place against such misuse—we cannot "make" the Bible say figurally anything it doesn't say literally elsewhere. Figural reading is not meant to discover something new that we didn't already know (the word for that is actually *heresy*). It is to see again what we already "know" in some surprising new place. So, for example, Anderson offers a reading of the Joseph cycle in Genesis as a story that presents the entire Torah in microcosm. God chooses the unlikely brother, Joseph, and incites the ire of his elder brothers, who try to murder him and then learn he is raised to power, before being mercifully offered grace instead of revenge. That's the electing God of Israel—choosing the unlikely, then offering mercy through that one to the jealous who had tried to undo God's chosen before they even know to ask for mercy. Anderson quotes a twelfth-century Cistercian homily to this effect: we Christian readers "yearn" for Jesus. "The great depth at which he is hidden and the diligence necessary in seeking him and the difficulty you will have in finding him will only make him all the sweeter to your taste."[13] Christian readers are desperate for more of Christ—for we have blood on our hands. And we find him surprising us anew in these texts, right where he promises to meet us. That blood, which we were desperate to hide, is actually our salvation.

There are problems deploying allegory, to be sure. But the bigger problem is this: we regularly read in ways designed to avoid Jesus. We read looking for something else, for some other purpose, however noble. And we miss the crucified victim at our hands, whose very blood not only condemns but also restores us.

12. Anderson, *Christian Doctrine and the Old Testament*, 77.

13. Anderson, *Christian Doctrine and the Old Testament*, 85, quoting Guerric of Igny, *Liturgical Sermons*, 2:81.

Delight is its own sort of rule. If a reading fails to delight, we should start over. A discordant reading—one that does not fit the words on the page, or the contours of the story, or the listening ability of those gathered to hear—does not delight. With allegory, as with biblical interpretation generally, we may not lie. But it is no lie to discover Jesus in the very scriptures that deliver him to us. It is, on the contrary, a delight.

The Moral Sense: What Do We Crave?

The Bible can be an odd place from which to draw one's ethics. It has stories that inspire to goodness, to be sure. It also has stories that no one should imitate—ever. A friend of mine's childhood story shows the Bible's moral oddity. His Sunday school class was supposed to respond to the teacher taking roll with a memorized Bible verse. So the child before my friend in the alphabet responded with "Judas went and hanged himself." And my friend responded next with "Go thou and do likewise." Wrenched out of context, the Bible can incite moral horrors. Christians know that no one should actually go and do likewise—so the discordance between our confession "This is the word of the Lord" and the text's plain sense can be played for laughs.

But scripture's moral admonitions can inspire horror even when not wrenched out of context, but when read perfectly well and appropriately in context. And that is the concern of Greg Boyd in a major new book on figural interpretation of the Bible, *The Crucifixion of the Warrior God*. Boyd's passion is the Bible's portrait of violence done by God's people. In an age like ours, in which religiously inspired violence is one of the great political anxieties, we Christians must show that the Bible itself forbids any such misreading. Boyd sees the apologetic harm that violent texts do—why should anyone take this book, this gospel, this God seriously? And he aims to show that the Bible itself undoes such violence. How so?

The heart of the Bible, for Boyd, is Jesus's nonviolent agape love for enemies. The climax of scripture is Jesus's revelation of God's breathtakingly beautiful character. So what do we do with the ream of texts that point the other way? Many Old Testament texts display the *herem*, the "ban"—God's command that nothing living in an opponent's camp can be spared. These are not inconsequential texts and they are not rare. As Philip Jenkins points out, the Bible has more of a violence problem than Islam's Qur'an does, despite the media's frequent suggestion otherwise.[14] What do we make of such texts?

We read them contrary to the letter. Boyd doesn't thrill to the language of "allegory," or even more obscurely "tropology" (the moral sense of scripture), but he argues it should be permissible, and indeed he deploys it.[15] He does so guided by ancient interpreters of the sort who have appeared throughout this book's pages, Origen especially. God does not intend such texts to be read literally, much less as moral models. They are, rather, accommodations by God to our infantile spiritual state. Boyd uses the analogy of a missionary to a people who know nothing of Christian faith.[16] They may have barbaric practices in place, like female genital mutilation. The missionary will not likely denounce such practices right away. She may have to bear with them in fact, while leading her hearers to a place of practicing something quite different more slowly than she would like. Patiently. Portraits in scripture that suggest anything less than the character of God revealed on the cross—self-sacrificial nonviolent love—represent divine accommodations, or "literary crucifixes," as Boyd often calls them. Such portraits represent masks that God deigns to wear in the meantime, before we are able to see more fully who God really is, as nonviolent love. They show how low God had to go to get to us. In fact, for Boyd, Origen and the allegorical interpreters of scripture don't go nearly far enough. They insist on christological interpretation but stop a step short of Boyd's preferred "crucicentric" way of reading—not just Jesus as God, but Jesus as God on a cross. And they tend to interpret scripture allegorically when it misrepresents God's metaphysical characteristics (changing, remembering, deliberating), not to correct for Boyd's preferred problem of the violence done by God's people. Boyd regularly insists he can find no one reading divine violence allegorically after the fifth century, when the church allied itself with imperial power and began to find such texts not repugnant but positively agreeable.

Boyd is absolutely right that our Christology had better impact our biblical hermeneutics, and in the case of the morally troubling texts of scripture, he shows us one powerful portrait of how this might be so. And he reads well major literary themes of the Bible, like divine accom-

14. Boyd relies heavily on Jenkins, *Laying Down the Sword*.

15. Boyd, *Crucifixion of the Warrior God*, 734.

16. This image first appears on p. 72 of vol. 2 of *Crucifixion of the Warrior God*, and frequently thereafter.

modation, in ways that throw light on particular passages. For example, he shows convincingly that portraits of God doing violence actually represent God "giving us up" to the chaos from which God normally shields us. Creation, from the beginning, has been a matter of God shielding us creatures from chaotic forces that would do us in. When scripture suggests God does violence, what it means is that God merely gives us up to the chaos that we prefer to God's presence (Rom. 1:24, 26, 28). Boyd is also refreshingly honest and clear as a thinker. He confesses he used to try to justify the Bible's violent portraits of God, but is no longer willing to do so. His bold book is a wager that we may have resources we did not know we had right there in our Bibles.

And yet there are places with which I must disagree with Boyd—disagreements that may be helpful for understanding biblical interpretation.[17] One major metaphor in the book is an imagined scene in which Boyd sees his wife from afar and witnesses her mistreat a homeless person, contrary to everything he knows of her character. He only subsequently discovers that his wife is part of a Department of Homeland Security sting operation and the homeless man is actually a terrorist in disguise. What appears to be an incorrect vision turns out, with further information, to make perfect sense. So it is with the Bible. We learn in Christ the more profound truth that explains the outwardly objectionable portrait we previously had.

I think this metaphor is flawed in significant ways. A better metaphor would be getting to know what one's spouse was like before one knew him or her. Think of poring over photos, hearing stories, watching video, visiting significant places, meeting relatives. There is an awakening to the depths of a person that deepens delight—you were like this? This happened here? Look at those clothes! You were so young! And yet there is also profound continuity, and so delight. Your grandmother is amazing! This family practice explains that thing you do. One can even see things one's spouse couldn't have seen about him- or herself. Boyd's farfetched analogy suggests that what we read in the Old Testament is absurd on its face. Origen is capable of such umbrage, but generally we Christians know better than to speak so disparagingly of the plain sense

---

17. There are other major disagreements that don't pertain to this book—namely, the hash that Boyd makes of Augustine (a convenient arch-villain in many a theological comic book) and lack of effort he makes to understand divine impassibility before blasting it for hundreds of pages.

of Israel's scriptures. Boyd at times tips over into heretical language for the Old Testament: the New "supersedes" the "inferior" Old; Christ's teaching is "altogether new"; it "dwarfs" all that came before, which is "cloudy," filled with "false conceptions" and "pre-Christian" notions of God, and so on.[18] We Christians decided, with good reason, we had to keep the book. And love it. It is no lie. It is, for all its complications, the truth about God.

Boyd builds much of his book on the Epistle to the Hebrews, which indeed uses more supersessionistic language to compare the covenants: Israel's temple, its scriptures, its relationship to God are all passing away—they are shadows surpassed in Christ. We Christians cannot do away with our New Testament either. And yet Hebrews is not the only portrait of the relationship between the covenant in Christ and the covenant in Israel. Remarkably, St. Paul's detailed engagement with God's faithfulness in Romans 9–11 is nearly absent in Boyd's account. It turns up as he argues against a simplistic portrait of Romans 9 on predestination, but almost not at all in Boyd's synthetic work. This is significant. Paul argues that God will be faithful to his promises whatever the current conditions that seem to suggest the contrary. The good news cannot be that God leaves his people Israel behind in order to save us gentiles. No, it must be that God has done a surprisingly faithful thing. For that's all God can ever do. God must be holding open the door for the full number of the gentiles to come in, in order then also to save his people Israel, for "all Israel will be saved" (Rom. 11:26). How will this work? Paul doesn't know. He dissolves into doxology: "O the depth of the riches and wisdom and knowledge of God! How unsearchable are his judgments and how inscrutable his ways!" (11:33). This apophatic note in St. Paul is nearly absent in Boyd's work. He seems to understand God rather transparently. But Christians know that even in Christ, especially at this climax of the covenant, God remains mystery. What we receive in Christ is trustworthy—God will not turn out to be different. And yet we have no place for presumption or arrogance over against previous generations of God's people. Boyd seems to hold objectionable Old Testament texts at arm's length, as far away as possible. It is hard to imagine him reading a

---

18. Boyd, *Crucifixion of the Warrior God*, 1:xxx ("supersedes"), 38 ("inferior"), 206 ("altogether new"), 49 ("dwarfs"), 408 and 1190 ("cloudy"), 408 ("false conceptions"), 839 ("pre-Christian," specifying Hosea). Boyd clearly spells out what other authors often disguise or leave implicit.

passage from the conquest in Joshua or the plagues in Egypt (or, for that matter, objectionable New Testament passages like Jesus's haranguing of the Pharisees in Matt. 23) before saying, "This is the word of the Lord." He would rather have to say the opposite—this is *not* the word of the Lord, this is God patiently bearing with his wayward people.

The problem is, where do we stop saying God is accommodating to our ugliness? Is Israel wrong to think it is chosen by God? The law, Boyd insists, was destined to fail; likewise God's work to make a nation of priests was lost from the beginning, and no nationhood is possible without violence.[19] Here Boyd seems to hold on to accommodation—a good doctrine—at the expense of others with which it should instead stand in tension. Namely, that God does not go back on God's promises, that what God demonstrates about God's self is true and reliable, and we don't now have to wonder in what way God is wearing a mask, crucifying himself literally, before one day revealing a greater truth. Or are we wrong to think that Christ is the savior of the world? Is that just one more mask before some fuller revelation?

Of course not, Boyd would say, and he would turn to me and ask how I read passages in which God commands the murder of every man, woman, child, and animal among an enemy. He offers one way of reading those passages—as literary masks, crucifixes. I have made similar suggestions about psalms of imprecation—that we read them, as Augustine does, as prayers to turn enemies into friends.[20] I would prefer to see descriptions of the conquest in spiritual terms—as God doing battle with our sins. Boyd is open to such a reading; he just does not pursue it with energy. We can have the strength of Boyd's readings—his willingness to read against the grain of the letter—without these weaknesses. The literal sense of conquest or genocidal passages is simply contravened by Christ's command to peace in the Gospels, so that now in Christ we may read those passages as descriptions of God's work to root out our sins and make us holy. We don't need to scissor these passages out. We can instead let them sit awkwardly alongside other texts whose literal sense contradicts them. And when asked which we'll follow, Jesus's people do not have to puzzle long. We follow the guy who loved and forgave his enemies. And as Boyd expertly shows elsewhere in his book, this was not anything he created from scratch. He was following a thread in Israel's

19. Boyd, *Crucifixion of the Warrior God*, 727.
20. "Allegory and the Jews," in *Praise Seeking Understanding*, 149–93.

own scripture—in which God abhors violence and longs for fullness of life for every creature.

But there is a more profound challenge still, in the moral sense of scripture. That is, why can I not bring myself to do what scripture asks? Jesus may be clear about his desire for his people with regard to violence, money, power, friendship, and a myriad of other things. So how come we, his people, follow him so poorly? In one way, it is literally clear what to do with Matthew 5: love our enemies as Jesus commands. But morally it is not so easy. Just try, on your own, not to sin, starting now. You won't make it far.

In a place that's less literally clear, but more morally encouraging, St. Paul gives a novel reading of Genesis's opening words. He is speaking to the Corinthians of the way the Holy Spirit transfigures the church from one degree of glory to another. This is not easy—for we are mere earthen vessels, however powerful and patient God is to work within us. And Paul quotes Genesis: "For it is the God who said, 'Let light shine out of darkness,' who has shone in our hearts to give the light of the knowledge of the glory of God in the face of Jesus Christ" (2 Cor. 4:6). The God who made everything from nothing can surely make saints even from such unpromising materials as us. And this is the key moral theme in the Bible—how God works to transfigure the likes of us sinners. Boyd has nary a mention of this theme in 1,300 pages, but anyone who has ever failed to keep a promise or tell the full truth knows better. Anyone whose government is spending trillions on violence and taking money from the poor and children and the elderly knows better. Anyone who can't, by sheer fiat, make right what is wrong in their own heart knows better. The primary problem isn't in the Bible. It's in me, and in the collection of me's called "church" and the collection of me's called "world."

The moral sense of scripture is not primarily, then, about apologizing for scripture's dangerous passages. It is about God's relentless work to make us holy. It is about God's patience and the Spirit's sanctifying inclusion of a stubborn, selfish, and lazy humanity in the repair of the cosmos. The God who made everything can surely do this, and infinitely more than we can ask or imagine (Eph. 3:20).

Anagogical: What Future Is Coming?

This final sense of scripture is traditionally about Christian hope. In John Cassian's famous illustration, Jerusalem is a city in Palestine literally, the church allegorically, the virtues that make us holy tropologically, and the city of God anagogically. Look at its ramparts! the psalmist enthuses. Walk around its towers! (Ps. 48). God dwells among his people here in this temple, in this city, the navel of the universe. When Christians claim that God dwells with us in Christ, we have a lot to learn from how the Jews regard Jerusalem. And we pray for its peace—now—not just eschatologically (Ps. 122).

Eschatology is its own field of Christian theology, having to do with the last things. This is one area in which we seem to have made a significant divergence from our Jewish forebears. Jews at the time of Jesus anticipated that at the end of all things the messiah would come and judge the living and the dead and deliver Israel. There is no salvation from the God of Israel that is nonbodily, so the dead would need to get their bodies back. Hence, some Jews tried to get buried as close to the Mount of Olives as possible—to be the first to see the messiah and the goodness of his deliverance. But just here we Christians propose an amendment to the minutes. The general resurrection has begun! we Christians say. But, strangely, it has begun with only one Jew. Jesus's resurrection is a sure sign the rest of us will be raised as well. And that the end of the world is here! It's just not here in full yet. Everything else we teach is something Jesus could have been passing on precisely as he learned it while bouncing on Mary's knee. This two-part hitch in the resurrection was exceedingly unexpected, but not unfaithful, of God.

Christian interpretation of the Bible has to have an accent on hope. Not because we see things getting better. That was the mistake of the early Constantinian church, of nineteenth- and twentieth-century liberal Christianity—an optimism that through our herculean efforts and great cleverness we could institute the kingdom Jesus preached. It failed. That doesn't mean the effort was altogether a waste—God will not forget any action to bring about the kingdom. We just lack the power to do what only God can do. And yet we can be confident that Jesus's reign *will* come in full. So Christian interpretation of the Bible cannot be hopeless, whatever the circumstances. Desmond Tutu used to preach, with apartheid-era security forces glowering at him from the back of the room, that he'd read the last page of the story—and we win! So he would invite the frowners to join the winning side. Jesus's side, that is, which forgives and does not avenge against enemies.

This may seem a strange place to put reflections of this sort, but it is a place for us to think about the vexed problem of Christianity and science. This has often been presented as a Manichaean struggle of the forces of light against the forces of darkness, in which for one side to win the other must be annihilated. Interestingly, both irreligious and religious types have used such apocalyptic imagery. Irreligious types have been saying religion must go away since the rise of modern science in the eighteenth and nineteenth centuries, but especially since the 9/11 attacks, when began a rash of "New Atheist" best sellers.[21] In the eighteenth century, when science was not yet an established academic field, when one had to be an Anglican clergyman even to teach at an English university, science launched itself into prominence by attacking religion as retrograde naïveté. They had plenty of evidence to offer, of course. So science has always coasted on its attack on religion—hooking into the prestige of faith like birds in a slipstream, to borrow one recent powerful image.[22] And yet science was not actually so new as that. It had been around as long as anyone had looked in the sky and wondered at what they saw, since anyone tried to ameliorate another's suffering, since we managed to tease out nature's secrets to make life better, to satisfy our desperately hungry curiosity. On the other side, fundamentalists have also insisted that one must choose either their side or science's, that faith and skeptical inquiry are a zero-sum game. To speak of an endless war between science and religion is, one author points out, like discussing a war between Israel and Egypt in the year 1600. Anyone who knows even a little knows those countries didn't exist as independent entities then. "Science" and "religion" as we think of them now are modern developments.[23] Far from always being at war, they have not always *been* in their current forms at all—in the great span of human existence they showed up yesterday.

In an earlier chapter I wrote of how the pelican has been a Christ symbol in Christianity for millennia, arguing we should remember this image and redeploy it. Such a view depends on the sort of analogical

21. Larsen, "War Is Over, If You Want It."
22. Wagner and Briggs, *The Penultimate Curiosity: How Science Swims in the Slipstream of Ultimate Questions*.
23. Harrison, *Territories of Science and Religion*.

imagination that Christians had for most of the church's life—that God is resplendent throughout his creation and we creatures do well to stop and notice and give thanks. For example, whenever the church would gather on a rainy day, I would use two preacher riffs. One, St. Francis would say that whenever it rains we should remember our baptism. And two, Christian friends in Sudan, when it rains, will exclaim, "God is blessing us!" It's my way of turning grumbling into praise. But many in science have worried that such religious observations about the natural order dull the senses, quench curiosity, and so are bad for science. Auguste Comte famously argued that this sort of religious wondering gets in the way of finding out facts.[24]

But scientists are people, not brains in vats. And they have this awkward habit of being inspired into their profession by their religious faith. Francis Collins, head of the human genome project, has made no secret of his evangelical faith, even offering a gentle defense of Darwinism in his testimony-like memoir.[25] As a pastor I have noticed that hard science students and practitioners and professors seem slightly more likely to be people of faith than their peers in the humanities, who tend to have more reductionistic views of humanity less burdened by awkward facts. Roger Wagner and Andrew Briggs make a similar observation about their Cambridge colleagues.[26] They tell the story of one Henry Acland, a physician who not only isolated the source of the 1854 cholera outbreak in Oxford, but also organized the city's medical response and campaigned passionately for new approaches to sanitation. He saw his passion for medicine in religious terms, as something to which God *called* him. He argued, in sync with then novel Darwinism, that whenever human beings became self-aware and God-aware, that's when they were in the image of God, and he accused a bishop who denounced Darwinism of "lying for God." Acland responded to Comte's critique with the story of William Harvey, discoverer of circulation, whose motivation was precisely his hunt for clues of the order and beauty by which God superintends creation. Harvey did not rely on his faith for his science. He did the science! But he did his work "believing . . . that there is purpose as well as harmony in the material world [and]

---

24. Wagner and Briggs, *Penultimate Curiosity*, 379.

25. Collins, *Language of God*. And to cheer once for the home team—he had his conversion in the Methodist church! See, Methodists? We can still do this!

26. Wagner and Briggs, *Penultimate Curiosity*, 265–73.

acted in this faith."[27] Fulminations on either side notwithstanding, religious interest does not necessarily stymie scientific curiosity. On the contrary, it has often inspired it.

We might see science here as a participant in what Jews often speak of as "the repair of the world." That the world is troubled seems beyond dispute. That science has contributed to that repair ought also to be beyond dispute. Science and technology have alleviated unimaginable amounts of misery (they have caused some too, but that's another story). As a pastor, I have strolled many rural church graveyards and noticed many family plots with a father and several stones for wives, with death dates conspicuously close to birthdates for children.

So why the antipathy to science from so many Christians? Precisely because of the sort of belittling we have heard from cultured despisers like the New Atheists. These interpreters treat Christianity like it's just stupid science, the Bible like it's a dated science textbook, Christians like the rubes and naïfs we fear we may indeed be. Our faith is founded on the resurrection of a dead Jew and his promise to make all things new. If you can believe that—for which there is scant scientific evidence indeed—you can believe a lot.

Part of the problem, Tom McLeish thinks, is the origin stories of Genesis appearing so early in our Bibles.[28] Both believers and skeptics alike have been tempted to treat Genesis 1–2 like it's a journalistic account of what happened in the cosmos's earliest moments—one to defend, the other to belittle. But McLeish points out there are actually dozens of creation stories in our Bible spread through both testaments. Some of these are, in fact, much friendlier a priori to modern scientific endeavors than Genesis may be—but even Genesis is friendlier than often assumed. McLeish is particularly taken with the Bible's Wisdom literature, in which Wisdom (the capital is intentional) is present with God in creation, delighting in the Creator's work, making all things according to divine rationality and order and love. Proverbs 8 speaks of wisdom as a young girl, spritely playing in the nascent cosmos, reflecting God's delighted manner in all things coming into being. Exploring that wisdom as creatures is no affront to God—it is, instead, to meet God's delight with ours. McLeish points also to psalms like the thirty-third, which speaks of the Word of the Lord by which God makes all that is, and the Breath of God's

27. Wagner and Briggs, *Penultimate Curiosity*, 380.
28. McLeish, *Faith and Wisdom in Science*, 70–74.

mouth by which he establishes everything (ancient Christians saw the Son and the Spirit in the Word and the Breath). Creation was not, then, a onetime act from which God walks away, as a superficial reading of Genesis could surmise. It is what God is always doing. Most impressively to McLeish, Job 28:1–8 offers a peek into the underworld of the sort only brave miners usually get, in which the creature sees the very foundation of the earth, and wonders at its order beyond our wondering.

But then order and structure are not the only attributes of the cosmos. The world is also shot through with disorder, chaos, unpredictability. McLeish knows this in his own work as a scientist, working with gels and studying the ways they act like solids or liquids or both. Turning back to the Bible, he attends to natural wonders that were once thought chaotic: comets (long since explained now), volcanoes (explained somewhat, but still unpredictable), and lightning (ditto). Creation seems perched on the edge between order and disorder, and this precarious position is precisely the source of life. Chaos is not entirely undone in the Genesis creation stories. It is rather held back, channeled, so that human beings can carve out a life. St. Paul is especially helpful for speaking of the way creation groans and quakes in its disorder and remaining chaos (Rom. 8:18–27). And then this is remarkable: the resurrection is the outbreak of God's new creation in the midst of the old. Christians are agents of this new creation—ministers of reconciliation, as Paul calls us (2 Cor. 5:18–20). We take part in mending the gap between creation as God dreams of it (for example, in the pacific creaturely relations of Isa. 11:1–9) and creation as it currently is (in which animals eat one another and the planet may die).

Scientists also participate in this ministry of reconciliation. Their work is not merely that of baleful duty, discounting previous theories as they peer with frowny faces into microscopes and telescopes, cracking jokes about believers at coffee breaks. They are helping God repair God's beloved creation. Many actually are fully aware of this and give thanks. In the world made right, any scientist peering in any microscope when she makes a discovery will sing the doxology. Many more than we imagine already do today.[29] McLeish writes of the joy of discovery in terms that anyone who has ever experienced a religious conversion will immediately recognize:

29. I take the image from a comment by David Steinmetz in church history classes at Duke, 1996–2001.

When . . . a new light shines on a previously dark part of the unknown world, something almost unspeakable happens. Scientists only very rarely write this down—it is almost too personal. But it is what we work for. Those miraculous moments when the fog clears and we know something for the first time really are "more precious than rubies," to borrow biblical language. A conversation I was recently enjoying with a very serious theoretical physicist wandered into this territory . . . about the intensely personal and frankly ecstatic moments of achievement (or are they moments of gift?) at which a physical principle at work is understood for the first time.[30]

McLeish speaks often of the delight that drives science. It looks below the surface into the depths, as we have recommended biblical study must do. It seeks explanations that are elegant, aesthetically pleasing, beautiful. When ideas are being nurtured, they require love, like a marsupial with its infant, born but not yet ready for stand-alone independence. And as a practitioner of religious language himself, McLeish can call on it to describe the scientific experience of seeing something for the first time before one shows what one sees to others. This is the ministry of reconciliation. It is taking part in God's renewal of all things in the cosmos, until God one day brings the new creation from heaven to earth, and knowledge of the Lord and of all his creation covers the earth as the waters cover the sea.

And that is anagogical interpretation of the Bible—reading it in light of the repair of the cosmos in which all people are invited to take part. A reading of the Bible that does not lend to the repair of creation is not a Christian one. We should go back and start over. Because God's profound longing is for the flourishing of all God's creatures. And our profound calling is to take part with God in bringing that about. Even to the point of the undoing of all decay—the decay of death—which is begun in Jesus's resurrection.

I have spent many hours now reading both ancient and modern biblical interpretation, and if I had to characterize their difference in one way, it would be this: the difference is in their delight. Ancient interpreters read like they're reading with joy. The text sits somewhat lightly in their hands, even as they bring the best linguistic and manuscript and scientific knowledge to bear on it that they can. They know their work is not done until their hearers are delighted as they are. Modern

30. McLeish, *Faith and Wisdom in Science*, 177.

interpretation much more often seems doleful, dutiful, as much fun as eating broken glass, like the false stereotype of the scientist mentioned above. Not always, of course. Ancient Christians have their polemical moments of denouncing Jews and others that make us reach for readings like Boyd's. Modern interpreters can break out in joy just as well as any other human being can. But in terms of overall tenor, our ancient forebears delighted in what they were doing. Contemporary interpretation, sequestered as it often is among academics endlessly niggling about details or authorial intent, insisting that for a thing to be true no interpreter must have noticed it until I did just this moment, is often miserable. But God's final word over creation is one of delight. All his promises, in Christ, are "Yes" (2 Cor. 1:20).

There is nothing to fear. So let us read . . .

For Further Study

Fowl, Stephen E. *Engaging Scripture: A Model for Theological Interpretation.* Eugene: Wipf & Stock, 2008.

Fowl surgically undoes the effort to divine an author's original intention and lays out a much more catholic vision for interpreting the Bible.

Lubac, Henri de. *Medieval Exegesis.* 3 vols. Grand Rapids: Eerdmans, 1998–2008.

More examples than anyone could ever want of how creatively and faithfully Christians interpreted scripture at multiple levels over the centuries.

Moberly, R. W. L. *Old Testament Theology: Reading the Hebrew Bible as Christian Scripture.* Grand Rapids: Baker Academic, 2015.

Christian scholars have long produced weighty tomes of Old Testament theology. This one has the virtue of actually reading the biblical texts themselves and giving them a greater voice than any scholarly construct.

Postlude

Doxological Science

A relative of mine is a young earth creationist. He's also a genius, having written textbooks in use in Ivy League universities (not in natural science, I should add!). After a round of debate once, I asked him why he holds this scientific belief despite near universal condemnation from science and religion. "Because all creation bears witness to Jesus," he said.

He is correct. All of creation, viewed aright, bears witness to the God who creates and redeems it in Christ. The more time I spend with allegory in ancient Christians' hands, the more I think our disdain or ignorance of it is related to our lack of a doctrine of creation. And that lack is at least partly due to our reception of Darwinism. Science's account of the natural world as descending over millions of years through random happenstance still sits at odds with Christian theology's trust in a God of order and harmony who creates for his own glory. It is extremely important to Darwinism that adaptations happen randomly, without a guiding hand. These adaptations happen all the time, and once in a while, by sheer accident (don't call it "grace"), one of these improves matters in competition for survival. How different from a Christian account that says God is perfect communion. God has no need of any other, and yet *as* perfect communion it is perfectly appropriate that God would create creatures like us with whom to share his love. In one account, life is premised on happenstance and bloody competition; in the other, it depends on benevolent mutual relationship.

No wonder so few try even to reconcile these two accounts. My cousin rejects one. Most of the modern world rejects the other. What do the rest of Christians do as they read biblical texts praising the

God whose "heavens declare" his glory as in Psalm 19, who comes forth from his tent like a bridegroom, like the sun charging across the sky, as in Psalm 19? When *we* lift up our eyes to the hills (Ps. 121), we have been trained to see sheer, pitiless randomness, not a "world charged with the grandeur of God."[1] But I'm guessing a "hallelujah" still escapes most lips in the presence of natural beauty. So how much of the Psalms do we ignore, or not take very seriously? They have been disqualified by science, and science is the great arbiter of truth in our age.

This book makes an argument about how to read the Bible—in a way that seeks to be surprised by Jesus, reading the text at multiple levels, for the sake of the church's health and the world's blessing. Modern critical approaches have dominated biblical studies in major universities over the last century or two with a very different set of goals. They have done great service to our reading of the Bible, yet I remember as a student constantly feeling left cold by these ways of study. This way of reading is barely a beginning of an approach to the literal sense. Let's ask about finding Christ in the Old Testament right up front, as the first question. Then we can argue over whether this or that reading was a good one, or whether Christ ought to be found some other way, or whether it is responsible to find Christ in this at all. This book emerges from the desire to imitate our ancient forebears again. But at times I'm not sure how a local church will take a sermon like those preached by Mary, Origen, Augustine, or Gregory. Yet I worry I'm holding something back from them by not trying. Isn't the whole gospel meant for the whole people of God? Who am I to deprive them of these riches, these depths? The Bible itself, I argue here, demands it.

Scientifically I have much, much less to add. As these things happen, I had magnificent humanities teachers and lousy science ones. Yet I can say why I rejected rejecters of Darwinism among my fellow Christians in the evangelical world (my "progress" toward the mainline was gradual and slightly begrudging). I didn't care for the paranoia engendered by rejecting Darwinism. To say that the whole thing is a lie would suggest that the entire scientific establishment at every university and research center and in every government in the world was in on a massive conspiracy. That was a bridge too far for me. And this is no minor issue. Medicine is based on Darwinism. Yet creationists turn up at the hospital

---

1. As in Gerard Manley Hopkins's poem "God's Grandeur," in *Selected Poems*, 20–21.

when they are sick. There is no non-Darwinist medicine from which to seek healing. When they make those trips, they put fossil fuel–based gas in their car, though they think dinosaurs couldn't have existed long enough ago to actually turn into fossil fuels. In other words, young earth creationists seem to me to draw all the benefits from modern science while rejecting its premise. And the scale of the cover-up required, the paranoia thereby engendered, is asking too much.

My cousin's desire to see Christ witnessed to in every rock is a good and holy and biblical desire. And Augustine had me ready for it. For him, the rock is always Christ, according to 1 Corinthians 10:4. In creative reading of the Bible, Paul says the rock followed the Israelites around in the wilderness. Moses is always talking to it or striking it or otherwise miraculously getting water from it to slake the thirst of a grumbling people. Elsewhere Jesus himself promised if the children stay quiet, the stones themselves will burst into song (Luke 19:40). See? The rocks bear witness to the glory of God. Why should we also insist that scientists cannot determine their age, or if that age is supposedly older than 4004 BCE they must all be lying?

Perhaps even more centrally, Augustine knows when to defer to someone with greater knowledge, so as not to undo his claim to graced knowledge.

Usually, even a non-Christian knows something about the earth, the heavens, and the other elements of this world, about the motion and orbit of the stars and even their size and relative positions, about the predictable eclipses of the sun and moon, the cycles of the years and the seasons, about the kinds of animals, shrubs, stones, and so forth, and this knowledge he holds to as being certain from reason and experience. Now, it is a disgraceful and dangerous thing for an infidel to hear a Christian, presumably giving the meaning of Holy Scripture, talking nonsense on these topics; and we should take all means to prevent such an embarrassing situation, in which people show up vast ignorance in a Christian and laugh it to scorn. The shame is not so much that an ignorant individual is derided, but that people outside the household of faith think our sacred writers held such opinions, and, to the great loss of those for whose salvation we toil, the writers of our Scripture are criticized and rejected as unlearned men. If they find a Christian mistaken in a field which they themselves know well and hear him maintaining his foolish opinions about our books, how are they going to believe those books in matters concerning the resurrection of the dead, the hope of eternal life, and the kingdom of heaven?[2]

One of the virtues of allegory is that it can allow multiple readings of the Bible to be true at the same time. A wooden literalist would have to say Genesis and a modern science book are the same thing. They are not. And with scripture we can offer another sort of interpretation. Historians can do all the creative work necessary about 1 Corinthians 10 or Luke 19 (did other Jews at Paul's time think the rock walked around the wilderness?). At the same time, the church can praise a God who is always shouting from every stone. A major New Testament scholar in the United States once waved off my work in private conversation: "I don't think we have to go looking for Jesus under every rock." Here I agree with my cousin: sure we do. In fact, we don't have to look. He's already there. When we read the Bible christologically, we are not smuggling Jesus in—we are discovering him there, to our and others' delight. To say otherwise is to fail to read Paul or Luke well. It's to miss that all creation hollers praise. It is to leave the world ungraced, uncharged by the grandeur of God, with no witness to the One who creates and redeems it in Christ.

Yet my cousin is mistaken to deny carbon dating, the age of the earth, the consensus of science. God's self-witness in his creation cannot hang by so thin a thread as a conspiratorial cover-up on a vast scale, like Bigfoot research or alien exploration or birther or truther theories. There is no need to fear science. I remember an Orthodox priest being interviewed on the radio once. He said this simple thing when asked about Darwinism: "I don't understand it, but I'm not afraid of it." His faith is secure. God is unafraid of what is going on in our test tubes. On the contrary, he delights in our delight in discovery. To suggest otherwise is, ironically, to accord too much trust in science. It is to say that all of modern science has to be proven wrong for Jesus to be Lord. No way.

I did not write this book because I can carry on this argument very long. Other luminaries can do that heavy lifting—John Polkinghorne, Alister McGrath, Sarah Coakley, Tom McLeish, and others are worthy reading for these matters. The most scorching denunciation of Darwinism I know is in the great novelist Marilynne Robinson's *The Death*

2. Augustine, *Literal Meaning of Genesis*, 42–43.

of Adam—brilliant reading. She worries that scientific Darwinism has never managed to separate itself from social Darwinism, in which the creatures at the top of the food chain are lauded for kicking down those that are genetically inferior (the Nazis were enthusiastic social Darwinists, it is often noted). If all creation is just the result of a great cosmic accident, then it seems human life is expendable, optional, subject to the whims and desires of those with the biggest army and checkbook. That can be a recipe for great tyranny. The rush to legal blessing of euthanasia in Western countries like Canada—likely unthinkable when there was more living memory of the Nazi atrocities—may prove evidence of this. Conservative Christians have long decried the abortion industry as another example of our willingness to dispose of unwanted life. I'm not sure they're wrong.

The church has sometimes been guilty of deploying a "God in the gaps," by which the lack of scientific explanation of phenomena is a place where we insert God's action or presence or cause. "We don't know why X happens; therefore God must be the explanation." But God is not the biggest creature around. God is distinct from his creation, in a way we cannot imagine. God is more like a playwright. God can act with a certain freedom that is not limited by his characters' freedom. This Creator/creature difference is key to imagining how accounts of the world like creation and evolution can each tell us some truths, both in their own ways. Hence, God is responsible for all things, but he will not be discovered the way created things are. For God to be at work, it is no threat to have a natural explanation. As in biblical interpretation, orthodox Christianity has always been happy with multiple causes, and modernity has always been nervous about any such suggestion. God invented and supervises and delights in photosynthesis and plate tectonics and gravity and meteors (I remember here a Jewish observer saying, when evidence of long-dried-up water was discovered on Mars, that God delights when his universe gets a little bigger). As we study such phenomena, we are giving praise to God, even if we are unaware. God is also, and in a complementary way, to be looked for where he has revealed himself: in Israel, in Christ, then derivatively in scripture and in creation—the latter two viewed through the lenses of the first two.

For too long among Christians, the divide has been between liberals who accept modern science and put distance between themselves and the Bible and conservatives who reject science and embrace the Bible. I find myself, by no grand plan, on the liberal side, if that means making peace with science, for the most part. Part of my love for allegory comes from its attentiveness to the letter of the Bible. I call it "christological literalism," in a phrase I hope others will also pick up and deploy. My fear about biblical fundamentalism is that it takes the Bible *not seriously enough*. It doesn't pay attention to the letter enough to notice that light and dark are created before the sun and the moon in Genesis. The authors and editors of the Bible could easily have smoothed out, removed, or otherwise explained away what look like discrepancies or contradictions in scripture. Why did the church leave the awkwardness untidied? The church was glad for the variety in the gospels, even the discrepancies and outright contradictions. Difficulties in the scriptures should not be feared, apologized for, or turned away from. They're *there*, so let's do business with them as reminders of Christ's lordship, not embarrassing cracks to be papered over, garbage to be hurriedly and nervously shuffled into the trash. For Origen, and ancient Christians after him, difficulty in scripture is a sign that the Bible *intends* us to read it figurally. A contradiction or a problem is actually a clue. God has left a surprise for us here—let us delight in finding what God means for us to see.

Evangelical and conservative theological circles often require signing of a statement of inerrancy or infallibility before teaching in their institutions or preaching in their churches. I have signed such statements before happily and would do so again, to the chagrin of my more liberal mainline colleagues. Why? The church fathers make enthusiastic noises about the perfection, beauty, and trustworthiness of scripture. They do not mean by that that we humans always read it correctly. They know we are sinners and can use it for harm as well as good (with their keener attention to heresy than ours, they had abundant evidence of its misuse). Yet the Bible is always true *when read right*—that is, read the way God wants us to read it. How is that? With reference to Christ. Even that is a contestable claim. But eventually all scripture, like all creation, all creatures, all of the natural order, bends the knee. Scripture is always read with certain rules in mind, whether by historical critics, heretics, evangelicals, or liberals. The ones from the ancient church we should borrow are these: God is the author of scripture. God is no fool. And God speaks to us in the church. God does not contradict himself.[3] Readings that violate such rules mean we have not yet read deeply enough.

---

3. I borrow here from Jenson, "What If It Were True?"

So I offer this exposition of what ancient Christians say about the Bible partly in hopes of helping us take every inch of the Bible more seriously. The way to do that is to be both more literal and more christological at the same time. And the goal is to offer praise. The Bible is not a science textbook. To read it as such is to do violence to it. It is the gift wherein God teaches us about himself and turns us into disciples. Isn't that enough? And let us remember the church's great heritage of birthing and celebrating scientists. I have heard churches spontaneously erupt into applause when a young person decides to go into ministry. Why not when they take up biology?

Ancient Christian biblical interpretation shows us one way forward past a ridiculous impasse of having to choose either the Bible or science. May both flourish, their tribes increase. And may the church offer praise of Christ until knowledge of the goodness of God covers the earth as the waters cover the sea.

For Further Study

Collins, Francis S. *The Language of God: A Scientist Presents Evidence for Belief.* New York: Free Press, 2007.

The author's evangelical faith breathes through this text as he marvels at what can also be known about God from the natural sciences and critiques his fellow Christians for ignoring or impugning the latter.

Hart, David Bentley. *Atheist Delusions: The Christian Revolution and Its Fashionable Enemies.* New Haven: Yale University Press, 2010.

Bombastically responds to stock modernist dismissals of Christian faith as anti-scientific.

Sacks, Jonathan. *The Great Partnership: Science, Religion, and the Search for Meaning.* New York: Schocken Books, 2014.

Britain's former chief rabbi explores the overlap between science and religion and clears away the misperceptions that can make for fear in both directions.

Bibliography

Allison, James. *The Joy of Being Wrong: Original Sin through Easter Eyes.* New York: Crossroad, 1998.

Ambrose. *Isaiah.* The Church's Bible. Grand Rapids: Eerdmans, 2007.

Anderson, Gary A. *Christian Doctrine and the Old Testament: Theology in the Service of Biblical Exegesis.* Grand Rapids: Baker Academic, 2017.

—————. *The Genesis of Perfection: Adam and Eve in Jewish and Christian Imagination.* Louisville: Westminster John Knox, 2002.

Athanasius. *On the Incarnation of the Word.* Crestwood, NY: St. Vladimir's Seminary Press, 2012.

Augustine. *Confessions.* Translated by Henry Chadwick. Oxford World Classics. Oxford: Oxford University Press, 2009.

—————. *Expositions of the Psalms 99–120.* Translated by Maria Boulding. In *The Works of Saint Augustine: A Translation for the 21st Century.* Hyde Park, NY: New City Press, 2003.

—————. *Instructing Beginners in Faith.* Translated by Raymond Canning. Hyde Park, NY: New City Press, 2006.

—————. *The Literal Meaning of Genesis.* Translated by J. H. Taylor. Ancient Christian Writers 41. Baltimore: Newman, 1982.

—————. *On Christian Doctrine.* Translated by D. W. Robertson. Upper Saddle River, NJ: Prentice Hall, 1958.

Aulén, Gustaf. *Christus Victor: An Historical Study of the Three Main Types of the Idea of Atonement.* Translated by A. G. Herbert. Eugene: Wipf & Stock, 2003.

Bader-Saye, Scott. *Church and Israel after Christendom: The Politics of Election.* Boulder: Westview Press, 1999.

Barber, William J., II, with Jonathan Wilson-Hartgrove. *The Third Recon-

struction: How a Moral Movement Is Overcoming the Politics of Division and Fear. Boston: Beacon, 2016.

Barth, Karl. *Church Dogmatics* IV/3. Translated by G. W. Bromiley. Edinburgh: T&T Clark, 1961.

Basil of Caesaria, St., and St. Gregory Nazianzus. *The Philocalia of Origen.* Translated by George Lewis. Edinburgh: T&T Clark, 1911.

Beasley-Murray, George R. *John.* Word Biblical Commentary 36. Waco: Word, 1987.

Boersma, Hans. *Scripture as Real Presence: Sacramental Exegesis in the Early Church.* Grand Rapids: Baker Academic, 2017.

Bonhoeffer, Dietrich. *Life Together.* Translated by Geoffrey Kelly. Vol. 5 of *Dietrich Bonhoeffer Works.* Minneapolis: Fortress, 2004.

Bossy, John. *Christianity in the West 1400–1700.* Oxford: Oxford University Press, 1985.

Boyd, Gregory A. *The Crucifixion of the Warrior God: Interpreting the Old Testament's Violent Portraits of God in Light of the Cross.* 2 vols. Minneapolis: Fortress, 2017.

Brueggemann, Walter. *Chosen: Reading the Bible amidst the Israeli-Palestinian Conflict.* Louisville: Westminster John Knox, 2015.

Burrell, David. *Deconstructing Theodicy: Why Job Has Nothing to Say to the Puzzle of Suffering.* Grand Rapids: Brazos, 2008.

Burtchaell, James. *The Dying of the Light: The Disengagement of Colleges and Universities from Their Christian Churches.* Grand Rapids: Eerdmans, 1998.

Butler, Cuthbert. *Benedictine Monachism.* London: Longmans, Green, 1919.

Byassee, Jason. "Andrew Walls: An Exciting Period in Christian History." *Faith & Leadership*, June 5, 2011, https://www.faithandleadership.com/multimedia/andrew-walls-exciting-period-christian-history.

———. "Can a Jew Be a Christian?" *Presbyterian Church and Messianic Judaism*, May 3, 2005, 22–27.

———. "If Death Is No Barrier." *Books & Culture*, January/February 2007.

———. "Jason Barr: 'Move Forward.'" *Faith & Leadership*, December 28, 2008, https://www.faithandleadership.com/multimedia/jason-barr-move-forward.

———. *Praise Seeking Understanding: Reading the Psalms with Augustine.* Grand Rapids: Eerdmans, 2007.

———. *Trinity: The God We Don't Know.* Nashville: Abingdon, 2015.

Cameron, Michael. *Christ Meets Me Everywhere: Augustine's Early Figurative Exegesis.* Oxford: Oxford University Press, 2012.

Cavanaugh, William T., and James K. A. Smith, eds. *Evolution and the Fall*. Grand Rapids: Eerdmans, 2017.

Chesterton, G. K. *Orthodoxy*. Chicago: Moody, 2009. Originally published 1908.

Clark, Elizabeth. "Uses of the Song of Songs: Origen and the Later Latin Fathers." In *Ascetic Piety and Women's Faith: Essays on Late Ancient Christianity*. Lewiston, NY: Mellen, 1986.

Collins, Francis S. *The Language of God: A Scientist Presents Evidence for Belief*. New York: Free Press, 2007.

Daniel, Lillian. *Tired of Apologizing for a Church I Don't Belong To*. Nashville: FaithWords, 2016.

Davis, Ellen F. *Getting Involved with God: Rediscovering the Old Testament*. Cambridge, MA: Cowley, 2001.

———. "Losing a Friend: The Loss of the Old Testament to the Church." *Pro Ecclesia* 9, no. 1 (2000): 73–84.

Demacopoulos, George E. *Gregory the Great: Ascetic, Pastor, and First Man of Rome*. South Bend: University of Notre Dame Press, 2015.

Dickson, Athol. *The Gospel according to Moses: What My Jewish Friends Taught Me about Jesus*. Grand Rapids: Brazos, 2003.

Dillard, Annie. *Teaching a Stone to Talk: Expeditions and Encounters*. New York: Harper & Row, 1982.

Dodd, C. H. *Parables of the Kingdom*. New York: Charles Scribner's Sons, 1961.

Elie, Paul. *The Life You Save May Be Your Own: An American Pilgrimage*. New York: Farrar, Straus & Giroux.

Evans, G. R. *The Thought of Gregory the Great*. Cambridge: Cambridge University Press, 1986.

Felski, Rita. "Suspicious Minds." *Poetics Today* 32, no. 2 (Summer 2011): 215–34.

Finn, Thomas. "It Happened One Saturday Night: Ritual and Conversion in Augustine's North Africa." *Journal of the American Academy of Religion* 58, no. 4 (1990): 589–616.

Ford, David. *The Future of Christian Theology*. Oxford: Wiley-Blackwell, 2011.

Fowl, Stephen E. *Engaging Scripture: A Model for Theological Interpretation*. Eugene: Wipf & Stock, 2008.

Frederiksen, Paula. *Augustine and the Jews: A Critical Defense of Jews and Judaism*. New Haven: Yale University Press, 2011.

Frei, Hans. "The 'Literal Reading' of Biblical Narrative in the Christian Tradition: Does It Stretch or Will It Break?" In *Theology and Narrative*:

Selected Essays, edited by George Hunsinger and William C. Placher, 117–52. Oxford: Oxford University Press, 1993.

Frymer-Kensky, Tikva, David Novak, Peter Ochs, David Fox Sandmel, and Michael A. Signer, eds. *Christianity in Jewish Terms*. New York: Basic Books, 2002.

George, Timothy. "Evangelicals and the Mother of God." *First Things*, February 2007, https://www.firstthings.com/article/2007/02/evangelicals-and-the-mother-of-god.

Girard, Rene. *Job: The Victim of His People*. Translated by Yvonne Freccero. Stanford: Stanford University Press, 1987.

Goldberg, Michael. *Jews and Christians: Getting Our Stories Straight; The Exodus and the Passion-Resurrection*. Eugene: Wipf & Stock, 2001.

Greenberg, Irving (Yitz). *For the Sake of Heaven and Earth: The New Encounter Between Judaism and Christianity*. Philadelphia: Jewish Publication Society, 2004.

Gregory the Great. *The Book of Pastoral Rule: St. Gregory the Great*. Translated by George Demacopoulos. Crestwood, NY: St. Vladimir's Seminary Press, 2007.

———. *Dialogues*. Translated by Odo John Zimmerman, OSB. Fathers of the Church 39. New York: Fathers of the Church, 1959.

———. *Forty Gospel Homilies*. Translated by Dom David Hurst. Kalamazoo: Cistercian, 1990.

———. *The Homilies of St. Gregory the Great: On the Book of the Prophet Ezekiel*. Translated by Theodosia Gray. Etna, CA: Center for Traditionalist Orthodox Studies, 1990.

———. *Morals on the Book of Job by S. Gregory the Great*. Translated by John Henry Parker. A Library of Fathers of the Holy Catholic Church. London: J. G. F. and J. Rivington, 1844.

Guerric of Igny. *Liturgical Sermons [by] Guerric of Igny*. Translated by Monks of Mount Saint Bernard Abbey. 2 vols. Spencer, MA: Cistercian, 1971.

Hankins, Davis. *The Book of Job and the Immanent Genesis of Transcendence*. Evanston, IL: Northwestern University Press, 2014.

Harmless, William. *Augustine in His Own Words*. Washington: Catholic University Press, 2010.

Harrelson, Walter J., ed. *New Interpreter's Study Bible*. Nashville: Abingdon, 2003.

Harrison, Peter. *The Territories of Science and Religion*. Chicago: University of Chicago Press, 2017.

Hart, David Bentley. *Atheist Delusions: The Christian Revolution and Its Fashionable Enemies*. New Haven: Yale University Press, 2010.

———. *A Splendid Wickedness*. Grand Rapids: Eerdmans, 2016.

———. *The Story of Christianity: An Illustrated History of 2000 Years of the Christian Faith*. London: Quercus, 2007.

Hauerwas, Stanley. *Unleashing the Scripture: Freeing the Bible from Captivity to America*. Nashville: Abingdon, 1993.

———. *With the Grain of the Universe: The Church's Witness and Natural Theology*. Grand Rapids: Baker Academic, 2013.

Hays, Richard. *Echoes of Scripture in the Gospels*. Waco: Baylor University Press, 2017.

———. *Echoes of Scripture in the Letters of Paul*. New Haven: Yale University Press, 1989.

Heclo, Hugh. *On Thinking Institutionally*. Oxford: Oxford University Press, 2011.

Hopkins, Gerard Manley. *Selected Poems of Gerard Manley Hopkins*. Dover, UK: Dover Thrift Editions, 2011.

Howell, James C. "Christ Was Like St. Francis." In *The Art of Reading Scripture*, edited by Ellen Davis and Richard Hays, 89–108. Grand Rapids: Eerdmans, 2003.

Janzen, J. Gerald. *Job*. Interpretation: A Bible Commentary for Teaching and Preaching. Atlanta: John Knox, 1985.

Jenkins, Philip. *Laying Down the Sword: Why We Can't Ignore the Bible's Violent Verses*. San Francisco: HarperOne, 2012.

———. *The Next Christendom: The Coming of Global Christianity*. 3rd ed. Oxford: Oxford University Press, 2011.

Jennings, Willie. *The Christian Imagination: Theology and the Origins of Race*. New Haven: Yale University Press, 2011.

Jenson, Robert. "What If It Were True?" *CTI Reflections* 43, no. 1 (2001): 3–16.

Johnson, Trygve David. *The Preacher as Liturgical Artist: Metaphor, Identity, and the Vicarious Humanity of Christ*. Eugene: Cascade, 2014.

King, J. Christopher. *Origen on the Song of Songs as the Spirit of Scripture: The Bridegroom's Perfect Marriage-Song*. New York: Oxford University Press, 2005.

Kullberg, Kelly Monroe, ed. *Finding God at Harvard*. Downers Grove, IL: InterVarsity Press, 2007.

Lamott, Anne. *Operating Instructions: A Journal of My Son's First Year*. Norwell, MA: Anchor, 2005.

Larsen, Timothy. "'War Is Over, If You Want It': Beyond the Conflict between Faith and Science." *Perspectives on Science and Christian Faith* 60, no. 3 (September 2008): 147–55.

Lash, Nicholas. *Theology on the Way to Emmaus.* London: SCM, 1986.

Leclercq, Jean. *The Love of Learning and the Desire for God: A Study of Monastic Culture.* Translated by Catharine Misrahi. New York: Fordham University Press, 1960.

Legaspi, Michael. *The Death of Scripture and the Rise of Biblical Studies.* Oxford: Oxford University Press, 2011.

Levenson, Jon. *Creation and the Persistence of Evil: The Jewish Drama of Divine Omnipotence.* Princeton: Princeton University Press, 1994.

———. *The Hebrew Bible, the Old Testament, and Historical Criticism: Jews and Christians in Biblical Studies.* Louisville: Westminster John Knox, 1993.

Lienhard, Joseph T. "Origen and the Crisis of the Old Testament in the Early Church." *Pro Ecclesia* 9, no. 3 (2000): 355–66.

Lipka, Michael. "The Most and Least Racially Diverse U.S. Religious Groups." Pew Research Center, June 2015, http://www.pewresearch .org/fact-tank/2015/07/27/the-most-and-least-racially-diverse-u-s -religious-groups/.

Louth, Andrew. *Discerning the Mystery.* Oxford: Clarendon, 1980.

Lowry, Eugene. *The Homiletical Plot: The Sermon as Narrative Art Form.* Louisville: Westminster John Knox, 2000.

Lubac, Henri de. *Medieval Exegesis.* Vol. 2, *The Four Senses of Scripture.* Translated by E. M. Macierowski. Grand Rapids: Eerdmans, 2000.

Macauley, Rose. *The Towers of Trebizond.* New York: FSG Classics, 2012.

Markus, Robert A. "The Jew as a Hermeneutic Device: The Inner Life of a Gregorian Topos." In *Gregory the Great: A Symposium,* edited by John C. Cavadini, 1–15. Notre Dame: University of Notre Dame Press, 1995.

Martens, Peter. *Origen and Scripture: The Contours of the Exegetical Life.* Oxford: Oxford University Press, 2014.

McCourt, Frank. *Angela's Ashes.* New York: Scribner, 1999.

McDermott, Gerald. *Israel Matters: Why Christians Must Think Differently about the People and the Land.* Grand Rapids: Brazos, 2017.

McGee, Gary. *People of the Spirit: The Assemblies of God.* Springfield, MO: Gospel Publishing House, 2004.

McGinn, Bernard. "Contemplation in Gregory the Great." In *Gregory the Great: A Symposium,* edited by John C. Cavadini. Notre Dame: University of Notre Dame Press, 1995.

McLeish, Tom. *Faith and Wisdom in Science.* Oxford: Oxford University Press, 2014.

Melito of Sardis. *On Pascha.* Translated by Alistair Stewart-Sykes. Crestwood, NY: St. Vladimir's Seminary Press, 2001.

Milbank, John. *Theology and Social Theory: Beyond Secular Reason.* 2nd ed. Oxford: Wiley-Blackwell, 2006.

Miller, Donald. *A Million Miles in a Thousand Years: How I Learned to Live a Better Story.* Nashville: Thomas Nelson, 2011.

Moberly, R. W. L. *Old Testament Theology: Reading the Hebrew Bible as Christian Scripture.* Grand Rapids: Baker Academic, 2015.

Moorhead, John. *Gregory the Great.* The Early Church Fathers. London: Routledge, 2005.

Murphy, Roland. "Song of Songs." In *New Interpreter's Study Bible,* edited by Walter J. Harrelson. Nashville: Abingdon, 2003.

Newsom, Carol. "Job." In *The New Interpreter's Bible,* vol. 4. Nashville: Abingdon, 1996.

Ochs, Peter. *Another Reformation: Postliberal Christianity and the Jews.* Grand Rapids: Baker Academic, 2011.

O'Connor, Flannery. *The Habit of Being: Letters of Flannery O'Connor.* New York: Farrar, Straus & Giroux, 1988.

———. *Mystery and Manners: Occasional Prose.* Edited by Sally and Robert Fitzgerald. New York: Noonday, 1957.

Origen. *On First Principles.* Edited and translated by John Behr. Oxford: Oxford University Press, 2018.

———. *Origen: On First Principles.* Translated by G. W. Butterworth. Gloucester, MA: Peter Smith, 1973.

———. *The Song of Songs, Commentary and Homilies.* Translated by R. P. Lawson. Ancient Christian Writers 26. New York: Newman, 1956.

Owens, Roger. "Don't Talk Nonsense: Why Herbert McCabe Still Matters." *Christian Century,* January 25, 2005, 20–25.

Percy, Walker. *Message in a Bottle: How Queer Man Is, How Queer Language Is, and What One Has to Do with the Other.* London: Picador, 2000.

Perry, Tim. *Mary for Evangelicals: Toward an Understanding of the Mother of Our Lord.* Downers Grove, IL: InterVarsity Press, 2006.

Peterson, Eugene. *The Message.* Colorado Springs: NavPress, 2002.

———. *Reversed Thunder: The Revelation of John and the Praying Imagination.* San Francisco: HarperSanFrancisco, 1991.

Quash, Ben, and Michael Ward, ed. *Heresies and How to Avoid Them.* Grand Rapids: Baker Academic, 2007.

Robert, Dana Lee. *Christian Mission: How Christianity Became a World Religion*. Malden, MA: Wiley-Blackwell, 2009.

Robinson, Anthony B. *Going Deeper, Reaching Wider*. Unpublished manuscript.

Rogers, Jonathan. *The Terrible Speed of Mercy: A Spiritual Biography of Flannery O'Connor*. Nashville: Thomas Nelson, 2012.

Sacks, Jonathan. *The Great Partnership: Science, Religion, and the Search for Meaning*. New York: Schocken Books, 2014.

———. *Not in God's Name: Confronting Religious Violence*. New York: Schocken Books, 2017.

———. "Philosophy or Prophecy? (Va'etchanan 5777)." *The Office of Rabbi Sacks*, July 31, 2017, http://rabbisacks.org/philosophy-prophecy-vaetchanan-5777/.

Sawyer, John F. A. *The Fifth Gospel: Isaiah in the History of Christianity*. Cambridge: Cambridge University Press, 1996.

Schreiner, Susan. *Where Shall Wisdom Be Found? Calvin's Exegesis of Job from Medieval and Modern Perspectives*. Chicago: University of Chicago Press, 1994.

Sedgwick, Eve. *Touching, Feeling*. Durham, NC: Duke University Press, 2002.

Seitz, Christopher R. *Figured Out: Typology and Providence in Christian Scripture*. Grand Rapids: Eerdmans, 1997.

———. *Word without End: The Old Testament as Abiding Theological Witness*. Grand Rapids: Eerdmans, 1998.

Smith, Gordon T. *Evangelical, Sacramental, and Pentecostal: Why the Church Should Be All Three*. Downers Grove, IL: InterVarsity Press, 2017.

Smith, James K. A. *You Are What You Love: The Spiritual Power of Habit*. Grand Rapids: Brazos, 2016.

Smith, James K. A., and Michael Gulker, ed. *All Things Hold Together in Christ: Faith, Science, and Worship*. Grand Rapids: Baker Academic, 2018.

Soulen, Kendall. *The God of Israel and Christian Theology*. Minneapolis: Fortress, 1996.

Steinmetz, David. "Miss Marple Reads the Bible: Detective Fiction and the Art of Biblical Interpretation." In *Taking the Long View: Christian Theology in Historical Perspective*. Oxford: Oxford University Press, 2011.

Strawn, Brent. *The Old Testament Is Dying*. Grand Rapids: Baker Academic, 2017.

St. Symeon the New Theologian. *On the Mystical Life*. Translated and introduced by Alexander Gollitzen. Crestwood, NY: St. Vladimir's Seminary Press, 1995.

Torjesen, Karen Jo. *Hermeneutical Procedure and Theological Structure in Origen's Exegesis*. Berlin: de Gruyter, 1986.

Trigg, Joseph W. *Origen*. The Early Church Fathers. London: Routledge, 1998.

Wagner, Roger, and Andrew Briggs. *The Penultimate Curiosity: How Science Swims in the Slipstream of Ultimate Questions*. Oxford: Oxford University Press, 2016.

Walls, Andrew. *The Cross-Cultural Process in Christian History: Studies in the Transmission and Appropriation of Faith*. Maryknoll, NY: Orbis Books, 2002.

———. *The Missionary Movement in Christian History: Studies in the Transmission of Faith*. Maryknoll, NY: Orbis Books, 1996.

Ward, Graham. "*Allegoria.*" *Modern Theology* 15, no. 3 (July 1999): 271–95.

Wells, Sam. *Improvisation: The Drama of Christian Ethics*. Grand Rapids: Brazos, 2004.

Wilken, Robert. "The Face of God for Now." In *The Spirit of Early Christian Thought: Seeking the Face of God*. New Haven: Yale University Press, 2005.

———. "Interpreting Job Allegorically: The *Moralia* of Gregory the Great." *Pro Ecclesia* 10, no. 2 (Spring 2001): 213–26.

———. *Isaiah: Interpreted by Early Christian Medieval Commentators*. Grand Rapids: Eerdmans, 2007.

Williams, Rowan. *Christ on Trial: How the Gospel Unsettles Our Judgment*. 2nd ed. Grand Rapids: Eerdmans, 2003.

———. "Doctrinal Criticism? Some Questions." In *The Making and Remaking of Christian Doctrine: Essays in Honour of Maurice Wiles*, edited by Sarah Coakley. Oxford: Clarendon, 1993.

———. "Language, Reality and Desire in Augustine's *De Doctrina.*" *Literature and Theology* 3, no. 2 (1989): 138–50.

———. *On Augustine*. London: Bloomsbury Continuum, 2016.

———. *A Ray of Darkness*. Cambridge, MA: Cowley, 1995.

———. *Resurrection: Interpreting the Easter Gospel*. New York: Morehouse, 1994.

———. *Why Study the Past? The Quest for the Historical Church*. Grand Rapids: Eerdmans, 2005.

———. *Wrestling with Angels*. Edited by Mike Higton. London: SCM, 2005.

Williams, William Carlos. *Asphodel: That Greeny Flower and Other Love Poems*. New York: New Directions, 1994.

Willimon, William H. *How Odd of God: Chosen for the Curious Vocation of Preaching*. Louisville: Westminster John Knox, 2015.

———. *A Peculiar Prophet: William H. Willimon and the Art of Preaching*. Edited by Michael A. Turner and William F. Malambri III. Nashville: Abingdon, 2004.

Winner, Lauren. *Mudhouse Sabbath: An Invitation to a Life of Spiritual Discipline*. Brewster, MA: Paraclete, 2007.

Wright, N. T. *Paul and the Faithfulness of God*. Minneapolis: Fortress, 2013.

———. *Surprised by Hope: Rethinking Heaven, the Resurrection, and the Mission of the Church*. San Francisco: HarperOne, 2008.

———. *Surprised by Scripture: Engaging Contemporary Issues*. San Francisco: HarperOne, 2015.

Wyschogrod, Michael. "Incarnation and God's Indwelling in Israel." In *Abraham's Promise: Judaism and Jewish-Christian Relations*, edited by R. Kendall Soulen, 165–78. Grand Rapids: Eerdmans, 2004.

———. "A Jewish View of Christianity." In *Abraham's Promise: Judaism and Jewish-Christian Relations*, edited by R. Kendall Soulen, 149–64. Grand Rapids: Eerdmans, 2004.

———. "Letter to Cardinal Lustiger." In *Abraham's Promise: Judaism and Jewish-Christian Relations*, edited by R. Kendall Soulen, 202–10. Grand Rapids: Eerdmans, 2004.

Zinn, Grover. "Exegesis and Spirituality in the Writings of Gregory the Great." In *Gregory the Great: A Symposium*, edited by John C. Cavadini. Notre Dame: University of Notre Dame Press, 1995.

INDEX OF AUTHORS

INDEX OF SUBJECTS

INDEX OF SCRIPTURE REFERENCES